The Political Future of Afghanistan

ISSUES AND PERSPECTIVES

The Political Future of Afghanistan

ISSUES AND PERSPECTIVES

Edited by

Arpita Basu Roy
Srimanti Sarkar

Maulana Abul Kalam Azad Institute of Asian Studies
Kolkata

in association with

KNOWLEDGE WORLD

KW Publishers Pvt Ltd
New Delhi

The **Maulana Abul Kalam Azad Institute of Asian Studies** (MAKAIAS) is an autonomous body under the Ministry of Culture, Government of India. Based in Kolkata, it was registered as a Society under the West Bengal Registration of Societies' Act of 1961 on the 4th of January 1993, with Prof. Nurul Hasan, the then Governor of West Bengal, as the President of the Society. It is funded by the Department of Culture, Government of India.

MAKAIAS is a centre for research and learning with a focus on social, cultural, economic and political / administrative developments in Asia from the middle of the 19th Century onwards, with special emphasis on their links with India, and also on the life and works of Maulana Abul Kalam Azad.

ISBN 978-93-83649-75-4

KNOWLEDGE WORLD

Published in India by

Kalpana Shukla
KW Publishers Pvt Ltd
4676/21, First Floor, Ansari Road, Daryaganj, New Delhi 110002
Phone: +91.11.23263498/43528107
Email: knowledgeworld@vsnl.net • www.kwpub.com

2011 FIPBA BEST PUBLISHERS AWARD (ENGLISH)

Printed and Bound in India

Contents

Contributors

Andrey Nikolaevich Medvedev is Director of the Centre of Political Technologies, *Polit Contact*, Moscow.

Abdul Hadi Khalid is the Former Deputy at the Ministry of Interior, Kabul, Afghanistan.

Ambrish Dhaka is Associate Professor in the School of International Studies, Jawaharlal Nehru University, New Delhi.

Anwesha Ghosh is Doctoral Candidate under the DAAD International Conflict Management Programme at the Willy Brandt School of Public Policy, University of Erfurt, Germany.

Bahram Amirahmadian is Visiting Faculty of World Studies, Tehran University, Iran.

C. Sheela Reddy is Associate Professor at the Indian Institute of Public Administration, New Delhi.

Diloram Karomat is Fellow at the Maulana Abul Kalam Azad Institute of Asian Studies (MAKAIAS), Kolkata.

Maqsudul Hasan Nuri is Adviser in the Centre for Policy Studies at COMSATS Institute of Information Technology, Islamabad, Pakistan.

Mirwais Balkhi is Director of the Research Department at the University of Afghanistan.

Mohammad Ashraf Rasooli is former Minister and Adviser to the President of Afghanistan, Sadarat Palace, Kabul, Afghanistan.

P. Krishna Mohan Reddy is Assistant Professor in the Department of History, Sri Venkateswara University, Tirupati.

Raghav Sharma is Assistant Professor at the Conflict Studies Programme, Willy Brandt School of Public Policy, University of Erfurt, Germany.

Sreemati Ganguli is former Fellow at the Maulana Abul Kalam Azad Institute of Asian Studies (MAKAIAS), Kolkata.

Venkat Lokanathan is Assistant Professor and Coordinator of the Masters Programme at the Department of Political Science, St. Joseph's College (Autonomous), Bangalore.

Vishal Chandra is Fellow at the Institute for Defence Studies & Analyses (IDSA), New Delhi.

Yow Peter Raiphea is Doctoral Student at the North-Eastern Hill University, Shillong.

Zubair Popalzai is Consultant at the BBC Monitoring (Reading), United Kingdom.

Introduction

Even after more than a decade of international intervention in Afghanistan, increasing insurgent attacks weaken the fledgling post-Taliban democratic state from inside while strategies of regional and sometimes extra-regional states threaten to destabilise and weaken it from the outside. A growing insurgency is visible in the lethal attacks on specified targets, weak governance leading to space for increasing Talibanisation, a disgruntled population confused and disillusioned with corruption and abuse of power, insecurities related to the drawdown of international forces remain some of the perceptible tendencies visible in contemporary Afghanistan. Therefore the question is whether Afghanistan's political future is at an impasse? There are both internal and external reasons to believe so and the challenges for stability in a country ravaged by more than three decades of war remain considerable. Efforts to guarantee stability continue to be undermined by the above-mentioned Taliban-led insurgency that has access to safe-havens across the border, as well as by the implications of a political settlement with the Taliban and other armed opposition groups. The international community is making attempts to offer a "narrative of opportunity" to counter the anxiety of withdrawal, instability and foreign interference in Afghanistan. Yet, concerns about the fatigued international community's long-term commitment following the transition abound.

The international approach to peace-building in Afghanistan can be critiqued but nonetheless one can claim that the period of intervention did see momentous deviation from the status quo which Afghanistan suffered previously. Continuities of the past and changes in the contemporary are likely to influence the Afghanistan of the future. At the current juncture Afghanistan is undergoing three defining transitions, which include the security transition from NATO-led ISAF to Afghan National Security Forces, a political transition that depends on negotiating a political settlement with the insurgency and a stable political leadership, and lastly the economic transition to leverage opportunities for cross-border commerce and people-to-people exchange. Ashraf Ghani has become the elected President for the National Unity Government in Afghanistan but the challenges before him are abundant. There are references to the need for a long-term commitment by way of sustained financial assistance and material support for Afghanistan. But whether anything concrete will emerge from the periodic interactions among numerous stakeholders is doubtful. Afghanistan's future seems to look more uncertain and in need of direct security assistance after 2014. The lack of clarity on the international presence in Afghanistan, its level of commitment, and its inability thus far to insulate Afghanistan from other regional pressures remain Afghanistan's prime concerns, and realisation is dawning that the sacrifices of the past decade could fizzle out if the country is not given sustained aid after 2014.

In analysing the protracted conflict in Afghanistan, one would find that the circumstances in which the conflict was waged, and the dynamics of its development and sustenance, significantly revolve around the external factors/actors involved in the process. The motivation, involvement and ethnic connections of the regional players involved in Afghan affairs is considerably responsible for the obliteration of the Afghan state which had lost all its vital institutions, the state structure and the historical consensus that it once had. On the other hand, the root cause of interference in Afghanistan by foreign powers was the political polarisation among the Afghan groups, which pushed them to seek external support to counterbalance their internal adversaries during the civil war. In the current context, such alarm of external involvement within Afghanistan still runs high. Many analysts (and policymakers) have reached the conclusion that the war has reached a stalemate, and that Afghanistan's future stability depends on a political reconciliation with the Taliban and their external supporters.

Debates on the correct political course in Afghanistan have taken place in various international forums. Although Afghanistan experimented with democracy as a panacea for its challenges, positive results still elude the country. Rather, manipulated elections, cabinet reshuffle, crisis in the parliament have emerged as new issues needing attention. Numerous conferences focus on Afghanistan's problems but immediate issues like security and stability are still unsettled. Uncertainties about the drawdown of troops and increasing reluctance of other major powers to remain actively engaged have added to the anxieties of a number of domestic and regional actors. Sometimes federalism has been suggested as the effective mechanism to deal with problems like ethnic diversity, regional divide and warlordism. The presidential system of government has also been under question, and some have favoured a strong Parliamentary system over the Presidential one. Many experts have argued that the only way to lead Afghanistan out of its present quagmire is to restore the country to its well-established and widely respected tradition of neutrality. The problem of fitting its traditional institutions into modern ones, a phenomenon that can be referred to as *Afghanisation*, has been highlighted as issues of great significance to the future of Afghan polity.

Most of the articles in this volume were presented at an international seminar organised by Maulana Abul Kalam Azad Institute of Asian Studies in collaboration with the Nelson Mandela Centre for Peace and Conflict Resolution, Jamia Millia Islamia University, New Delhi and attended by several Afghans and other international scholars in the region and beyond. Some other essays were commissioned later on. The purpose was to critically examine the functioning of the political arrangement and gaze into the future to build alternative political scenarios factoring in the role of various stakeholders such as the different ethnic groups, the insurgents, the warlords, the traditional political institutions in Afghan society. The role of regional and extra-regional powers in any possible political future was also taken cognizance of in order to give a direction to Afghanistan out of the spell of uncertainty. Most of the discussions that took place during the Seminar were extremely relevant till date and therefore the necessity of bringing out the volume became implicit. While portions of the publication may have become dated as changing dynamics have afflicted the region and the seminar was held in 2012, yet some of the debates remain critical to the contemporary dynamics. The discussions in this volume, therefore, have revolved around the following themes: evaluating the international state-building project and political arrangement, federalism and the problem of ethnic diversity, Parliamentary/Presidential forms of government, and question of neutrality of Afghanistan, the problem of traditional and modern political institutions, resurgent groups/Talibs, regional and extra-regional powers in Afghanistan's political future.

International support for state-building and stabilisation has often failed to achieve its goals, and may have unintended or even counterproductive consequences. The poor prospects of success and unpredictable consequences of external support are what is highlighted in Zubair Popalzai's article *Understanding the Aberration of the Liberal Ontology of International State-Building*. It explains how international state-building frameworks of intervention and regulation are more than just a set of policy practices revolving around the narratives of security, development and democracy. They shift the focus away from government to governance, sharing or co-producing sovereignty understood as administrative regulatory control. They serve as a framework for the rationalisation of the projection of power and have proved to be an apologia for the limits of the ability of international state-builders to build states. Viewed as a bureaucratic exercise amenable to Western technical support, focused on building institutional capacity to enhance sovereignty, international state-building reinforces fragility and deprives the state of the autonomy to establish a framework for development. He discusses this aberration in the context of Afghan state-building and argues that it is essential to give the state the necessary space to establish itself, and a state's ability to govern independently will enable it to establish international relations on the basis of its national interests.

Afghanistan's political history displays resistance to centralised governance as most Afghans continue to be suspicious of national governments in Kabul. Analysts have argued that Afghanistan is likely to function better under some kind of a federal political system, in which significant power is wielded at the provincial and local levels. Raghav Sharma in his article *Afghanistan's Ethno-Political Challenges: A Case for Federal Arrangements* captures the subtle shift in the conflict discourse of Afghanistan from one centring exclusively on ideology to one towards ethnicity. While recognising the multiple challenges posed by the myriad actors having diverging ethnic aspirations, the author contends that federal institutional arrangements hold a credible potential to prevent conflict from becoming intractable in Afghanistan. According to him, misplaced "fears of federalism" had prevented the proper development of the federal structures in the Afghan society. He argues that the key to the end of the Afghan conflict, thus, lay in the institutionalisation of sociocultural autonomy that would make local political structures and actors more accountable. Federal institutions hold the prospect for modulating and transforming the Afghan conflict towards a more meaningful social reconciliation and a much enduring peace over a period of time.

The influence of Islam on the development of political discourse in Afghanistan is abounding. The analysis spans several historical periods and events from pre-colonial times to the twenty-first century. It discusses the frequent use of the institution of jihad to mobilise the masses against foreign occupation or intervention. The enforcement of *shari`ah* has also been exploited in order to extend government control through judicial courts and the educational system. Ambrish Dhaka in his article *Islam and the State in the Constitutional History of Afghanistan* tries to locate the ontology of the state in Afghanistan with reference to the position of Islam in the history of constitutional development of the state. Since long, the clergy had utilised Islam as a geopolitical tool to instigate the tribes on the periphery to oppose the state itself. Thus the author, by carefully defining concepts like "political Islam," "Islamic Statehood in a Tribal Society," "Islam in the constitution" in the specific context of Afghanistan supported the need to understand the true tenets of Islam which is invariably different from the juxtaposed misinterpretations by various groups, including the extremists.

Afghanistan has a weak central government, nomadic structure of society, an extreme form of Islam along with, more importantly, the rule of the mafias and the warlords and the prevalence of drug trafficking. Bahram Amirahmadian in his article titled *Afghanistan's Political Institutions: A New Approach* discusses the unsolved "crisis triangle" in Afghanistan comprising the vicious network of drug mafias and the Taliban or the extremists. He contends that the functioning of two contradictory forces, one supporting the opening up of Afghan society to the West and the other against it, has created a situation of equilibrium in Afghanistan that had resulted in this "crisis triangle." Furthermore the traditional and tribal social structure of Afghan society helps sustain this fool proof system which has more subsystems under it. He argues that all initiatives to deal with the Afghan problem should take into account the social structure of the country and that the central government has minimal authority within the traditional system. The increasing strength of the hard-line Islamic Taliban movement poses a threat to the Afghan state system exposing the dismal state of political affairs combined with social and structural fetters.

The year 2014 has been an extremely significant year in terms of the political and security transition in Afghanistan. Maqsudul Hasan Nuri in his article titled *NATO's Withdrawal from Afghanistan: Post-2014 Scenarios* builds probable scenarios that he feels are likely to prevail after the withdrawal of the US troops in 2014 and categorises them into positive and negative ones. While he contends that there is a probability of a "peaceful" or rather a "neutral" Afghanistan in which the different ethnic groups will coexist and share power in collusion with one another after complete exhaustion of their moral and material strengths, the author did not allay the fears of a sordid scenario. He also contends the probability of a civil war-like situation to erupting in Afghanistan once the NATO-led ISAF forces leave. The chance of the Taliban regaining its stronghold in post-2014 Afghanistan, where the government remains essentially weak and the regional players are busy promoting their interests, portrays a bleak picture of Afghanistan rather than a bright one. The only way to allay this situation is a measured attempt to engage with the neighbours and take forth the nation-building process in a more meaningful way.

In another essay dealing with the post-2014 situation, Vishal Chandra in his article titled *Where is Afghanistan Headed?* questions the critical process of security transition from Western to Afghan forces which coincides with the round of presidential and parliamentary elections in the country in 2014-

15. According to him the future course of Afghanistan will largely depend on the outcomes of both these transitions—military and political—that will either result in the return of the old warring politics along predictable socio-political fault lines, or make way for a somewhat fragile but relatively stable and manageable Afghanistan. However, the author contends that with the uncertainty building up over post-transition Afghanistan, the prospect of a stable political system continuing after 2014 appears somewhat bleak. The emerging internal political configuration suggests reopening of old fault lines as multiple centres of power jostle for space and clout at both national and local levels in view of a waning American intervention. A drift into another round of chaos and anarchy, complemented by alternating phases of limited stability and unabated turbulence are likely to be the scenario in post-transition Afghanistan.

Another marginal group in Afghanistan who are to be severely affected by a civil war or the return of the Taliban are the Afghan women. Since the overthrow of the Taliban in 2001, women and girls have made significant progress, returning to the public sphere and to school in large numbers. Women leaders are playing important roles not only in advancing the rights of women and girls, but also in rebuilding their country. There is a fear that Afghanistan could easily slip backward after the transition. C. Sheela Reddy in her article titled *Women and the Political Future of Afghanistan* makes an elaborate explication of the situation of Afghan women in health, education and employment sectors. According to her, the role and position of women in the Afghan society has its own repercussions in the political future of the country. Over the years the Afghan women have fought vehemently for their rights with the support of international donors, various Afghan officials, activists and NGOs, but women are yet to go a long way to reap benefits from the changes taking place since 2001. Every genuine attempt to improve the conditions of the Afghan women, the author argues, should give due recognition to the Afghan culture and her unique religious dispositions and refrain from the imposition of the so-called "Western" concept of women's rights.

Music has played a key role in the cultural identity of Afghanistan. Diloram Karomat in her paper titled *Music as a Factor in Political Stabilisation of Afghanistan* has argued that music has a role to play in the reconstruction of Afghanistan as it has a powerful appeal. Sufism, she argues, had a continued impact through the ages. And in the post-Taliban period, music of all kinds became a space for promoting particular ideologies and position of authorities for stabilising Afghanistan. By carefully highlighting the geostrategic uniqueness of Afghanistan—as a country at the crossroads of civilisations, a land "in between" the East and the West and a territory contested by political powers—with multicultural influences essentially inevitable in Afghan society, the author emphasises the potency of music as a powerful agent for political stability of the country. It captures the evolution and transformation of traditional music in Afghanistan very well. The article thereby conjoins an interesting account of ethnomusicology with political relevance.

Afghanistan's geopolitical location has been very critical in shaping its political history. Its own internecine conflicts have had a deep impact on the region where animosities within Afghanistan and among regional players created the space for extra-regional actors to interfere. The USA happens to be a major extra-regional power in the political dynamics within Afghanistan for quite some time. Venkat Lokanathan in his article titled *US Policy towards Afghanistan and Options for India* makes a critical assessment of the US policy towards Afghanistan in the backdrop of the 9/11 attacks and the Global War on Terror with the support of a coalition of willing countries that has in turn a significant impact on the international security environment of the world, and the region in particular. While critically measuring the US geostrategic interests in Afghanistan as well as that of India in Afghanistan, the author contends that a three-pronged strategy is likely to be adopted to engage with Afghanistan. However, he argues that the biggest challenge in this case will be to separate the collective and conflicting interests of both India and Pakistan in Afghanistan, for which the US has to determine the way to either maintain simultaneous engagements with all the three players, namely, India, Pakistan and Afghanistan, or to keep them at bay on board collectively.

In analysing the conflicting imperatives of the tripartite relations between India, Pakistan and Afghanistan, Anwesha Ghosh in her article titled *Conflicting Imperatives of India and Pakistan in Afghanistan* examines the dynamics of the triangular relationship between these three countries and assesses the competitive role played by India and Pakistan in Afghanistan. She specifically evaluates the role of the neighbouring countries in Afghanistan where a political vacuum was likely with the withdrawal of US troops in 2014. Arguing from a realist viewpoint, Ghosh linked the political future of Afghanistan to the rivalry between India and Pakistan. India's capacity to deal with Pakistan will be a determining factor affecting stability and peace of the region as a whole. Afghanistan, she argues, is a litmus test for India's ascendance as a regional and global power for which a critical understanding of the conflicting imperatives of this tripartite relationship is indispensable.

Saudi Arabia happens to be another key player in Afghanistan and its role in the Afghan conflict predates the Osama connect. Saudi Arabia supported the Afghan resistance movement against the Soviet occupation along with the US and Pakistan which included official and unofficial aid. Unlike Iran, with support of the Shia groups within Afghanistan, Pakistan and Saudi Arabia funded the Wahabi leader and these pro-Wahabi leader and these pro-Wahabis would eventually form the core of the Taliban leadership. Mirwais Balkhi in his article titled *Saudi Arabia's Long-Term Policy Towards Afghanistan: The Consequences* attempted a study of Saudi Arabia's policy towards Afghanistan by mapping the long history of Saudi Arabia's engagement in Afghanistan. Historically, the Saudi-Afghan relationship seems to stand hard against the changing global conditions by virtue of its oil-diplomacy and Islamic moorings; but, of late, especially in post-communist Afghanistan, the role of Saudi Arabia seems to have been largely affected by the prevailing international, regional and national situations where major powers are actively playing a key role. Given such a situation, the author contends that Saudi Arabia's Afghan policy is in poor shape and requires a careful re-envisioning along the lines of Islam, economics and security.

The Shanghai Cooperation Organisation—comprising Russia, China, Kazakhstan, Kyrgyzstan, Tajikistan, and Uzbekistan—some observers believe has ambitions to be a regional counterpoint to NATO. P. Krishna Mohan Reddy in his article titled *Afghanistan's Political Future and the Shanghai Cooperation Organisation* interestingly depicts the larger geostrategic interests of the great powers namely China, Russia and the US through a critical analysis of the relationship between Afghanistan and the Shanghai Cooperation Organisation. The SCO, which is primarily driven by China and Russia, aims not only to balance but even counter the American influence not only in terms of NATO in the Eurasian region but also in Afghanistan. The Bonn Conferences held between 2001 and 2011 had been significant in a way, because it eventually marked the increasing dependence of Afghanistan on the SCO for political, economic, and strategic benefits in the future relegating the sole dependence on US. The author thus tries to draw a scenario whereby during the post-NATO withdrawal period, both Russia and China will have a meaningful role to play.

India is an important regional power and India's extensive economic activity and investments in Afghanistan have played an important role in helping the government of Afghanistan in the post-2001 period. Yow Peter Raiphea in his paper *India in Afghanistan: The Saga of India's Role in Afghanistan's Political Future* attempts to examine the role of India in Afghanistan's reconstruction and developmental activities. He explains why India should continue helping Afghanistan towards a peaceful, prosperous and stable democratic country. In doing so the author puts forth the various options that India has with respect to Afghanistan from a geostrategic perspective. He further reinforces the need for understanding the unique socio-political setting of Afghan society and establishing contacts with important domestic players in the country.

By highlighting the broad features of a parliamentary system which pre-empts cooperation and coordination among the three branches of the government, Mohammad Ashraf Rasooli in his research note argues that it as an apt system for Afghanistan over the presidential system which can bring about the much desired sovereignty to the people. In his note titled *Parliamentary System for Afghanistan: Advantages and Disadvantages* Rasooli explains how the new political regime in Afghanistan combines the major characteristics of both parliamentary and presidential system of government. Decrying absolute separation of power as practically unrealisable, the author calls for an arrangement of partial separation of powers under a parliamentary system which would prevent centralisation of power or authoritarian overtures of different institutions and promote rule of law and thereby help the practice of democracy in Afghan society.

By drawing instances from the various European countries which restored neutrality through no common rules and ways, A. N. Medvedev flagged some of the key prerequisites for permanent neutrality of Afghanistan in his research note entitled *Neutrality as Institution of International Law: The Case of Afghanistan* and extensively deals with the need for Afghanistan to restore its status of permanent neutrality in the region. In doing so, he carefully identifies the various domestic and international pre-determinants for ensuring neutrality in the country and thereby maps the geopolitical landscape of the region at large. Increasing inter-regional trade and cooperation in the region can act as a positive change that can pull the war-torn country out from its stigma of being the centre of insecurity for the last thirty years. Sreemati Ganguli in her article titled *Silk Road Comes to Afghanistan Again* exemplifies the geostrategic significance of Afghanistan located along the ancient Silk Road that stretched from China to the Mediterranean through India and today's Central Asia. Through an annotation of the various Silk Road initiatives that have been undertaken since 2001, the author tries to show the way Afghanistan can act as a vital node between South and Central Asia. Ganguly's research note in a way highlights Afghanistan's enduring toils in the field of trade and connectivity.

A crucial issue in the post-2014 dynamic in Afghanistan is the preparedness of its security forces after the international withdrawal. Abdul

Hadi Khalid in his article *Withdrawal of Foreign Troops from Afghanistan and Preparedness of Its Security Forces* talks about how the security transition in Afghanistan and the withdrawal of the foreign troops from the country forms a crucial part of the US security strategy in Afghanistan. By carefully mapping the various geostrategical dynamics that are at play, the author lists four probable scenarios that are likely to prevail in post-2014 Afghanistan. Abdul Hadi's article, in a sense, lays down a critical road map of the future of Afghanistan in post-US withdrawal situation. Thus the trends and uncertainties of Afghanistan have been highlighted through the various papers in this volume. Some also come in the form of recommendations to the problems in order to counter any possible political deadlock. The identification of a common framework for cooperation on Afghanistan and connectivity at various levels remain imperative to avoid any political impasse. The voices from within Afghanistan and the region help understand the varying nuances of the Afghan situation.

Abbreviations

ADB	Asian Development Bank
AIG	Afghan Interim Government
ANA	Afghan National Army
ANDS	Afghanistan National Development Strategy
ANIM	Afghanistan National Institute of Music
ANP	Afghan National Police
ANSF	Afghan National Security Force
ASEAN	Association of Southeast Asian Nations
AWEC	Afghan Women's Education Centre
AWN	Afghan Women's Network
BRO	Border Roads Organisation
CAR	Central Asian Republic
CAREC–ADB	Central Asia Regional Economic Cooperation–Asian Development Bank
CC	Cooperative Council
CCA	Constitutional Commission of Afghanistan
CDC	Centre for Disease Control and Prevention
CEDAW	Convention on the Elimination of all Forms of Discrimination Against Women
CIA	Central Intelligence Agency
CIS	Commonwealth of Independent States
CJCS	Chairman of Joint Chiefs of Staff
CNPC	China National Petroleum Corporation
CSTO	Collective Security Treaty Organisation
DEA	Drug Enforcement Agency
DFID	Department for International Development
DOD	Department of Defence
ECO	Economic Cooperation Organisation
EU	European Union
FATA	Federally Administered Tribal Areas
FFP	Fund For Peace
FSI	Failed States Index
FTO	Foreign Terrorist Organisation

GCC	Gulf Cooperation Council
GDP	Gross Domestic Product
HuA	Harkat-Ul-Ansar
HUJI	Harkat-ul-Jihad-al-Islami
HuM	Harkat-Ul-Mujahideen
IBL	Institutionalisation Before Liberalisation
IBRD	International Bank for Reconstruction and Development
ICCR	Indian Council for Cultural Relations
IDB	Islamic Development Bank
IDLG	Independent Directorate of Local Governance
IED	Improvised Explosive Device
IMF	International Monetary Fund
INA	Immigration and Naturalisation Act
ISAF	International Security Assistance Force
ISI	Inter-Services Intelligence
ITPF	Indo-Tibetan Police Force
IWA	Integrity Watch Afghanistan
JC	Judicial Commission
KGB	*Komitet Gosudarstvennoy Bezopasnosti*
KhAD	Khadamat-e Aetela'at-e Dawlati
LeT	Lashkar-e-Taiba
MCC	Metallurgical Corporation of China
MFA	Ministry of Foreign Affairs
MMR	Maternal Mortality Rate
MoWA	Ministry of Women's Affairs
MSR	Modern Silk Road
NAM	Non-Aligned Movement
NAPWA	National Action Plan for Women of Afghanistan
NATO	North Atlantic Treaty Organisation
NDS	National Directorate of Security
NGO	Non-governmental Organisation
NIE	National Intelligence Estimate
NSP	National Solidarity Programme
NWFP	North-West Frontier Province
OEF	Operation Enduring Freedom
OIC	Organisation of Islamic Cooperation
OSCE	Organisation for Security and Cooperation in Europe
PC	Provincial Council
PDPA	People's Democratic Party of Afghanistan
PRC	People's Republic of China

PRT	Provincial Reconstruction Team
R&AW	Research and Analysis Wing
SAARC	South Asian Association for Regional Cooperation
SCO	Shanghai Cooperation Organisation
SDGT	Specially Designated Global Terrorists
SOF	Special Operations Forces
TIP	Turkistan Islamic Party
TTP	Tehrik-e-Taliban Pakistan
UAE	United Arab Emirates
UK	United Kingdom
UN	United Nations
UNAMA	United Nations Assistance Mission in Afghanistan
UNDP	United Nations Development Programme
UNGA	United Nations General Assembly
UNICEF	United Nations International Children's Emergency Fund
UNIFEM	United Nations Development Fund for Women
UNOCAL	Union Oil Company of California
UNODC	United Nations Office on Drugs and Crime
UNSC	United Nations Security Council
US	United States
USAID	United States Agency for International Development
USFOR-A	United States Forces Afghanistan
XUAR	Xinjiang Uyghur Autonomous Region

1. Understanding the Aberration of the Liberal Ontology of International State-Building

Zubair Popalzai

The Failed State Syndrome

From Afghanistan to Zimbabwe, the area covering some 50 weak or failing states, which according to some commentators[1] are home to "two billion" disenfranchised people, is seen to be at the heart of the entire complex of global problems today. International state-building, which seems to be centred on building the institutional capacity of the weak or failed states[2] to enhance their domestic legitimacy and international sovereignty and thus enable them to overcome their weakness or failure, is now seen as key to addressing the management of global commons, the global challenges of poverty, insecurity, refugees and HIV/AIDS among other issues, which arguably emanate from failing or failed states. In no fewer than 10 proposed Congressional bills and various reports of the State Department Office, the United States (US) deals with the subject.[3] It has become the central theme in Western foreign policy discourses and the focus seems to be, and will remain, on building states, at least in theory.

From Liberalism to Neo-Liberal Functionalism

Contrary to our understanding of nation-states as sovereign political entities which do not require the stamp of international approval, which are built on domestic consensus and enjoy popular legitimacy, international state-building approaches today framed within the notions of development, democracy and international security concerns are a shift away from the liberal ontology towards a neo-liberal post-representational framework. Instead of being, as it was and should be, a liberal citizen-centred agenda, international state-building, which often comes in the form of external intervention, is an imposition of the normative vision of good state. It internationalises domestic politics in a way which legitimises the entire enterprise as a project independent of representational forces in society through the focus on formal principles of administrative governance and not on political or legal justifications.

Since sovereignty is an attribute of statehood, current state-building frameworks, which use this concept to measure state weakness and failure, operate on the assumption that providing support to the functional capacities of the state will provide answers to state weakness or failure and thus enhance state sovereignty. State failure seems largely to be understood as failing to meet one's national and international obligations defined in a set number of ways. The goal of much of the current state-building theory and practice is, therefore, not to build states as we know them traditionally—independent and self-governing—but rather to build the state's functional capacity and enhance its sense of responsibility.

From this point forwards, I will take a look at some of the definitions of weak, failed and collapsed states. A succinct literature review will follow to locate my argument. I will then discuss how present-day international state-building discourses revolve around new definitions and understandings of the key attribute of state-hood, sovereignty. I will explain that sovereignty is no longer seen as an indivisible right but rather as capacity and responsibility. I will conclude with some practical recommendations.

Weak, Failed and Collapsed States

State weakness, failure, and collapse have been defined in a number of ways which are often overlapping and controversial. A state can be defined as weak when it lacks the "capacities to penetrate society, regulate social relationships, extract resources, and appropriate or use resources in determined ways."[4] Where these capacities are high, states are, in Mann's terms, possessed of "infrastructural power."[5] Weak states, which lack this infrastructural power, are rather based on despotic power as state officials centralise, or try to centralise, decision-making rather than embed it in society.[6] State failure, on the other hand, is difficult to define authoritatively and the distinctions drawn by scholars between state weakness and failure are controversial at best because the difference between a weak state and a failed state can be eroded by time and practice.[7] The Crisis State Research Centre defines state failure as "a condition of 'state collapse'"—for example, a state that can no longer perform its basic security and development functions and that has no effective control over its territory and borders.[8] In a failed state, "the structure, authority (legitimate power), law and political order have fallen apart and must be reconstituted in some form, old or new."[9] Rotberg notes that, in failed states, "ruling cadres increasingly oppress, extort, and harass the majority of their own compatriots while privileging a more narrowly based party, clan, or sect."[10] Armstrong and Rubin conceptualises state failure as "the transformation of public power into privately held and often fragmented power" although "sometimes individuals within a regime fragment and disperse power to weaken resistance to their regime and entrench themselves."[11] At the other spectrum, commentators like John Warnock are of the view that the concepts of "rogue" and "failed" states in the British and American foreign policy have served as instrumental tools to intervene in the internal affairs of weaker countries unilaterally for self-serving purposes through regional organisations such as the North Atlantic Treaty Organisation (NATO) and international organisations such as the United Nations (UN).[12] From Warnock's point of view, a '"successful"' state in the eyes of Western powers would be one with a "liberal democratic government, a high standard of living and a free market economy and more or less aligned with the United States."[13] A collapsed state is a "rare and extreme version of a failed state" where "the structure, authority (legitimate power), law and political order have fallen apart and must be reconstituted in some form, old or new."[14]

The Sovereignty Vacuum

International state-building seems to have become a policy solution to the problem of the functional sovereignty of the state also described as the "creeping sovereignty gap."[15] The old form of state sovereignty—indivisible right—is seen as "a licence for arbitrary power"[16] and the focus is on sharing sovereignty to perform functions in weak, failing or failed states. Ghani and Lockhart, for example, suggest that "double compacts" be used as a mechanism between the international community and the national governments of failing countries for organising aid and other interventions. They propose that a sovereignty index to measure state effectiveness should be compiled on an annual basis allowing the UN and the World Bank to directly intervene should a state fail to fulfil the requirements of a function.[17] In fact, Fund for Peace (FFP) has already set up a Failed States Index (FSI) running for the ninth year. Every June, it compiles a list of states judged to be "failed" and the judgements are based on 100 variables. Zooming in on Somalia and Afghanistan, Englehart also suggests that intervening in the name of democracy is inadequate if the crisis lies with the state's institutions and that a minimally functioning state is required for the promotion of democracy to bear fruit.[18] Krasner[19] and Fearon and Laitin[20] also argue for the internationalisation of sovereign state functions to bridge the gap between the functional demands considered necessary and weak, or absent, state capacity. The functionalist and institutionalist approach to international state-building is probably best articulated in Roland Paris' influential Institutionalisation before Liberalisation (IBL) thesis.[21]

This framework, which is premised on redefining sovereignty, building capacity and partnership, is such that it prevents the establishment of strong relations between the state and society. The state, which is the object of intervention, needs to administer good governance, framework of rule of law and so on instead of pursuing political or independent goals. The institutions of the state seem to be little different from local administrative bodies, conduits of policy, rather than autonomous policymaking units. International state-building approaches seem to overshadow individual freedoms inherited by birth and transform politicians largely from representatives of their constituents into individuals performing administrative tasks or, even worse, unable to do anything. While government officials blame international actors for limiting their autonomy in national policymaking and thus their ability to deliver services, international actors cite corruption and the lack of capacity of the government as a reason for the shortcomings and failures of the project. Local level state authorities blame national level authorities whereas national level authorities shift the blame to international actors. Neither local actors nor external state-builders seem to be accountable to the citizenry, who seem to have assumed the role of helpless monitors of state policies instead of being active participants in policy discussions and policymaking processes. They are the mere recipients of international generosity.

The focus on institutions and capacity-building is both pragmatic and an apologia for the limits of the ability to build states. It is pragmatic because transferring technical skills on how to operate a central banking system, for example, is arguably easier and manageable than building an education system or developing the media sector which involve cultural sensitivities. It is an apologia because institutionalism constructs the problem in a specific way and locates the solutions as out of the hands of external actors or the world market. It roots the problem in the institutions and culture of the state being built.

Sovereignty as Responsibility

Responsibility, the first key concept in the state-building discourse, presents sovereignty as a product of an external framework of institutional regulation. Sovereignty is not seen as autonomy because the rights of sovereignty today are conditional and its responsibilities are seen to be flexibly constructed. Sovereignty as responsibility marks the internationalisation of sovereignty and constructs the legitimacy of external judgement as to whether these responsibilities are met. As such, sovereignty is now an attribute, marking or designating inequality and inverting the liberal rights framing of equality. It is no longer an attribute that separates a state as autonomous or independent and is an aberration from its traditional liberal meaning. Instead, it is founded on external intervention and regulation.

International state-building enables the exercise of external influence in a manner to which the traditional understanding of sovereignty as absolute right and freedom is no longer a barrier. As the elites of the state and the international community, including the international financial institutions, enter into "partnerships" or tacitly share "sovereignty"—the latter is redefined from an indivisible right and freedom to capacity-building to deliver services and to a responsibility to accept policy options put forward by the Western states. As the rhetoric of partnership makes every domestic and international actor a stakeholder, international state-building becomes a new framework for the internationalisation of the domestic sphere at all levels of government.

Contrary to earlier forms of governance which allowed governments to make decisions at their own discretion, the redefinition of sovereignty as responsibility, i.e., having the responsibilities of sovereignty rather than its political rights, undermines state legitimacy in the eyes of the citizenry and has implications for major national policy processes. The legitimacy of the state in question is often associated with its willingness and ability to promote Western-style democracy and comply with international diktats or risk being subjected to selection bias. Of course, the convenient categorisations of rogue or failed state do not apply to certain states like Saudi Arabia, for example, which have mutually beneficial economic ties with major Western countries. In weak states like Afghanistan, sovereignty as responsibility results largely in a donor-client relationship which excludes the citizenry and renders the state unable to overcome dissent. As the state's domestic policymaking realm is internationalised while the state itself is held responsible for weaknesses and failures, the citizenry grow more disenfranchised and withdraw their support for the state. The experience of nation-building in post-World War II Europe and Japan, for example, demonstrates that nation-building based on the consent of citizens and legitimacy of rules and policies that the citizens themselves make, is more likely to be enduring than the ones imposed by force or through personalities even if it is in the form of "empowering" or "freeing." The problem becomes worse when civil and political structures of the state being built are bypassed by duplicative and parallel structures set up by intervening countries.[22]

Sovereignty as Capacity

Sovereignty as capacity is the second key concept in international state-building discourses today. This concept suggests that if state capacity is built, its sovereignty will be enhanced. Afghanistan is a good example. The frameworks of intervention and regulation were premised on the ideas of institutional and societal capacity-building and empowerment to build the sovereignty of the Afghan state, i.e., building its functional capacity. Once a confused effort at state-building was initiated, it interpreted the economic, social and political problems of state-building in bureaucratic and administrative terms, amenable to Western technical assistance. It was assumed that the political landscape would normalise itself automatically if the focus remained on functional capacity-building.

Technical assistance, which often comes up as the ugly face of the developed world to the underdeveloped world, has reportedly accounted for almost 40 per cent of the development assistance received by Afghanistan. International technical cooperation has emerged as the predominant form of assistance, the bulk of which has made use of expatriate expertise largely in an unsustainable fashion. Hundreds of international consultants, many of whom had no knowledge of the workings of the Afghan government or the necessary skills and expertise, have been brought into Afghanistan to train and coach their local replacements while performing line functions. In many cases, the consultants are preoccupied with line responsibilities while the training and development of Afghan capacities is minimal or non-existent. Most veteran Afghan civil servants cannot speak the English language to communicate with their mentors or effectively operate modern equipment like computers. Only a small percentage of young Afghans working for international organisations such as the UN and non-governmental organisations (NGOs) and studying at universities in other countries have benefitted to some extent. Even in their case, the higher salaries and benefits offered by donors have drawn Afghan nationals away from the government and bid up the cost of scarce domestic talent, thus creating a parallel bureaucracy of poor cousin versus the rich cousin working for $ 50 to $ 250 and $ 700 to $ 5,000 dollars or more respectively, and with it mutual resentment. Afghanistan reportedly had 240,000 civil servants in 2001. By 2004, all the talented ones had left to become drivers for multilateral organisations and NGOs which paid salaries several times greater than their government salaries.

A common view is that much of the technical assistance is not coordinated with the Afghan government and is "poorly coordinated among the donors themselves."[23] As Michailof says, "the widespread use of uncoordinated and non-strategically targeted technical assistance is neither fiscally nor politically sustainable."[24] A major World Bank review concluded that "technical assistance tends to be donor-driven and peppered around at high cost with little effective involvement from national decision makers and only marginal impact in terms of lasting capacity-building."[25] Of all technical assistance to Afghanistan, which accounts for a quarter of all official development assistance to the country, only 37 per cent was provided through coordinated programmes.[26] Sometimes, consultants working in one ministry are funded by, and accountable to, several different donors.

Where there is arguably no capacity, state functions are contracted out to international firms,[27] which weaken the corresponding branches of the state whose legitimacy is crucial to its functioning. The security sector is a major example. Whereas the US-led coalition forces rebuilt private militias commanded by local commanders to help fight the remnants of the Taliban and Al Qaeda (during the early years of the military intervention) and protect supply convoys and military bases, almost all major international organisations and foreign embassies rely on the security services provided by private security companies, which are often the same former militia fighters.

International state-building on the cheap or "Empire Lite," as Ignatieff calls it,[28] combined with the focus on functional capacity-building reduces the entire approach into a patronising exercise that ends up failing to build capacity or sovereignty. As such, it is a "therapeutic" approach which does not result in building sovereign states but rather in what Chandler calls "phantom states" whose governing institutions may have extensive foreign support but lack social and political legitimacy.[29] For Chandler, whose arguments inform this article, the transformation of the institution of sovereignty has blurred the division between "domestic government and international governance" and the influence of donors and international financial institutions have been formally distanced from responsibility. "Yet, the shell of sovereignty, the state form, especially international legal sovereignty, formal independence in international law is stressed."[30] As he puts it, "the problematic of state-building is therefore that of how Western governments, policymakers and civil society activists can resolve the wide-ranging problems facing citizens of governments of the non-Western world."[31] However, since international state-builders see the state as both an object of intervention and the subject of its own transformation, the burden of weakness (of the Afghan security forces, for example) or failure is shifted on the locals only.

Recommendations

If state-building can become more than a framework for the rationalisation of international interventionist policies and if it can genuinely be a process for building states capable of governing themselves and making autonomous decisions, international state-builders will have to subject their policies to revision and their assumptions to questioning. States need more autonomy to play an interventionist role to help establish a framework for development, overcome conflict and legitimise them. The contradictory effects of international state-building, as a framework, are an aberration from liberal ontology and need to be recognised and reversed.

The language of partnership to build capacity to deliver services and thus enhance legitimacy and sovereignty of the state is abstract and, in fact, a reproduction of the same set of challenges. The concept of partnership should mean mutual accountability and the establishment of working relations based on respect, fulfilment of commitments, transparency of development objectives, and accountability for decisions, actions and results. Inequality of power relations among states is a fact, but it should not result in a patronising relationship between powerful Western actors and states subjected to reconstruction. It is interesting that the more unequal the partners, the more notions of partnership and equality are stressed, but the true meaning of partnerships, as they stand today, can be understood "in the way decisions are made, responsibilities are reported and money is channelled, spent and accounted for throughout the aid system down to the community."[32]

National leaders and international state-builders should share risks and responsibilities of state-building failure. Effective partnership and mutual accountability is about much more than just sharing sovereignty and producing reports; it is also about partnerships in development, acting on promises, transparency, and making citizens producers of policy, not its monitors or, even worse, its recipients. When there is no shared vision among the different parties about how responsibilities can become collective accountability, it is difficult to move beyond the establishment of purely technical mechanisms to a form of accountability that is "felt."[33] Recasting relationships in these terms may lead to revising policies on conditionality, including giving greater responsibility to the state in question in defining conditions and making decisions, and in new ways in which to manage and resolve disputes. Only then can a semblance of partnership be created as the state's ability to predict aid flows and plan and prioritise on the basis of unique contextual needs will increase.

It is imperative for international actors to understand the specific dynamics of state-building, and to integrate the broader social and political context in programme design. International actors should only seek to help develop nationally driven strategies and not dominate them or be overly prescriptive about policies. Good practices for mutual accountability can include methods such as direct support to the national budget, aligning donor interests with that of the government, enabling the government to prioritise and predict donor support for its priority programmes, developing indicators to measure value for money in development aid and genuinely enabling the citizenry to participate in setting priorities, making decisions and holding the government and donors to account. Domestic political agendas in foreign countries do not always go well with what would be the best practice, but donors must recognise that undermining budgetary processes through service-delivery decisions, poor coordination, off-budget financing and administrative overheads, undermines the social contract between the state and the citizenry. It is also necessary to give the state space to establish itself and to ensure that local ownership leads to locally grown institutions. A state's ability to govern independently will enable it to establish international relations on the basis of its national interests and exercise its sovereignty as its indivisible right.

Notes

1. Ashraf Ghani and Clare Lockhart, *Fixing Failed States: A New Framework for Fixing a Fractured World* (New York: Oxford University Press, 2008), p. 3.
2. See Call and Cousens, "Ending Wars and Building Peace: International Responses to War-Torn Societies," *International Studies Perspectives,* 1-21 (9), 2008, p. 4; and Francis Fukuyama, *State-building: Governance and World Order in the 21st Century* (New York: Cornell University Press, 2004), p. 55.
3. Stuart E. Eizenstat, John Edward Porter and Jeremy M. Weinstein, "Rebuilding Weak States," *Foreign Affairs*, 84 (1), p. 134.
4. Migdal S. Joel, *Strong Societies and Weak States: State-Society Relations and State Capabilities in the Third World* (Princeton and New Jersey: Princeton University Press, 1988), p. 4.
5. Michael Mann, *The Sources of Social Power: A History of Power from Beginning to AD 1760,* vol. I (Cambridge: Cambridge University Press, 1986), pp. 450-99.
6. Aidan Hehir and Neil Robinson (eds.), *State-Building: Theory and Practice* (London and New York: Routledge, 2007), p. 4.
7. Read, for example, Hehir and Robinson, 2007.
8. Crisis State Research Centre, "Crisis, Fragile and Failed States: Definitions used by the CSRC," Crisis States Workshop, London, March 2006.
9. I. William Zartman, "Introduction: Posing the Problem of State Collapse," in I. W. Zartman, (ed.), *Collapsed States: The Disintegration and Restoration of Legitimate Authority* (Boulder: Lynne Rienner Publishers, 1995), p. 1.
10. Robert I. Rotberg (ed.), *State Failure and State Weakness in a Time of Terror* (Washington DC: Brookings Institution Press, 2003), p. 6.

11. Andrea Armstrong and Barnett R. Rubin, "The Great Lakes and South Central Asia" in Simon Chesterman, Michael Ignatieff, and Ramesh Chandra Thakur (eds.), *Making States Work: State Failure and the Crisis of Governance* (Tokyo: United Nations University Press, 2005), p. 83.
12. John W. Warnock, *Creating a Failed State: The US and Canada in Afghanistan* (Winnipeg: Fernwood Publishing, 2008), pp. 22-23.
13. Warnock, *Creating a Failed State*, 2008, p. 24.
14. Zartman, "Introduction: Posing the Problem of State Collapse," 1995, p. 1.
15. See, for example, Ashraf Ghani, Clare Lockhart and Michael Carnahan, "Closing the Sovereignty Gap: An Approach to State-Building," UK Overseas Development Institute Working Paper, London, September 2005.
16. Ashraf Ghani and Clare Lockhart, no. 1, p. 10.
17. Ibid., p. 229.
18. Neil A. Englehart, "In Defense of State Building: States, Rights, and Justice," *Dissent*, 4 (213), 2003, pp. 18-22.
19. Stephen D. Krasner, "Sharing Sovereignty: New Institutions for Collapsed and Failing States," *International Security*, 29 (2), Spring 2004, pp. 5-43.
20. James D. Fearon and David D. Laitin, "Neotrusteeship and the Problem of Weak States," *International Security*, 28 (4), Spring 2004, pp. 5-43.
21. Roland Paris, *At War's End: Building Peace after Civil Conflict* (Cambridge: Cambridge University Press, 2004).
22. Ashraf Ghani and Clare Lockhart, no. 1, p. 30.
23. 2006 Survey on Monitoring the Paris Declaration: Afghanistan, OECD, p. 6.
24. Serge Michailof, "Fixing Failed States: An Unconventional Agenda Based on Lessons Learned from the Afghan Fiasco," Discussion Paper prepared for the "Failed States Symposium," University of La Verne College of Law, April 15-17, 2010, p. 10.
25. "Review of Technical Assistance and Capacity-Building in Afghanistan," Discussion Paper for the Afghanistan Development Forum, World Bank, April 26, 2007, p. 1.
26. "Survey on Monitoring the Paris Declaration: Afghanistan," OECD, 2006, p. 5.
27. For example, central procurement services in Afghanistan were contracted out to Bearing Point, Crown Agents (UK) and others.
28. Michael Ignatieff, *Empire Lite: Nation Building in Bosnia, Kosovo, Afghanistan* (London: Vintage Books, 2003), p. 126.
29. David Chandler, *Empire in Denial: The Politics of State-Building* (London: Pluto, 2006), p. 9.
30. Ibid., p. 10.
31. Ibid., p. 5.
32. Bianca Suyama, *Mutual Accountability in Aid Relationships: Making Aid Work for the Poor* (London: Care International, 2008), p. 2.
33. Ronald E. Fry, "Accountability in Organisational Life: Problem or Opportunity for Nonprofits?" *Nonprofit Management and Leadership*, 6 (2), 1995, pp. 181-95.

2. Afghanistan's Ethno-Political Challenges: A Case for Federal Arrangements[1]

Raghav Sharma

> The painful lesson of Afghanistan's history has been that strong centralised government in any form will only lead to the hegemony by one group, whether ethnic, linguistic or religious, and abuse by the ruling group at the expense of justice for all citizens of Afghanistan.[2]
>
> Many who know the ground reality in Afghanistan would agree that federalism is not only unnecessary under the circumstances, but it would also serve as a recipe for deeper divisions among the diverse ethnic groups in Afghanistan and would lead to a subsequent disintegration of the country.[3]

Introduction

Notwithstanding passionate and often diametrically opposed views which characterised much of the debate regarding the institutional mold in which a Post-Taliban Afghan state should be cast, Article 1 of the Afghan Constitution adopted in 2004—emphatically endorsed by the United States (US), the world's largest federal democracy—declared: "Afghanistan shall be an Islamic Republic, independent, unitary and indivisible state."[4] Fears of political-geographical fragmentation engendered by civil war and acute anxiety to rein in regional political-military power holders, so as to foreclose interference by neighbouring countries, coupled with prevailing conventional wisdom that regards the centralised state as the guarantor of unity and stability, helped to entrench the idea of a unitary state in a heterogeneous society constitutionally.

The reign of Amir Abdur Rahman Khan signifies perhaps the first violent rupture with Afghanistan's traditional political culture, characterised until the 1850s by a considerable measure of local autonomy.[5] Abdur Rehman achieved a high degree of political unification and administrative centralisation. But all that came at a high cost, vividly captured in a pointed observation of Kashimbekov:

> The military occupation of Uzbek populated lands of today's Afghanistan by Afghan troops, the atrocities committed by the

> conquerors, led not only to passive resistance of the local population (not just Uzbeks, but also Turkmens and Tajiks) … but also numerous attempts at rebellions whose aim was to get rid of the enslavers' yoke through armed struggle.[6]

Thus, the excessive force required to put in place and defend an excessively centralised system marked a radical departure from established traditions. Regions became more vulnerable and their relative insulation from political collapse at the centre was steadily eroded.[7] The sharp memory of violence accompanying this process coupled with the general legacy of violence, disruption and breakdown wrought by the civil war, colours much of the subsequent socio-political discourse.

Today, a decade after the US-led military intervention in 2001 and eight years since the adoption of a new Constitution in 2004, Afghanistan continues to wrestle with challenges it had hoped to swiftly master through a centralised state. Worse, it is wracked by an insurgency, made more potent by a growing governance deficit. Commenting on the ineptness of an excessively centralised system,[8] a recent study to assess the state of local governance observed: "Development planning and budgeting at the provincial level is dysfunctional. This is largely a result of the highly centralised nature of these processes, which leaves provincial administrations unable to make development decisions in line with local needs."[9] Poor delivery of services is grimly borne out in the detail: "Last year the execution rate was 37 per cent for public services."[10]

Governance deficits assume heightened significance in an environment characterised by growing insecurity and political uncertainty. They serve to rekindle socio-political polarisation primarily along ethnic lines. Recent conflicts and developments are perceived in reference to a checkered historical canvas of varied conflicts and distrusts. Hence, the strong sense in contemporary discourse that existing ethnic cleavages so violently aggravated in recent years during the civil war, represent an ancient order of things in Afghanistan. Consider in this context the statement of Fauzia Kufi, Member of Parliament, concerning ethnicity and conflict:

> I am surprised when people think it [ethnicity] is an issue that has emerged in the last thirty years. It [ethnicity] goes back to the period of the monarchy. Look at who killed King Nadir Shah? It was a Hazara student from Habibia High school. What made him kill? It was a result of the fact that the other ethnic groups did not have the opportunity to take "revenge" or challenge in any way those who ruled over them … when groups are

ruled exclusively by certain individuals, or other groups, then everybody would like to struggle for power.[11]

Thus, for Kufi, ethnic fault lines have been part of Afghan socio-political life long before the recent civil war but they remained dormant because of an absence of opportunity for political assertion. It is noteworthy that in all previous power struggles the Tajiks and Ghilzai Pashtuns usually aligned themselves with one of the contenders for power, i.e., Durrani Pashtuns. The only notable exception to this was the eight-month rule of Habibullah Kalakani, who installed himself as Amir following the overthrow of Amanullah Khan. Two points need to be taken note of here: first, Habibullah couched his rule and opposition to Amanullah's reforms in religious and not ethnic terms. He directed his appeal to, and enlisted the support of, notables in the religious clergy such as Hazrat of Shor Bazaar, head of the Mujadidi family and the Naqshbandiya sufi order. All of them were opposed to Amanullah's reforms.[12] Habibullah skilfully played upon tribal cleavages between the Ghilzai's and Durrani Pashtuns.[13] The nature of these political alignments and realignments centred around Islam and its socio-political formations. The need is to critically examine the factors that allowed and aided transformation of the conflict fault line predominantly along an ethnic axis.

Ironically, the Afghan jihad with Islam as its rallying cry, after realising two of its primary objectives—ousting the Soviets from Afghanistan and Dr. Najibullah's government—very soon paved the way for ethnicity to supplant Islam. Rangin Dafdar Spanta's pointed observation in this context merits consideration: "… as everyone was Muslim, Islam lost its relevance and ethnicity gained prominence as a tool to gain access to power."[14] The linguistic cleavage between Dari and Pashto too could not serve as a rallying point either, since Dari in large measure served as a medium of communication across ethnicities; it is for instance the mother tongue of Hazara ethnicity.

As the power sharing agreement brokered by Rawalpindi unravelled, an agonising period of civil war followed and various Mujahideen factions splintered along ethnic lines. Thus unfolded the subtle transformations in the fault line of conflict from one centred on ideology (Islam) to ethnicity. Spanta aptly draws attention to the reason for the potency of ethnicity as a powerful mobilising tool. But along with that must be borne in mind the historical-cultural frame in which the elite operate. It sets the limits within which ethnicity can be deployed and mobilisation around it can occur. In the Afghan case, ethnicity was grafted onto both the real and the perceived sense of denial-deprivation and it resonated as a mobilisational strategy and also helped to rekindle traces of long past internal socio-political tensions and conflicts.

It would be pertinent at this point to draw attention to the fact that it was not a power struggle *per se* that was new to Afghanistan. The significant detail is that the power struggle came to be underpinned by a new kind of dynamics, engendered by the sheer scale and intensity of violence and external involvement on an unprecedented scale. Ordinary Afghans were drawn into protracted violence on a scale never before possible or thinkable. For the first time in over 200 years, the struggle for power involved the non-Durrani and non-Pashtun elite. Never before in Afghanistan's history of over 200 years had there been an explicit challenge to the exclusive legitimacy of the Durrani elite who regarded their right to rule as preordained.

The outbreak of civil war following the collapse of Dr. Najibullah's regime in April 1992 became the opportune moment when means and opportunity for renegotiating with the implicitly established socio-political contract converged. It was characterised by an unofficial hierarchy of sorts in which Pashtuns, more specifically the Durrani Pashtuns, came to be at the top. The reinstatement of the old order was challenged in the light of the radically altered circumstances. The political assertion of ethnicity was reinforced by gradual polarisation in the social support base of various Mujahideen parties. It was accompanied by an experience of autonomy of the kind unknown since the mid-nineteenth century and the perception of empowerment and emancipation that it generated. All this was accompanied by the arming of local populations on an unprecedented scale. Perhaps the most notable and striking case in this context concerns the traditionally non-arms bearing groups like the Uzbeks and Hazaras.

Dramatic transformations in the socio-political dynamic, briefly dwelt upon above, altered perceptions regarding as to who possesses the legitimacy to rule, as well as how such rule is to be exercised, necessitate a need to revisit notions regarding the historically unitary-centralised nature of the Afghan state. Moreover, the present over-centralised system is feeding the crisis of legitimacy further accentuated by the growing governance deficit and creating a niche for sharpening of ethnic cleavages. The argument that this chapter seeks to state in the section that follows is that federal institutional arrangements, as opposed to mere decentralisation within a unitary framework, provides a more viable institutional mechanism to manage and negotiate the challenges thrown up by the imperative need of a modern state in a heterogeneous social setting.

Before stating the case for federalism[15] it would be useful to briefly spell out what is intended and meant by the term "federalism." First of all, there is no clear consensus on the definition of federalism.[16] For our purpose, Will Kymlicka's definition succinctly marks the basics of of federalism:

> ... A political system which includes a constitutionally entrenched system of the division of powers between a central government and two or more sub-units, defined on a territorial basis, such that each level of government has sovereign authority over certain issues.[17]

Such fundamental underpinnings in federal arrangements are usually protected through additional measures, namely, special procedures to amend the written Constitution embodying federal features (these can range from requiring a simple majority as in Canada and Switzerland to a special majority in both legislative chambers as is the case in India, the US and Malaysia, in addition to ratification of amendments by a majority or all constituent units, or referendums) and an independent constitutional or Supreme Court to resolve disputes that may arise.[18]

The primary concern of the chapter is to evaluate the potential of federal arrangements for providing institutional frames for negotiating critical challenges in a heterogeneous society severely strained by a legacy of protracted war. Kymlicka's definition is useful in that it underscores the key feature of federalism—in instructive contrast to unitary systems that may be administratively decentralised—which is characterised by constitutionally guaranteed delegation of powers to different levels of government as opposed to voluntary delegation of powers which can be revoked unilaterally.[19] Also, federalism recognises that sovereignty does not rest exclusively with the central government, but is divided between several levels and spheres of governance.[20] Third, growing recognition of the significance of local governance structures for the vitality of democratic systems could be read as an affirmation of the principles of federalism. Some of the implications of the propositions just outlined would become clear in the sections that follow.

What Federalism Can Achieve and Decentralisation Cannot

> The government, in preserving the principles of centralism, shall transfer necessary powers, in accordance with the law, to local administrations in order to accelerate and improve economic, social as well as cultural matters, and foster in developing national life.[21]
>
> (Article 137)

In the year 2005 the Afghan Government took steps to devolve certain admistrative powers to the provincial and district levels. These measures were conceived and crafted keeping in mind the unitary character and spirit of the state envisaged in the Constitution.[22] These steps were precipitated in considerable measure by the pressing need to improve the governance record, as also by a tacit recognition of the gap that persisted despite fervent proclamations of a centralised unitary state due to the sheer inability in actual practice to administer the countryside directly from Kabul.

Thus, to begin with, Provincial Councils (PCs) were established in 2005, a step viewed positively by Afghans, as it translated into enhanced accessibility to government agencies, seen increasingly as service providers. Field studies indicate a greater willingness on the part of people to contact PC members to resolve local issues in preference to members of parliament.[23] Despite that, the PCs remain extremely feeble and ineffective. The principal reason for that is to be seen in the poor constitutional placement of the PCs.[24] The financial support provided for the PCs is meagre and their role is primarily that of being an advisory and consultative body.[25] The desperate need to put some life into agencies of local governance led to the establishment of the Independent Directorate of Local Governance (IDLG) in 2007. Although set up with the intention of decentralising administration and bolstering support for the government by improving service delivery, it has in fact "resulted in increased power for the President's office"[26] as "its reporting line directly to the President's office has rendered it a highly politicised institution and its methods tend to reinforce rather than reduce central control."[27]

It is not much of a surprise then that decentralisation measures have failed to improve governance and the political system at all levels continues to be controlled by Kabul. Decentralisation evades the issue of local ownership and is devoid of financial and administrative muscle. The grave paradox in this context is that even as the President's Office garners more and more arbitrary power, it stands more vulnerable and increasingly less effective. As ever, more power is effectively concentrated in the office of the President, lack or failure of service delivery is blamed on the central government, i.e., President's Office, as it controls appointment of governors at the provincial and district levels who are entrusted with oversight of administration[28] as also the Director of the IDLG entrusted with an "important role in creating a local governance plan for Afghanistan and building legitimacy for the Afghan government at the local level."[29] Furthermore, the system is rendered fragile as the discretion exercised by the President's office in appointments has helped institutionally entrench a patronage network, tied to interests of the individual in office as opposed to the state.

Second, absolute concentration of authority in the office of the President leaves little scope for meaningful participation by the people or their representatives. It also carries far-reaching reverberations for two key processes, namely, the direction of the flow of aid for the reconstruction process and plans for reconciliaton with the Taliban. In relation to both these issues, the international community is an important actor. The peace process is perceived as not merely controlled by President Karzai, but also as reflective of a certain ethnic bias in line with the Taliban's own attitude towards the non-Pashtuns while in power and a silent expression of President Karzai's own ethnic Pashtun lineage.[30] The larger flow of international aid to insurgency wracked and predominantly Pashtun provinces in the southeast[31] has further strengthened feelings of ethnic denial and deprivation.

In critique of the international community's approach which has aggravated the state of affairs, Tom Koenings remarked that "there is a need to believe in and strengthen Afghan institutions, especially its Parliament, but the international community has no strategy for this … at the provincial level everyone talks to the Governor and not to the Provincial Councils, while at the national level there is not enough dialogue with the Parliament, reducing the importance of parliamentary institutions."[32] This growing marginalisation of the legislative pillar of the state is increasingly pitting it against the executive.[33]

Therefore, mere administrative decentralisation has had little success in addressing people's needs and creating a sense of ownership for government initiatives. The large disturbing fact is that it is alienating people and creating an atmosphere where all kinds of conflicts get easily projected as ethnic expressions. The current situation calls for an urgent need to reconfigure the current institutional framework that clearly entails looking beyond mere administrative decentralisation.

Federalism: An Institutional Mechanism to Negotiate Challenges

The failure of the state to respond to the citizen's needs and aspirations is experienced and perceived against the backdrop of the internal socio-political canvas, which lends a strong ethnic tinge in almost all responses and judgements of citizens concerning their government's performance.

> Ethnic differences [between the *khalq* and *Parcham* factions of the ruling PDPA] led to a collapse of the communist regime, after which ethnic issues emerged strongly as every ethnic group tried to become stronger, get more freedoms and gain a greater say in the decision-making process of the country. Today the most significant topic in Afghanistan's political

> and social discourse is ethnicity. Ethnic issues existed prior to the coming of the communists to power but those days there was no opportunity to address this issue and frustration in this regard always existed. When the time came many of the political demands of people got ethnicised and thus ethnic demands became political demands. Hence the issue of federalism is very important in Afghanistan today and it is the only arrangement that can address this issue.[34]
>
> Since the control of the centre has been the main cause of friction and tensions between different Regions, thereby threatening national solidarity and integrity, the distribution of functions between regions and the Centre should be reviewed and so arranged that only such subjects and functions as will engender the minimum suspicion and friction among different groups are allowed in the hands of the Federal Government.[35]

Kabul has been the repository of symbolic political legitimacy, military, administrative and financial power and hence also the focal point of struggle in the civil war. Control of Kabul was vital for acquiring political legitimacy as also negotiating a place in the new order. Virtually nothing has changed in this respect even today. Nevertheless certain altered ground realities mark significant shifts, namely, the enlarged field of political participation has fostered new notions regarding who should rule and how such rule is to be exercised; heightened expectations of the state as a service provider; longing for a share in determining policies that affect people's lives; and a strong demand for security. A response to these complex set of challenges that are crucial for establishing legitimacy of the Afghan state necessitates a need to reconfigure the present institutional mechanisms.

Federal institutional arrangements and a parliamentary form of government appear better suited to respond to the prevalent expectations and situations. The current presidential form of government vests all executive authority in the office of the president. The role of the legislature is severely circumscribed. The president can appoint two vice-presidents,[36] but they do not enjoy any substantial executive powers,[37] rendering the office largely symbolic. Furthermore, a parliamentary federal arrangement allows for meaningful participation by groups in government, not just at the regional but also at the national level. Given the immense heterogeneity of Afghan society, a parliamentary set-up will encourage political actors to broaden their appeal by moderating their agendas so as to win greater support through broader cross-ethnic coalitions. The heterogeneity of provincial composition is likely to create a fluctuating coalition of interests, ensuring thereby that no single group is completely excluded. These stands, in striking contrast to presidential forms of government, in the words of Amin Saikal and William Maley,

> … typically produce many disgruntled losers intent on challenging or undermining the victor. In addition, they can also put too much formal power in the hands of the winner, leading to personalised politics in which lesser politicians fight viciously over access to the president. Yet, paradoxically, the actual powers of the president are often less than they appear on paper, while his responsibilities are heavy and the expectations that citizens have of him are unrealistic. It is all too easy to create a job that no one could do adequately. This is precisely what has happened to President Karzai.[38]

In a parliamentary set-up, even groups that are not part of the government can have some meaningful participation as an opposition in the legislative process. It would also provide for greater legislative oversight on the executive as in a parliamentary system "the fusion of executive and legislative power in parliamentary systems is based instead on the democratic notion that by placing the executive in the legislature and making it constitutionally responsible to the legislature which itself is democratically elected, coherent but controlled and accountable federal policies will be possible."[39]

Other significant implications flow from a clear constitutionally defined and guaranteed division of powers and autonomy at the sub-national level. To begin with, such a division allows communities to exercise greater control through elected local representatives over everyday cultural, welfare and security issues, i.e., education, health services, social welfare and local policing. This places the most immediate concerns of groups, in this case groups centred around ethnic identity—culture, local security and basic services—under greater local control. That would help modulate and correct the rampant perception of deliberate denial and deprivation on the basis of ethnicity and thus strengthen their stakes in the system.

Second, a clear constitutional division of roles and powers between the different tiers of government can help improve service delivery, as that would make for greater local control over resources, planning and implementation in line with local needs. It would also pave the way for greater accountability on the part of local actors and structures, as a directly elected government will find it hard to direct all blame for poor performance on to the Centre, thus reducing the pressure on a fragile Centre. Furthermore, a directly elected provincial government can help draw in politically active actors who currently operate outside the ambit of the state's institutional structure to demonstrate their real political weight. Often such actors provide much needed basic services and resources to people in their constituencies and thereby entrench their patronage networks and local power base deeper.[40]

Third, federal arrangements allow minority groups at the national level to constitute their own government at the provincial level and administer their own affairs. Developing multiple points of access to pursue claims can help reduce feelings of exclusion amongst minority groups.[41] Moreover, federalism involves a duplication of governmental functions at the level of the constituent units of the federation. Thus, it also multiplies job opportunities in the government bureaucracy, allowing for the pursuit of claims at levels other than the central level, especially so if the government in power at the Centre is not too strongly identified with a particular group.[42] Claims made by groups or individuals by virtue of belonging to a particular group can be meaningfully addressed through provisions for access to independent courts. Such an arrangement helps deflect heat from an already fragile Centre, and thus at least partially correct perceptions of ethnic denial and deprivation.

Fourth, as the case of federal polities such as Nigeria and India demonstrate, the capitals of federated units, endowed with greater political and financial muscle, emerge as alternative urban and developmental magnets. This can help rectify problems of excessive resource concentration in one metropolis,[43] which presently finds a stark reflection in the fact that Kabul is home to 13.9 per cent of the country's total population.[44]

Fifth, since a federal arrangement would normally vest jurisdiction of the constituent units of government over natural resources such as land and water that constitute one of the most common causes of conflict, it would help check localised disputes from attaining a pan-national character. A case in point is the violent turn that disputes between Pashtun Kuchi nomads and the Hazaras have taken over conflicting claims for access to summer pastures. Though the dispute is largely localised, being most intense in the provinces of Bamian and Maidan Wardak, a sharp national focus has been imparted over such issues given the overwhelming jurisdiction enjoyed by the government in Kabul. This has served to magnify ethno-political challenges as the issue and mobilisation around it spreads outside affected areas, lucidly demonstrated by "ratio of nationwide protests, often carried out by individuals who have never seen nomads or pastures in their whole life,"[45] thus generating greater friction in an already overheated Centre.

Sixth, a division of sovereignty amongst two or more levels of government can mute the potency of ethnicity as a political weapon, as issues are likely to get framed in terms of Centre-province relations. An institutional arrangement of such a nature would thus structure incentives for provincial elite to forge coalitions across ethnic lines to bargain with the Centre. Alternatively, potential alignments among provincial elite could be triggered, pitting small units against big ones or resource-rich units against resource-poor ones, thus reducing the salience of ethnicity as the paramount fault line.

Seventh, institutional structuring of access to state power and resources under a federal arrangement will generate intra-ethnic competition in homogenous provinces, while in mixed provinces it can encourage formation of cross-ethnic political coalitions at the sub-national level.[46] These are not far-fetched possibilities given the remarkable ability displayed by the Afghan political elite over the years to cobble together such coalitions. A lucid illustration of intra-ethnic cleavages playing out can be observed in violent trends in South Afghanistan where up to 70 per cent of the violence is believed to stem from local disputes.[47] These findings in a Department for International Development (DFID) study, based on a communication with key United Nations Assistance Mission in Afghanistan (UNAMA) personnel, elaborating on the undercurrents of this violence, observes that:

> At the root of this violence are the grievances of communities or social groups over perceptions of exclusion from the district or provincial public administrations. For instance, in Kandahar, the Noorzai tribe perceives itself as being virtually excluded from government offices, which are seen to be monopolised by rivals … As a response the tribes members have frequently affiliated themselves with the Taliban and subsequently attacked government targets not because they wish to destabilise the state as a whole but press their own equitable to public resources and positions.[48]

Eighth, the heterogeneous character of a large proportion of the constituent units that make up Afghanistan[49] throws up both opportunities and challenges. The opportunities presented are twofold, namely: it can help curb the strength of ethno-national elite claiming to speak for an entire ethnic group, as co-ethnics spread across constituent units and forge coalitions determined by more immediate considerations of everyday life requirements rather than ethnicity. It also allows for a test of the real strength of parties laying claim to representing the legitimate interests of an ethnic group. The ethnolinguistic mosaic as it exists also deters any realistic proposition of secession along ethnic lines. Furthermore, it is pertinent to point out that in spite of groups like the Uzbeks, Tajiks and Turkmens having ethnic brethren in neighbouring states, there is little desire for political union, as social structures and values, which play an important role in judging social performance, have been altered in the Central Asian Republics under Soviet experience. Moreover, the political elite operating amongst these groups would stand to lose their political space under any political union. This in large measure accounts for why political-geographical fragmentation of the country during the civil war of the 1990s did not fructify into secession.

However, this heterogeneity also raises a serious challenge. It creates sub-national minorities that could possibly find themselves directly placed under a government dominated by a group who might otherwise be a minority at the national level. Instituting adequate safeguards to protect their interests is vital; else it defeats the raison d'être of putting in place a federal arrangement, which aims to create a more inclusive order. A good case in point is that of Pashtuns settled in the Northern Provinces of Afghanistan. Failure to check reprisals against Pashtuns following the collapse of the Taliban[50] has generated a feeling of disenfranchisement among ethnic Pashtun minorities in the North, which is being successfully played upon by the Taliban. It is here that mechanisms for protection and redressal of grievances through the federal government should be instituted with vigour and determination. That could, for instance, take the form of delegating authority to a special officer, or setting up a minority commission reporting directly to the federal government.

Conclusion

Given the nature of Afghanistan's own political structures, social ethos and certain recently altered ground realities, federalism can serve not only as an effective institutional mechanism to accommodate and recognise diversity but to also harness varied energies and resources for sustaining a larger political framework. Its capacity to respond to both the fact and perception of denial and deprivation predicated on ethnicity, far from fanning fires of secession, has the potential to strengthen and firm up the interests upholding the system. Foremost, it tames and modulates conflicts up to manageable limits.

Conversely, as situations in Pakistan and Sri Lanka demonstrate, it is invariably the refusal of states to recognise identity and demands organised around them, that stability and national unity come under threat. However, federal arrangements are not an end in themselves. Meaningful and sustainable peace requires that such arrangements must be reinforced by building an inclusive national identity informed and inspired by a quest for social reconciliation.

Annexure 1

S.No.	Name of Province	Major Groups	Languages Spoken #	Religion
1.	Badakshan	Tajik, Uzbek, Kyrgyz	Dari (80.6%), Pushtu (0.9%), Uzbek (12.5%), Turkmen (0.6%), Others (5.3%)- Kyrgyz, Pamiri, Missing (0.2%)	Sunni and Shia
2.	Badghis	Tajik, Pushtun, Baluch, Turkmen, Uzbek	Dari (56.4%), Pushtu (39.7%), Uzbek (0.8%), Turkmen (2.4%), Balochi (0.4%), Missing (0.3%)	Sunni
3.	Baghlan	Tajik, Pushtun, Hazara, Uzbek	Dari (70.4%), Pushtu (22.4%), Uzbek (5.9%), Pashai (0.1%), Nooristani (0.1%), Other (0.8%), Missing (0.3%).	Sunni, Shia
4.	Bamian	Hazara, Tajik and Pushtun (minority—Latter only in Kahmard)	Dari (97.9%), Pushtu (1.6%), Others (0.1%), Missing (0.4%)	Shia, Sunni
5.	Balkh	Tajik, Pushtun, Uzbek Hazara, Turkmen, Arab, Baluch	Dari (50%), Pushtu (26.9%), Turkmen (11.9%) and Uzbek (10.7%), Others (0.2%), Missing (0.1%)	Sunni, Shia
6.	Daikundy	Hazara, Pushtun, Baluchi, Sayeed	Dari (84.5%), Pushtu (13.6%), Turkmen (0.1%) and Balochi (0.1%), Others (1.5%), Missing (0.3%)	Sunni
7.	Farah	Tajik, Pushtun, Baluch	Dari (41.3%), Pushtu (57.2%), Balochi (0.7%), Others (0.2%), Missing (0.6%)	Sunni
8.	Faryab	Uzbek, Pushtun, Tajik, Turkmen	Uzbek (53.5%), Dari (27%), Pushtu (13.1%), Turkmen (5.8%), Others (0.3%), Missing (0.3%)	Sunni

9.	Ghazni	Pushtun, Tajik	Pushtu (51.2%), Dari (46.4%), Uzbek (0.1%), Others (1.5%), Missing (0.7%).	Sunni, Hindus* and Sikhs*
10.	Ghor	Tajik, Pushtun	Dari (97.2%), Pushtu (2.4%), Uzbek (0.1%), Others (0.2%)	Sunni
11.	Helmand	Pushtun, Baloch, Hazara	Pushtu (92.1%), Dari (4.5%), Balochi (1.1%), Uzbek (0.1%), Others (1.6%), Missing (0.5%)	Sunni, Shia
12.	Herat	Tajik, Pushtun, Uzbek, Turkmen	Dari (73.4%), Pushtu (24.2%), Uzbek (0.2%), Turkmen (0.7%), Balochi (0.6%), Missing (0.8%)	Sunni, Shia
13.	Jawzjan	Uzbek, Turkmen, Tajik, Pushtun	Uzbek (34.3%), Turkmen (36.9%), Pushtu (15.9%), Dari (10.7%), Others (0.9%), Missing (1.3%)	Sunni
14.	Kabul	Tajik, Pushtun, Hazara, Uzbeks	Pushtu (60.4%), Dari (39%), Pashai (0.4%), Missing (0.2%)	Sunni, Shia, Hindus and Sikhs
15.	Kandahar	Pushtun, Tajik, Baloch	Pushtu (94.3%), Dari (0.8%), Balochi (1.4%), Others (0.2%), Missing (3.4%)	Sunni, Shia, Hindus and Sikhs
16.	Kapisa	Tajik, Pushtun, Pashai	Dari (49.1%), Pushtu (29.8%), Pashai (17%), Uzbek (0.4%), Turkmen (0.3%), Balochi (0.1%), Others (3.3%)	Sunni
17.	Khost	Pushtun, Tajik	Pushtu (99.4%), Dari (0.2%), Balochi (0.1%), Missing (0.3%)	Sunni
18.	Kunar	Pushtun, Tajik, Pashai	Pushtu (91.1%), Dari (0.1%) and Uzbek (0.4%), Pashai (2.2%), Nooristani (4.2%), Others (1.7%), Missing (0.3%)	Sunni

19.	Kunduz	Tajik, Hazara, Uzbek and Turkmen	Pushtu (41.3%), Dari (26.2%), Uzbek (20.1%), Turkmen (10.8%), Missing (1.5%)	Sunni
20.	Laghman	Pushtun, Pashai, Tajik and Gujjars	Pushtu (57.8%), Pashai (29.9%) Dari (11.6%), Others (0.7%), Missing (0.1%)	Sunni
21.	Logar	Pushtun, Tajik	Pushtu (60%), Dari (39.8%), Missing (0.2%)	Sunni
22.	Nangarhar	Pushtun, Pashai, Tajik, Gujjar	Pushtu (92.1%), Pashai (4.2%), Dari (3.2%), Turkmen (0.1%), Missing (0.2%)	Sunni
23.	Nimroz	Baloch, Pushtun, Tajik and Uzbek	Balochi (60.9%), Pushtu (27%), Dari (7.8%), Uzbek (2.8%), Others (0.1%), Missing (1.4%)	Sunni
24.	Nuristan	Nuristani	Dari (0.1%), Pushtu (1.0%), Uzbek (0.4%), Nuristani (84%) and Pashai (11.6%), Others (2.3%)	Sunni
25.	Paktia	Pushtun, Tajik	Pushtu (95.4%), Dari (4.3%), Missing (0.2%)	Sunni
26.	Paktika	Pushtun, Uzbek, Tajik	Pushtu (93.2%), Uzbek (1.9%), Dari (4.4%), Missing (0.6%)	Sunni
27.	Panjshir	Tajik, Hazara	Dari (98.1%), Pushtu (1.0%), Missing (0.9%)	Sunni
28.	Parwaan	Tajik, Pushtun and Hazara	Dari (70.2%), Pushtu (27.8%), Turkmen (0.1%); Other (0.1%), Missing (1.8%)	Sunni
29.	Sar-i-Pul	Uzbek, Pushtun, Arab, Tajik	Dari (62.6%), Uzbek (22.6%), Pushtu (11.6%), Turkmen (0.3%), Balochi (0.2%), Others (2.4%), Missing (0.4%)	Sunni

30.	Samangan	Uzbek, Tajik, Pushtun, Hazara, Arab	Dari (69.4%), Pushtu (4.6%), Uzbek (25.2%), Missing (0.8%)	Sunni
31.	Takhar	Uzbek, Tajik, Pushtun, Hazara	Uzbek (45.6%), Dari (44.2%) and Pushtu (7.7%), Balochi (0.7%), Others (0.7%). Missing (1.1%)	Sunni
32.	Uruzgan	Pushtun (90%), Tajik	Pushtu (93.1%), Dari (6.2%), Uzbek (0.3%), Missing (0.5%)	Sunni
33.	Wardak	Pushtun, Tajik, Hazara	Pushtu (69.2%), Dari (27.5%), Uzbek (0.6%), Other (2.4%), Missing (0.4%)	Sunni
34.	Zabul	Pushtun, Tajik	Pushtu (84%), Dari (0.2%), Missing (15.7%)	Sunni

Note: The province-wise distribution of ethnic, linguistic and religious groups has been drawn up based on the National Area Development plans drawn up by the Ministry of Rural Rehabilitation and Development (MRRD) in collaboration with the United Nations Assistance Mission in Afghanistan (UNAMA) as well as the household listing survey undertaken jointly by the Central Statistical Office (CSO) and the United Nations Population Fund for Afghanistan (UNFPA) between 2002 and 2005. The MRRD plans can be accessed at: http://www.mrrd-nabdp.org/Development%20Plans.htm. The figures provided are informed approximations based on field surveys, carried out by the MRRD and UNAMA. The Households listing survey was accessed by the author but is not available in the public domain.

*MRRD provincial profiles do not list religious minority groups, namely, the Hindus and Sikhs in development plans but they have been included here based on the author's first-hand knowledge during his engagement as an aid worker in 2010.

#Figures listed here are based on a survey report entitled "Afghanistan: A Socio-Economic and Demographic Profile," Central Statistics Office (CSO) and United Nations Population Fund (UNFPA), 2005, Kabul, p. 33. As per the findings of this household listings survey undertaken by CSO and UNFPA between 2002 and 2005 the population percentage according to the main languages spoken is as follows: Dari (38.1 per cent), Pushto (48.7 per cent), Uzbaki (7.2 per cent), Turkmani (1.8 per cent), Balochi (0.5 per cent), Pashai (1.3 per cent), Nooristani (0.7 per cent), Others (0.8 per cent), Missing (0.8 per cent). The statistics listed under the "Missing" head are of a small number of districts which could not be accessed due to unfavourable security situation. This UNFPA survey was undertaken as part of the pre-census stage preparations which would serve as a guideline for census which was scheduled to begin in 2008, but was postponed owing to a deteriorating security situation.

Notes

1. The term "federal arrangements" has been borrowed from the work of Daniel J. Elazar who uses it to emphasise the adaptability of the federal principles to particular situations, which as federal polities demonstrate, can be applied in more than one way. For further details refer to Daniel J. Elazar, *Exploring Federalism* (Tuscaloosa and London: The University of Alabama Press, 1991), pp. 6-7.
2. M. Nazif Shahrani, "Not 'Who?' but 'How?': Governing Afghanistan after the conflict," *Federations: Special Issue on Afghanistan*, October 2001, p. 8 at http://www.institute-for-afghan-studies.org/AFGHAN%20CONFLICT/Federalism/Federations%20Magazine%2010-26-01.pdf (Accessed on January 5, 2012).
3. Omar Zakhilwal, "Federalism in Afghanistan: A Recipe for Disintegration," *Federations: Special Issue on Afghanistan*, October 2001, pp. 8-11 at http://www.forumfed.org/libdocs/Federations/V1afgh-af-Zakhilwal.pdf (Accessed on January 5, 2012). Mr. Zakhiwal currently occupies the office of Finance Minster in President Hamid Karzai's cabinet.
4. The Constitution of the Islamic Republic of Afghanistan, January 26, 2004.
5. Amin Saikal, *Modern Afghanistan: A History of Struggle and Survival* (London: I. B. Tauris, 2004), p. 38; and Thomas Barfield, *Afghanistan: A Cultural and Political History* (Princeton and Oxford: Oxford University Press, 2010), p. 147. Memories of having enjoyed a period of autonomous rule continue to persist strongly. In a focus group discussion the author had with local Shura members of Yakowlang district in Bamian province, participants recalled the period as one characterised by "just rule." In particular, attention was drawn to the names of two rulers, Shaibur Rana and Shahi Qalandar, who, it was claimed, were rested in the graves in the local cemetery of Yakowlang. Author's focus group discussion with Yakowlang Shura Members, Yakowlang, Bamian, September 12, 2011.
6. Quoted in Amin Saikal, no. 5.
7. Thomas Barfield, no. 5, pp. 162-63.
8. A study undertaken by the World Bank on the need for administrative reform in Afghanistan underscores the excessively centralised character of planning, with 44 per cent of the country's civil service being located in Kabul. For further details refer to "Afghanistan: Building an Effective State, Priorities for Public Administration Reform," *The World Bank*, Kabul, 2008, p. 5 at http://siteresources.worldbank.org/AFGHANISTANEXTN/Resources/305984-1213128265371/5090855-1213128292963/AFstatebuilding.pdf (Accessed on January 8, 2012).
9. Douglas Saltmarshe and Abhilash Mehdi, "Local Governance for Local Needs: Key Findings and Policy Options for Afghanistan," *AREU Policy Note Series*, July 2011, p. 3 at http://www.areu.org.af/EditionDetails.aspx?EditionId=547&ContentId=7&ParentId=7 (Accessed on January 10, 2012).
10. Podcast: "Local Government Is Failing to Meet Local Needs," Recording of an AREU Press Conference, June 22, 2011 at http://www.areu.org.af/EditionDetails.aspx?EditionId=544&ContentId=7&ParentId=7 (Accessed on January 10, 2012).
11. Author's interview with Ms. Fauzia Kufi, Member of Parliament, Badakshan province, Kabul, October 16, 2011.
12. Angelo Rasanayagam, *Afghanistan: A Modern History. Monarchy, Despotism or Democracy? The Problems of Governance in the Muslim Tradition* (London: I. B. Tauris, 2003), p. 22.
13. Thomas Barfield, no. 5, pp. 192-95.

14. Author's Interview with Dr. Rangin Dafdar Spanta, National Security Advisor to the President of the Islamic Republic of Afghanistan, Kabul, October 16, 2011.
15. "Afghanistan: The Constitutional Loya Jirga," December 12, 2003, *International Crisis Group*, Kabul/Brussels, p. 2. at http://www.crisisgroup.org/~/media/Files/asia/south-asia/afghanistan/B029%20Afghanistan%20The%20Constitutional%20Loya%20Jirga.pdf (Accessed on January 11, 2012). The International Crisis Group notes that the results of the constitutional commission's public consultations held over the course of the drafting process revealed that while federalism was favoured in parts of the north, participants of the southeast strongly supported a constitutional monarchy. The author observed a similar trend over the course of his interactions in Afghanistan between 2010 and 2011, as also in discussions with Afghan students whom the author had the opportunity to teach in 2011 at the University of Erfurt, Germany. It was observed that a large number of people belonging to non-Pashtun ethnic groups expressed a preference for a system that gives them greater autonomy to manage their own cultural affairs and address developmental needs. This trend is visible in the stance taken by the political elite of the country with leaders from ethnic and sectarian minorities being most vociferous in demands for federal arrangements. The most recent and explicit display of the same was witnessed in a meeting in Berlin on January 11, 2012 between US lawmakers and Ahmad Zia Massoud, Younas Qanooni, Dr. Abdullah Abdullah, Amarullah Saleh, Atta Mohammad Noor (all belonging to the predominantly Tajik Jamiat-i-Islami party), Gen. Abdul Rashid Dostum (Head of the Jumbish-i-Milli which has a strong constituency amongst the Uzbeks and Turkmens), Haji Mohammad Mohaqiq (Shia leader from Kandahar). Notably there were no Pashtun leaders and expectedly the meeting drew severe criticism from the Afghan government. For further details refer to "Berlin Meeting, Such Actions Should not Be Repeated: MoFA," *Daily Outlook Afghanistan,* January 12, 2012, at http://outlookafghanistan.net/news?post_id=3094 (Acessed on January 15, 2012).
16. Comprehensive theoretical reflection on the origins, nature and meaning of federalism deserves an independent work in its own right. Therefore the definition cited in this paper merely reflects a broad understanding of federalism generally practised. For further reflections on the concept of federalism refer to Daniel J. Elazar, no. 1; and William H Riker, "The Origin and Purpose of Federalism," in John Kincaid (ed.), *Federalism: Historical and Theoretical Foundations of Federalism*, 1 (London: Sage Library of Political Science, Sage, 2011).
17. Will Kyymlicka, "Minority Nationalism and Multination Federalism" in John Kincaid (ed.), *Federalism: Historical and Theoretical Foundations of Federalism*, 1 (London: Sage Library of Political Science, Sage, 2011), p. 230.
18. Ronald L. Watts, *Comparing Federal Systems* (Second Edition) (Montreal and Kingston: McGills University Press, 1999), p. 100 and 105.
19. Ibid., p. 231, and Daniel J. Elazar, "Federalism vs. Decentralization: The Drift from Authenticity," in John Kincaid (ed.), *Federalism: Historical and Theoretical Foundations of Federalism*, 1 (London: Sage Library of Political Science, Sage, 2011), p. 82.
20. Katherine Adeney, *Federalism and Ethnic Conflict Regulation in India and Pakistan*, (New York: Palgrave Macmillan, 2007), p. 34.
21. The Constitution of The Islamic Republic of Afghanistan.
22. The Constitution of 2004 in this regard displays remarkable contiguity with the earlier Constitutions of 1964, 1977 and 1987—all of which stress the "unitary" character of the state.

23. Sanjay Ruprelia and Ruth Rennie, "Governance and Development in Afghanistan," in Ruth Rennie (ed.), *State Building, Security and Social Change in Afghanistan* (The Asia Foundation, 2008), p. 132, at http://asiafoundation.org/resources/pdfs/2008surveycompanionvolumefinal.pdf (Accessed on January 15, 2012).
24. Articles 139 and 140 respectively spell out the role of the PCs as follows: "participating in the attainment of development objectives of the state, and improvement of the affairs of the province and advising the provincial administration on related issues. The provincial assembly shall perform its duties with the cooperation of the provincial administration" and "organise activities and attain active participation of the people in provincial administration."
25. Podcast, no. 10.
26. Ibid.
27. Douglas Saltmarshe and Abhilash Mehdi, no. 9.
28. For a more detailed reflection on the effects of central control over appointment of Governors, refer to Martine Van Bijlert, "Between Discipline and Discretion: Policies Surrounding Senior Sub-national Appointments," Briefing Paper Series, AREU, May 2009, pp. 7-8 at http://www.areu.org.af/Uploads/EditionPdfs/923E-Subnational%20Appointments-%20BP-print.pdf (Accessed on January 11, 2012); Zubair Babarkhail, "Residents Stage Protest Demo Against Governor," *Pajhwok Afghan News*, May 24, 2007 at http://www.rawa.org/temp/runews/2007/05/24/residents-stage-protest-demo-against-governor.phtml (Accessed on January 4, 2012).
29. Colin Cookman and Caroline Wadhams, "Governance in Afghanistan: What We Leave Behind," Centre for American Progress, May 2010, p. 11 at http://www.americanprogress.org/issues/2010/05/pdf/afghangovernance.pdf (Accessed on January 8, 2012).
30. The author often encountered such views by common Afghans as also by a section of the political elite during his work and interaction as a Humanitarian Aid Worker in 2010 as well as by a section of the political elite the author interviewed between August and October 2011.
31. "Quick Impact, Quick Collapse: Dangers of Militarized Aid in Afghanistan," *Oxfam International*, January 2010, pp. 3-4 at http://www.oxfam.org/sites/www.oxfam.org/files/quick-impact-quick-collapse-jan-2010.pdf (Accessed on January 16, 2012).
32. Tom Koenings, Parliamentarian, Bundinis, Green Party, speaking as a panelist at an International Conference on Afghanistan on "Ten Years After Petersburg: Where Does Afghanistan Stand Today?" Berlin, November 23, 2011.
33 Sultan Barakat, "DFID Understanding Afghanistan: Synthesis Report," *Recovery and Development Consortium*, DFID, November 2008, p. 55.
34. Author's interview with Dr. Abdul Latif Pedrom, Member of Parliament, Badakshan Province and founder member and leader of the Kangra-i-Milli (National Congress Party), Kabul, September 2, 2011.
35. Statement of Lt. Col. Ojukuwu to diplomatic representatives of the UK and the USA, September 1996: Eastern Nigerian Viewpoint, Eastern Nigeria, Ministry of Information, Enugu, 1966, 42. Quoted in Donald L. Horowitz, *Ethnic Groups in Conflict* (Berkeley and Los Angeles: University of California Press, 2000), p. 615.
36. Afghanistan currently has two vice-presidents: Field Marshal Qasim Mohammad Fahim, an ethnic Tajik from the Jamiat-i-Islami party and Abdul Karim Khallili, an ethnic Hazara leader from the Hizb-i-Wahadat party have been appointed as first and second vice-presidents respectively.

37. As per the provisions stipulated under Article 60 of the Constitution, executive authority can only be exercised by the office of the first vice-president "In case of absence, resignation or death of the President" and by the second vice-president "in the absence of the first Vice-President."
38. Amin Saikal and William Maley, "The President Who Would Be King," *The New York Times*, February 6, 2008 at http://www.nytimes.com/2008/02/06/opinion/06saikal.html (Accessed on January 12, 2012).
39. Ronald L. Watts, no. 18, p. 84.
40. During the author's field visit in October 2011 to Shiberghan, capital of Jowzjan province and a stronghold of General Dostum's Jumbish-i-Milli party, it was observed over the course of interviews and informal interactions with the local populace that while the government was blamed for lack of development and job opportunities, General Dostum and his party were credited with not merely empowering Uzbeks and Turkmen in particular but also for providing jobs in local administration and in the party's TV station *Ayna*, organising computer training sesssions for the young, among a host of other initiatives.
41. Donald L. Horowitz, *Ethnic Groups in Conflict* (Berkeley and Los Angeles: University of California Press, 2000), p. 617.
42. Will Kyymlicka, "Multi-nation Federalism," in Baogang He, Brian Galligan and Takashi Inoguchi (eds.), *Federalism in Asia*, (Cheltenham, UK: Edward Elgar, 2007), p. 39.
43. Daniel J. Elazar, no. 1, p. 252.
44. *Afghanistan: A Socio-Economic and Demographic Profile*, Central Statistics Office (CSO) and United Nations Population Fund (UNFPA), 2005, Kabul, p. 1.
45. For a brief but incisive account of the Hazara-Kuchi conflict, refer to Fabrizio Foschini, "The Kuchi, Hazara Conflict, Again," in *Afghanistan Analysis Network*, May 27, 2010 at http://www.aan-afghanistan.org/index.asp?id=764 (Accessed on January 7, 2012). The issue has also served to politicise members of the Afghan diaspora along ethnic lines, with many vociferously campaigning for their ethnic group and accusing the government of deliberate inaction and even of connivance with their Pashtun brethren. Refer to "Kuchis Must Leave Hazarajat: Protestors in Brisbane," *Hazaristan Times*, June 13, 2010 at https://hazaristantimes.wordpress.com/2010/06/13/kuchis-must-leave-hazarajat-protesters-in-brisbane/ and "Protest Against Kuchi Invasion of Behsud," *Hazaristan Times*, May 30, 2010 at https://hazaristantimes.wordpress.com/2010/06/13/kuchis-must-leave-hazarajat-protesters-in-brisbane/ (Accessed on January 7, 2012).
46. Donald Horowitz dwells upon this point at length using the case of Nigeria, which following the Biafra war, restructured the component units of the federation, which involved a proliferation in the number of states, which on the one hand gave more autonomy to the minorities and on the other brought to the fore subdued cleavages amongst groups which had earlier been overridden by a struggle between a Muslim majority North and Christian south. See Donald L. Horowitz, no. 41, pp. 603-6. In contrast the bipolar character of the Pakistani federation until its dissolution in 1971, strenghtened the fact and perception of denial-depriviation of the Eastern wing by the Western unit, whose ethnic and linguistic diversity cleavages were muted by a larger unit. For further details, refer to Katherine Adeney, no. 20, pp. 137-62. In our case, of the 34 provinces that constitute Afghanistan today, only the province of Nuristan is recorded as being ethnically homogeneous. In the other provinces the number of ethnic groups range from two to seven. Similar diversity can be seen with respect to the languages spoken. While provinces like Kandahar, Khost, Nangarhar, Paktia, Paktika, Zabul, and Panjsher are overwhelmingly comprised of one

ethnic group, and are likely to witness increased intra-ethnic competition, the other provinces display remarkable levels of ethnolinguistic diversity. For a more detailed survey, refer to the "National Area Based Development Plan" of The Ministry of Rural Rehabilitation and Development. These plans developed in collaboration with UNAMA, involved an extensive consultation process with local communities, covering social, economic and demographic conditions at the province and district level. They provide us a broad but insightful window into the country's diversity and equip us better to understand the accompanying social complexities and means to respond to those. These plans can be accessed at http://www.mrrd-nabdp.org/Provincial%20Development%20Plan.htm and http://www.mrrd-nabdp.org/DDP_1.htm (Accessed on January 15, 2012).

47. Sultan Barakat, *Understanding Afghanistan*, no. 33, p. 22.
48. Ibid.
49. For a province-wise distribution of the ethnic linguistic and religious groups, refer to the Table in Annexure 1.
50. For further reference, see "Paying for the Taliban's Crimes: Abuses Against Ethnic Pushtuns in Northern Afghanistan," *Human Rights Watch*, April 2002, 14 (2c), at http://www.hrw.org/reports/2002/afghan2/afghan0402.pdf (Accessed on January 16, 2012).

3. Islam and the State in the Constitutional History of Afghanistan

Ambrish Dhaka

Religion is considered as a motivational force in nation-building. But, in the case of Afghanistan it has been a misrepresented fact. The role of Islam in defining the state of Afghanistan has been undisputed. But, it never went into defining the citizenship based on religion. The identity of state and its organs remained well-defined as only a Muslim could be the head of the state. However, the citizenry in Afghanistan remained within the realm of tribal identity. The Pashtuns, Tajiks and Hazaras being the larger groups, have a transnational geocultural identity that makes it imperative for them to retain ethnic identity across the national framework. It is also imperative to preserve their Lebensraum in a scarcity driven contest for land and water. The resources in an agrarian society are few and individuals or kinship groups are not the competent units to defend themselves. The usual reference to ethnicity is *qwoum* or the ethnos that brings in a greater sense of security. Islam is the principal basis of state law in Afghanistan since the first Constitution. The inter-ethnic discords are the usual instances where mullahs and qazis get the upper hand, for the rest of the times intra-tribal disputes are often subject to customary laws.[1] Islam provides the basis for universalisation of values and norms for a typically secluded Afghan society. Their nomadic segment of population is more reliant on these norms while contracting trade with the settled peoples. Thus, the pre-existing mode of universality somewhat precludes the influence of putative secular and modern culture. The inheritance of conflict at this level often finds reverberations in ideological elements of Islamic culture, which become the symbol of protest. For instance, when the negation of the West is in question—a case herein—the veil or burqa has often been a case of body-politic raked up both by the feminists and the mullahs. However, the history of Afghanistan is not devoid of various efforts made by the monarchy to substitute this universality of religion with secular symbols and the legal structure that were in consonance with Islam. But this ended largely with a backwash effect, with the return of a more fundamentalist form of governance. The dilemma is also augmented by the fact that the Afghan state has often been supported or weakened by imperial powers to suit their geopolitical objectives. And the external conditioning of the state has allowed the clergy and the Khans to increase their power stakes opposed to central authority. The change in this dynamics came when Amir Abdur Rahman Khan tried to create an Islamic state by liquidating the ethnoscapes. The geocultural sources of power were disturbed by introducing a hostile population in a region. Hence, the Ghizai Pashtuns were forcefully taken to the north and the Tajiks were encouraged to settle in the towns of southern Afghanistan. The aim was to create a counterbalance locally and make the state a sole recourse to justice. The situation of the Hazaras became worse as their highlands were forcefully given to Kuchi Pashtuns and the dispute on land-use often became a sore point for inter-ethnic tensions. Thus the period from 1880 to 1900 witnessed the territorialisation of national ideology, symbolised by the Sharia under Islam, and it also became a source to legitimise the use of violence.[2] Islam faces another peculiar condition due to its historic-geographical conditions. The rejectionist view towards elitist Islam has also been one of the important subaltern features in Afghanistan and it got somewhat reinforced through resuscitation of tribal customs, which counteract the sophistry of religion.[3]

This chapter tries to locate the ontology of the state in Afghanistan with reference to the position of Islam in the history of constitutional development of the state in Afghanistan. It has been one of the challenges for Afghan monarchs to blend modernity with Islam, and it has often been a geopolitical tool for the clergy who took it as a motive to instigate the tribes on the periphery to oppose the state. Islam played a vital role in defining the legitimacy of this opposition by terming it as jihad, the holy war. It reflected as a religious duty for every Afghan to direct his force against the central authority of the time. Jihad has been a term that has been ideologically cultivated by state and clergy, often to legitimise their use of violence to oppose the state.

Political Islam and the State

Islam is portrayed as an organic religio-political system.[4] There is an absence of differentiating markers between religion and Muslim society. Sovereignty rests with God and the political organisation of society is based on religious laws and traditions. There is a conceptual difference between politico-theological dogma and the actual political structures of Muslim societies throughout history, and this gap is politicised and capitalised on by radical Islamic movements, such as Wahabism and Salafism.[5] The ontology of Islam is dichotomous in the sense that it is at one level concerned with the interpretation of Quranic verses, *hadith* and *fiqh* in order to polarise power in favour of its institutions; and, on the other hand, the source of power emerging from the single authority of the Caliphate over the Muslim world brought Empires within Islam's grasp that invariably resisted autonomous localisation of these religious scriptures. Therefore, there remained an inherent tussle for power between the religious authority, the clergy and the Amir who represented society, which is the secular source of power. The necessity to declare an official religion serves the clergy's interest. The clergy are entrusted with the task of creating the ideology for the ruling class. The monopoly over interpretations of the text and their adaptation to suit ruling class interests is one of the important functions of the clergy. However, the contest emerges if the state tries to create secular foundations of power by vesting new structures of knowledge with the advent of private business and capitalism that weakens the bargaining power of the clergy. Normative Islam refers to the ideological structures as governed by the religious scholars, but empirical Islam refers to the sustainable idea of Islam amid daily problems of social place, work and communication. These two are in a dialectical relationship and often betray geocultural constructivism. Thus, the praxis of Islam remains a normative order as well as a communal consciousness, which paves the way for an easy access to the politicisation of the masses. The de-Islamisation of consciousness among the masses has often been resisted, as it remains the sole counter-force against the state, which has largely been authoritarian. Therefore, the induction of democracy has been an anomaly where the balance of power exists between the state authority, people and the clergy. The role of Islam in the ideological orientation of the masses essentially reflects the prevalence of class interest, which is quite distinct from the Islamic social order prevailing at a time in a Muslim society. The functional role of Islam in retaining a particular social order has been accommodated by tribal societies, where mullahs often are on the periphery of jurisprudence and the customary laws take precedence before the Sharia. However, the set of boundaries that are needed to retain these tribal orders are definitely the contribution of Islam within these societies, as they would defend its inviolability in the name of Islam. The ideological foundations of Islam are based on the inclusive membership of *Umma* and the positional interrelationship among the religious authorities. The role of Arabic language in providing the historical cultural continuity has been significant, which has retained its identity despite the transition to modern times. The popular idea of authority imbibes these elements in order to retain its influence over the masses. If there is any diversion from these, it gives an opportunity to the clergy to call for resisting the transformation of authority, often leading to religious revolt. This is vital to maintain a legitimate institution of power in the opinion of the masses. Therefore, the absence of democracy in Islam has made divine right the liable course for seeking this sanction to use power, and the clergy is entrusted to validate the divine right of the ruler.

Political Islam and the rise of fundamentalism in South Asia occurred on two accounts that invariably had an impact on Afghanistan. The resistance to syncretic culture of Indo-Islam grew under the aegis of Sheikh Ahmad Sirhindi (1563-1624).[6] This was seen as an effort to reject the Hindu-Muslim convergence of beliefs and practices and sowed the first seeds of distrust in the subcontinent. Second was the rise of the Marathas, the Sikhs and the British as a new ruling power that prompted Shah Walliullah to ask Ahmed Shah Abdali for intervention in India. Thus, the Muslim rule and its quest for power in Hindustan became the raison d'être for Islamists who found fundamentalism as the organising principle for resistance against central authority. Syed Ahmed Barelvi dedicated his life to arousing Pashtun tribes for jihad against the Sikhs. The Indian Sepoy Mutiny became the testing ground for Islamists, who appealed to Dost Mohammed, the Amir of Kabul, to send men and resources in defeating the British. However, the Amir maintained neutrality. The presence of the British in the South Asian subcontinent polarised the Muslim world in South Asia into two camps: the modernists, who were willing to work with the British in order to improve the social and economic well-being of elite Muslim class; and the orthodox, rallying around Deoband, who believed in subaltern forms of social organisation which would pay heed to their fatwas and strictures. It largely revealed that the rural-urban divide was fast emerging in South Asia. In Afghanistan, too, the influence of the modernists was growing in cities such as Kabul and Herat, whereas centres like Kandahar and Mazar-e-Sharif were becoming focal points for orthodox mullahs. The bent towards puritanism was seen by many as an attempt by the clergy to dominate over the political affairs of the state and it was around the same time that the boulevard of Islamic power was crumbling under various indigenous and external pressures. The role of religion in shaping Afghanistan's external polity has been a unique factor that has contributed to externality of Islam within the daily lives of ordinary Afghans. They believed that call for jihad essentially means an extraterritorial concern, whereas the tribal concept of *badal* and *pore* are intra-territorial concerns. The effort to bail out Afghanistan was made by Amir Abdur Rahman Khan. He divided the whole country into provinces and brought tax structures to regulate the socio-economic life of the nation. These efforts to detribalise society paved the way for introducing the constitutional judicial system superseding customary informal laws. Again, the externality of Islam was a maintained fact because even though the Sharia became the basis for adjudicating the cases, it was noted that people would reach court only when they had failed to reach an agreement in the informal courts.[7]

Therefore, a need for universalisation of norms that would serve as the common basis for territoriality brought political Islam to the fore. The role of Islam in defining the nature of the Afghan state has been perennially enshrined in successive Afghan Constitutions. The quest for a modern state putatively rejects tribalism and religious fundamentalism. But the decades of the twentieth and twenty-first centuries have witnessed marked proclivity towards pan-tribal identities and religious-nationalism as a basis for state formation. Therefore, the question of modernisation is still a quest in Muslim countries and Afghanistan falls in the same block. This seems more astounding when secularism is considered to be the basis for a nation-state. The dichotomy of a secular versus theocratic state has several manifestations in the form of regional, stratified interests that have grown into movements for political identities, or subnational territorialisation. Nation-building based on religious exegesis and a "revisionist" exercise brought in the clergy as a very strong negotiator between the state and society. This allowed Sharia to be the basis for common law, so far as the central authority was concerned. However, the tribal or customary laws remained privileged in the tribal areas. The influence of the Sharia remained largely an urban phenomenon in Afghanistan.[8] The link between fundamentalism and the Sharia invariably brings in the clergy and its desire to control state power. But Olivier Roy also cautions about the juridical autonomy of the Sharia.[9] In fact, it is being considered supreme to both state and society. It therefore has the ability to take suo moto cognition of needs for transformation and modification based on empirical social facts. The clergy negotiate these modifications based on *fiqh* and *hadith* in an evolutionary process. The state might contend that this supremacy of Sharia as the right to own a law is the basis of legitimacy of use of power and its putative sovereignty. If that is subject to Sharia then state sovereignty is subject to Sharia, which invariably makes the clergy the most powerful class in defining the sovereignty of the state.

Islamic Statehood in a Tribal Society

The modern state struggled to dispose of secular laws in lieu of the Sharia during the early years of state formation in Afghanistan in the twentieth century. It also invited questions on the basis of spirituality that itself could be part of the debate on religion. However, a major difference lay in the secular nature of law and the degree of secularity. The Alim did not seek state as a guarantor of law; for him it was his clientele, and society remained as the guarantor. Similarly, it has been society which can be a negotiator of the strategic balance of power between the state and the clergy. The state might try to destroy this balance through the use of force as happened during the times of Abdur Rahman Khan; but it has been seeking support depending on financial resources, from the clergy or the traditional leadership of society, namely, the kinship structures of tribes, headed by Khans and Sardars. The legitimacy in this context represented the kingship personified in the image of a good ruler. A ruler claimed superiority over the clergy class, not only in terms of intellect but also the force of strength so that he could fend off all social opposition. This superiority at times has been betrayed by tyranny, which has been an invariable feature of an Islamic state. However, the state seldom tried to annihilate the clergy by declaring totalitarian order. The exception has been the case of the Shiite clergy in Iran which reigned supreme, and as a matter of fact has effected modifications in the Sharia, which largely rendered it as a symbol of inherently secular innovations. The Soviet intervention disturbed the triumvirate equation between the state, society and the clergy. The mujahideen found state power indispensable; so the role of the clergy got minimised or imbibed through self-styled political Islam, just as in the case of the rise of the Taliban. The other situation had been to create a state which remains elitist in nature, just like those in the Middle East and the law remained largely the prerogative of the state with the clergy only supporting it. This was a serious challenge because the clergy were not dependent on the state and could rally the Khans to destabilise the state as the incident of Hazrat of Shor Bazaar revealed.

Rural life in Afghanistan has been contemptuous of the state's presence in their village environs. The village tried to defend their collective economy against the state. The very idea of the state was attested with two facts, the law and the revenue. Both have been ordained by Islam in the form of the Sharia and Zakat. These portrayed the state as a rentier organisation, which interfered with kinship structures through laws and extracted financial rewards without any penalty. The Afghan state did not emerge out of the tribal confederation, which was based on religious nationalism; nor did it have any liquidation of ethnic identities. It was a coalition of ethnic groups that brought out statehood in the name of Afghanistan, which would serve their interest beyond territories. So, the quest for state building was thoroughly externalised and to that extent Islam had a cohesive role. The tribes too had their relative differentiation in accordance to their size and geographic location. Pashtuns commanded influence beyond Afghanistan into Pakistan and part of India as well. No other tribe could claim such a geographical spread. Therefore, the Pashtuns were able to interchangeably deploy Islam and Pashtun hegemony for majoritarian interest. But Afghanistan did not emerge out of consciousness of the majority. It emerged as the consensus of all. Therefore, the Jirga system remained of prime importance due to its role in establishing statehood in Afghanistan. Nadir Shah, the Musahiban ruler in 1929, invoked a similar Jirga after the tribal revolt that uprooted Amanullah Khan, the visionary. According to Olivier Roy, the state in Afghanistan essentially rested on the periphery. This meant that within the village *raum* (German geographic term used for local environment, derived from lebensraum), the state was seen as a counter-agency. The growth of the state during the Musahiban period created a middle class largely attached to the bureaucracy. This class had an achievistic structure[10] capped at the top by the ascriptive structure signified by the King and his family. Tribal minorities were more feudal in their set-up and had been quick in grabbing these opportunities, as they could not confront the state which essentially remained Pashtun. Therefore Tajik, Farsiwan and Uzbek gained ascendancy in the bureaucracy and the military. The Pashtuns of Kabul and Herat were also quick to join the set-up. This created a spatial dichotomy between state territory and a territorialising state; the former being the core and the latter being the periphery. The territorialising state had been at a truce with tribalism and this was more visible in the highland regions of central and eastern Afghanistan. The state territory has been one where the dichotomy persists. This space has been contested by Islam and secular institutions. Here the word secular might convey the wrong sense. The more apt explanation could be seen as something closer to the Methodist school which included religion as a co-factor whilst administering state prerogatives.

The role of Islam has been to provide geocultural reference to the wide-ranging diversities in Afghanistan. The diversities ranged from ethnic, tribal, non-tribal, urban, rural, settled to nomadic and several others. Islam served as the binding element that transposes peripheries which were strongly identified with boundaries. According to Louis Dupree (1973), this pluralism had its own variant of a segmentary religious class. The village mullah, alim, ulema, pir, sayyed and the Islamists represent their manifestations in accordance to their clientele.[11] Based on these set of relations, Islam became visible in different manifestations. The popular Islam was defined by the village mullah, who performed rites of birth, marriage and death. The devotional aspect was visible in the form of pir and sayyed, who denoted the spiritual symbolism or might refer to particular practice of devout singing. The legal or orthodox Islam was ordained by the ulema, who tried to define the law during times of dispute over land, material wealth and women.[12] These disputes generally witnessed the presence of ulema as a consultative body to the tribal chiefs. The last one showed up the Islamists as a manifestation of the identity of a state based on Islam. The urban environment has been much affected more through this form of authority. The fiscal arm of this variant of Islam has also been quite strong as it often shared revenue from the urban environs in the form of funds and donations. Among the symbols, the mosque remained the most visible form. The system of values that permeated through the institutions of madrasa and mosque had been the only mode of universalisation of values among rural Afghans. The institution of madrasa was very fundamental to Afghan society since the early period of Islam. It was a religious school run by a maulvi, who taught the pupil (talib), all major stages of Quranic learning, the *hadith*, the Quran, theology and languages. Most of these teachers have been receiving degrees from mainland South Asia. The mosque was the central point for the diffusion of these values and defined the gradient from the umma to the non-believers. The individual in the form of mullah represented this popular or subaltern form of Islam. The property attached to mosque was wakf land, but there was scarcity of these resources in Afghanistan. The village religion was largely functional towards conservation of norms, so emulation was the larger order. The urban spheres also involved interpretation, which functioned as a political variable. This involved jurisprudence and hence the next in hierarchy was the Qazi, the interpreter of the law. The Qazi might not have the necessary force to implement the law, so the tasks usually rested with Khans and Maliks, who wielded power. As the locals entrusted them with the duty of resolving intra-tribal affairs, they also managed to secure a space from the state.

The role of Islam in providing the peripheral bind to tribal affairs remained an important characteristic. It also represented a significant point of interaction between those who were members and those who were non-members. This structure of tribal zones brought a specific role to Islam. It appeared as a secular instrument in a sense that the carrier of Islamic tenets was the mullah who served as a contact point between the tribe and the bureaucracy. The usual status of the mullah was below the tribe, but necessarily above the statist class.[13] These tribal orders have been strictly patriarchal. The status and legal rights of women were severely curtailed. The right to property was also limited. The tribal codes of honour and protection were generally held in high esteem and the Sharia often found itself counterpoised to these laws. Popular Islam in rural Afghanistan inculcated symbolism around charismatic personalities, their magical curing powers, the *mazaars* (tombs) for *ziarat* and the collective tribal worship of a *pir* (maraboutism). All this symbolism was very distinct when compared to the Salafist or the Wahabist form of Islam, which emerged out of the political connotation of Islam. Therefore, modern Islamists often confronted traditional Islam.

Sufism aims to reach the polar ends of religious manifestation, the esoteric (zahir) and the exoteric (batin). It tries to remain fundamentally hooked to tenets of Quran and *hadith*, but its implementation is purely circumstantial. Sufis have maintained a distinct identity in three schools (*tariqa*), namely, *naqshbandi*, *qadiri* and chisti. It believes in teacher-pupil relationship (pir-murid). Their goal is to practise spirituality by reciting verses for God. Sufis have been producing religious literature as well, which has found ready acceptance amongst the masses. Authors such as Rumi from Balkh and Jami from Herat have been highly regarded in Afghanistan. Sufis have played an important role in sanctioning or decrying an action of authority. Most of the Sufi traditions are carried out by notable families through generations, such as the Mujadidi family belongs to the Naqshbandi tariqa, while the Gailani family belong to the Qadiri tariqa. These families have been the negotiating agents between the tribes and the state. Quite often, the state tried to buy their favour in order to stabilise its regime. Revolts in the countryside often found their collusion with the dissatisfied. The ulema raised a revolt in 1928 against Amanullah Khan which resulted in his abdication.

Islam in the Constitutions of Afghanistan

The status of Islam was preconceived in Afghanistan's Constitution because of their long history of religious warfare in South Asia. The three Anglo-Afghan wars contributed to the buffer psyche among Afghan rulers, and Islam was the sole unifying force to carry that sense across numerous tribal groups. Therefore, the Jirgas have been held at times to approve the methods of governance, including the Constitutions. The 1923 Constitution was a reflection of nationalist awakening in Afghanistan after successfully negotiating independence after the third Anglo-Afghan War. Mahmood Tarzi and Shah Wali Khan were the two pioneering figures who brought institutional modernisation as state objectives to Afghanistan. They were also known as constitutionalists. Their role in creating symbols of nationalism deserves mention. It was the print media through which they tried to create public opinion in favour of the modernist ideas of monarchy.[14] But modernity never meant accepting the West. In fact, there was an intense critical approach towards imperialist powers and their relations with the dwindling Ottoman Empire. Pan-Islamism was a recourse to fight these hegemonic drives. It had an impact on the first Constitution of Afghanistan, which was promulgated by King Amanullah Khan in 1923. Articles 2 and 3 of the Constitution declared Islam as the religion of Afghanistan, and the followers of other religions were to be protected. The royal succession was preserved. Article 4 makes it incumbent upon the King to rule in accordance with the Sharia. He was also the protector of the religion (Article 5). But the concept of citizenship was defined without discrimination or with preference to none. Citizenship rights and personal freedom were guaranteed under law (Articles 9-11), which included the right to education (Articles 14, 15), and the right to property (Article 19). Citizens were made duty-bound towards the Sharia (Article 16) and courts were mandated to dispense justice in accordance with the Sharia along with civil and criminal laws (Article 21). It was also indicated that all future amendments would take into account the laws of Sharia (Article 72). However, the 1924 Mangal revolt created a situation which hijacked the promulgation of the Constitution. The Loya Jirga was convened in the same year to discuss the amendments to the Constitution. Article 2 was modified with the addendum that the Sunni Hanafi code is the basis of the religion of Islam and that Hindus and Jews must pay the special tax and wear distinctive clothing. Article 9 was amended to the effect that citizenship was privileged to being a Sunni Hanafi Muslim and it shall be the reference to all judgements of individual's rights and freedoms.[15] All the Constitutions have been invariably ratified by the Loya Jirga. They represent the widest possible acclaim through representation of the elite of major ethnic groups.[16]

The 1931 Constitution was a result of a serious backlash from the religious revolt. Nadir Shah, realising the sensitivities, brought religion to the forefront while outlining the new Constitution. It was written in September 1931 and published in December 1932. Amin Saikal prefers to term it as the process of "national gradualism," which betrays conservatism in domestic politics and neutrality in the international arena.[17] It begins with Article 1 stating that "Islam is the sacred religion of Afghanistan" and the state follows the Hanafi doctrine. It also declared that the king can only be a Sunni Hanafi and among the subjects (Hindus and Jews) there is a degree of permissibility in their citizenship subject only to the tenets of Muslim society. Article 6 preordained the oath in the name of Allah. A very important law had been Article 16 which declared that "a person's residence is inviolable." The effort to balance secular education with Islamic learning was made by introducing Article 22, which required all educational institutions to teach in accordance with Islamic principles. Article 27 provided for the Shura (National Assembly), which represented the will of the people. Article 29 spoke of elected members to the Shura from Kabul and the provinces. There was also a provision for an Elder's Council (Article 65) and provincial councils in each province (Article 69).[18] Article 73 was explicit in stating that "no one can occupy a Ministerial position unless he/she is a Muslim and an Afghan citizen." The 1931 Constitution retained its function for long, but was gradually amended during the reign of Zahir Shah. The rights of women were gradually reinstated, and the seclusion and veil were disregarded in 1959 with the support of Prime Minster Daoud.[19]

The 1964 Constitution was a path-breaker as it formally established separation of the monarchy from the government. It provided for a constitutional monarchy with the king as the executive head. The legislature, which was hitherto known as the Shura, was now made bicameral. The people were elected by direct territorial representation. For the first time, it institutionalised the Loya Jirga with the king as its head. The hallmark of the 1964 Constitution was an independent judiciary and the creation of formal courts to dispense justice by upholding the supremacy of the Afghan Constitution.[20] It paved the way for electing the two-house (Wolesi and Meishrano) Jirga, and also at the provincial levels and the city councils. As a result, popular elections were held in 1965, which brought to the fore divergent ideological groups into the political arena of Afghanistan. The People's Democratic Party of Afghanistan (PDPA) leaders, Taraki, Karmal and Amin were seen as pro-Soviet. The Khalq was largely the subaltern rural-based political group, led by Taraki; whereas the Parcham was the Dari-speaking elite group led by Karmal and was largely Kabul-based. The Khalq believed in class warfare; but the Parchamites believed in moderation. The revolutionary stand of Khalq was declared anti-Islamic, anti-communist and unconstitutional.[21] The 1964 Constitution paved the way for political parties, though the 1965 elections were held on the basis of parties, and in 1967 the Afghan Parliament passed the political parties bill, but king Zahir Shah refused to promulgate it. While Louis Dupree pointed out to the "parliamentary individualism" as one of the sources of power to anarchic chiefs and mullahs, the absence of political parties has been considered by many commentators as a major factor behind the failure of parliamentary democracy introduced under the 1964 Constitution.[22]

Constitutional development after the Saur revolution in 1973 brought out the rivalry between the Republicans and the Islamists. Islam was put at the back burner and a number of socio-economic reforms were introduced, which threatened the traditional elite, including the clergy. Daoud, after proclaiming Afghanistan as a republic after the Saur Revolution, promulgated a new Constitution in 1977, which spoke of a one-party system. The provisional Constitution of 1980 was the first Marxist Constitution for Afghanistan. Before that, immediately after the April 1978 revolution, in May, a programme was released with the name, "Basic Lines of the Revolutionary Duties of the Democratic Republic of Afghanistan." It spoke at length on the objectives of the Saur Revolution, and the subsequent provisional Constitution tried to imbibe all Marxian maxims for a just and egalitarian society. The provisional Constitution bearing these tenets in its evolution recognises three kinds of ownership, namely—public, private and cooperative. The PDPA had given priority to land reforms which went against the feudal class by restricting them to 30 jerib (6 hectares) under Decree 6 and 8 of 1978. The haste with which it was implemented led to resistance among the traditional elite. The 1990 Constitution promulgated by Mohammad Najibullah aimed at reconciliation with the Mujahideen forces but failed to break ice as the latter could smell victory at the behest of the Central Intelligence Agency (CIA) and the Inter-Services Intelligence (ISI).

The 2004 Constitution

The 2004 Constitution, apart from formally creating a head of the state and the parliament, was entrusted with a significant task of defining the law and its enactment suitable to Afghan environs. The Judicial Commission (JC) and Constitutional Commission of Afghanistan (CCA) were set up to formulate the judicial apparatus for the Afghan state. The Preamble of the Constitution declares Afghanistan to be a religious nation believing in the faith of Islam. Articles 1-3 define Afghanistan to be an Islamic state though it eliminates the confines of Sunni Hanafi sect, which earlier used to be the condition. The important element in the 2004 Constitution is revealed in Article 4, which mentions numerous ethnic groups. This clearly highlights the ethnic basis of the Afghan society that is defined by the unitary concept of Afghan citizenship. The ethno-federal basis of the Afghan state is also visible in the acknowledgement of the third official language other than Dari and Pashto, wherever there is a need (Article 16). This clearly marks a shift from previous Constitutions, which largely depended on Islam as the sole basis of the Afghan state. The national anthem of Afghanistan (Article 20) is in Pashto, but it emphasises the naming of all major tribal groups, meaning the relegation of Islam and bringing ethnic pluralism to the fore. Article 35 allows the practice of faiths and formation of associations, but it subjects all such acts to be bound by law and not in contravention to Islam. This permits judicial subjectivity in interpreting what is permissible and not contrary to Islam. Articles 62 and 63 retain the necessity of the Afghan president to be a Muslim and take oath in the name of Islam. Articles 110-115 formally institutionalise the Loya Jirga along with the National

Assembly (comprising the Upper and the Lower Houses). This might bring in the theological stricture in the state apparatus, if they find it difficult to get it passed in the National Assembly. Articles 116-135 represent the various norms adopted for establishing the judiciary. It mentions in Articles 130-131 that the Sunni Hanafi code shall be a residuary law where there is absence of formal constitutional law, and marks the distinction with the mention of Shia laws wherever needed.[23]

Conclusion

February 2007 was in a way a reversal when the town of Musla Qala was seized by the Taliban, decapitating the state authorities. The major slogan for the Taliban this time was not Islam and Sharia, but poppy. The Taliban proclaimed to Pashtun farmers that as long as they are in power no one could destroy their poppy fields. The call was not to bring an Islamic order, but to reinstall the ethno-geopolitical balance of power, which was allegedly in favour of northern Afghans. The districts of Helmand, cities of Qalat, Ghazni, Kunar, Kandahar, Jalalabad and Uruzgan were claimed by the Taliban forces at that time. Although they were flushed out later by the British forces by 2009, it brought out the stark reality of equipotential chances of war taking on ethnic colours, in the same way as the Islamisation had become the reigning ideology. The jihad does not turn into Pashtunwali. This tactical hedging of motives gives the Taliban an added advantage. It has tried to hide behind the ethnic facade, whenever their atrocious acts have been criticised. The relentless opposition of Afghanistan's 2004 Constitution has been the bulwark of their anti-state policy. They insist on bringing in the rule of Sharia oblivious to the fact that the present Constitution, like its predecessors, has also been categorical in stating that "no law shall contravene the tenets of Islam" (Article 3). Then what makes them a persistent opponent to the Constitution? The "red lines" announced by then Secretary of State, Hillary Clinton, in January 2011 in the aftermath of the London Conference held in January 2010, brought forth the possibility of reconciliation on wide-ranging issues of governance, including power sharing, with the Taliban. However, the mask of a moderated Taliban simply could not hold for long and the killing of former President Rabbani in September 2011, showed that the Taliban still retains the ethnic grudge against the other ethnic groups. This revealed that Islam would be given a bypass and the hegemonic ethnocracy, serving the interest of the majoritarian groups shall be the norm. The rest of the minority would be subject to the gaols in the name of being un-Islamic, a.k.a. anti-nationalists. Fear looms large among the smaller minorities from the Hazaras onwards.[24] The genuine spirit of justice could only be held on to, if all groups have equal stakes in state power. The tenets of Islam do not differentiate, but power does not run across ethnic groups, it runs along kinship groups in Afghanistan. Therefore, Islamism per se is juxtaposed with tribal authorities, and invariably, the extremists have found themselves on the wrong side of the polity, whence they are seen as a threat to tribal organisation of power. No doubt the aim of Afghan reconstruction was not to bring back tribal polity instead of an Islamic one. But, if the effort to sustain the progressive momentum is not maintained, then, certainly, the reversal would be of the worst kind, undoubtedly, and women, children and the minorities would bear the maximum impact.

Notes

1. Ashraf Ghani, "Islam and State-Building in a Tribal Society Afghanistan: 1880-1901," *Modern Asian Studies,* 12(2), 1978, pp. 269-84.
2. Conrad Schetter, "Ethnoscapes, National Territorialisation, and the Afghan War," *Geopolitics*, 10, 2005, pp. 50-75.
3. James M. Caron, "Afghanistan Historiography and Pashtun Islam: Modernization Theory's After-image," *History Compass,* 5 (2), 2007, pp. 314-29.
4. Anthony D. Smith, "Ethnic cores and dominant ethnics," in Eric Kaufmann (ed.), *Rethinking Ethnicity: Majority Groups and Dominant Minorities* (London: Routledge, 2004), pp. 15-26.
5. Asta Olesen, *Islam and Politics in Afghanistan* (Surrey: Curzon Press, 1995).
6. Husain Haqqani, "India's Islamist Groups," in *Current Trends in Islamist Ideology* 3, February 16, 2006, at http://www.currenttrends.org/research/detail/indias-islamist-groups.
7. Christina Jones-Pauly and Neamat Nojumi, "Balancing Relations between Society and State: Legal Steps toward National Reconciliation and Reconstruction of Afghanistan," *The American Journal of Comparative Law*, 52 (4) Autumn, 2004, pp. 825-57.
8. Thomas Barfield, *Afghan Customary Law and Its Relationship to Formal Judicial Institutions* (Washington, DC: United States Institute for Peace, June 26, 2003).
9. Olivier Roy, *Islam and Resistance in Afghanistan* (Cambridge, UK: Cambridge University Press, 1990), p. 10.
10. Achievistic and ascriptive social structures, are sociological terms, for example, caste is ascriptive but class is achievistic. Similarly, here bureaucracy based on merit is achievistic and monarchy is ascriptive.
11. Louis Dupree, *Afghanistan* (Princeton: Princeton University Press, 1973).
12. Larry Goodson, "The Fragmentation of Culture in Afghanistan," *Alif: Journal of Comparative Poetics* (18), 1998, pp. 269-89.
13. Political term used to define the persons who represent the state in the countryside, derived from Statism (in Japan).
14. Thomas Ruttig, *Afghanistan's Early Reformists*, AAN Occasional Paper, Afghanistan Analysts Network, 2008.
15. "The 1923 Constitution," Afghanistan Legal Document Exchange Centre (ALDEC), at http://afghantranslation.checchiconsulting.com/.

16. M. Jamil Hanifi, "Editing the Past: Colonial Production of Hegemony Through the 'Loya Jerga,'" *Afghanistan, Iranian Studies,* 37 (2), June 2004.
17. Amin Saikal, *Modern Afghanistan* (New York: I. B. Taurus, 2004).
18. "The 1931 Constitution," Afghanistan Legal Document Exchange Centre (ALDEC), at http://afghantranslation.checchiconsulting.com/.
19. Deniz Kandiyoti, *The Politics of Gender and Reconstruction in Afghanistan*, Occasional Paper 4, United Nations Research Institute for Social Development, 2005.
20. J. Alexander Thier, *The Making of a Constitution in Afghanistan*, LSE Research Online, 2010, 2006.
21. Mohammad Hashim Kamali, "Law in Afghanistan: A Study of the Constitutions, Matrimonial Law and the Judiciary," *Social Economic and Political Studies of the Middle East and Asia*, no. 36, August 1997.
22. Louis Dupree, *Afghanistan Continues Its Experiment in Democracy: The Thirteenth Parliament is Elected*, American Universities Field Staff Reports, 1971.
23. "The 2004 Constitution," Afghanistan Legal Document Exchange Centre (ALDEC), at http://afghantranslation.checchiconsulting.com/.
24. Kenneth Katzman, *Afghanistan: Politics, Elections, and Government Performance*, Congressional Research Service, 2009.

4. Afghanistan's Political Institutions: A New Approach

Bahram Amirahmadian

There is an unsolved "crisis triangle" in Afghanistan comprising drugs, terrorism and extremism. Drugs are produced by peasants and farmers, but their trade is controlled by the drug mafias. These mafias are active in various spheres from banditry to local and international politics. This is an important network that works in a foolproof system and consists of many subsystems employing a lot of people all around the world, who hail from Afghanistan. The network is well-oiled and protected and any attempt to give this system the slip faces its wrath. In the last ten years, the United States (US) and its allies, in spite of the most modern weaponry, technology and international support at their disposal, have not succeeded in controlling these mafias. The Taliban, drugs and terrorism still exist. The Taliban exists because of many factors and one of the important factors is the tribal, traditional and social structure of Afghan society. All initiatives to deal with the Afghan problem should take into account the social structure.

Afghanistan, like some other countries, is grappling with some important national issues. In Afghanistan two forces have been playing significant roles. There are forces that would like to engage with the West, to improve governance with intellectuals playing a key role. Many in the Karzai government belonged to this group. The other group is against the opening up of the Afghan society to the West and the international community. Those affiliated to this thinking would like to govern the country under the principles of Sharia. They want to keep the Afghan society isolated and patriarchal. They abhor nationalism and try to fight it from within, and would like to spread Islam as a world society. The Taliban and the extremists belong to this group. Women have no rights in such a society and are under the shadow and control of males in the family. Since the beginning of the twentieth century, the country has been struggling to solve these problems and arrive at a compromise. Afghanistan, due to its ethnic composition and geography, has the potential to disintegrate. This challenge created an equilibrium in Afghanistan, that resulted in the present situation. The lack of a powerful and authoritative central government in Kabul, existence of effective local governments and traditional structures in the regions, and a weak communication network in the country, besides a complicated ethnic composition, are the main reasons for instability. Foreign military forces in Afghanistan, and clashes between them and the Taliban make the situation more difficult.

Islamic Structure

In Islamic thought, Islam covered all the territory in which Muslims lived. Since historic times, Islamic territory expanded from the Arabian Peninsula in many directions. This territory was called *Thughur-al-Islam* (traditional Islamic frontlines). The Muslim populations which were living in this territory were called *Ummat*. The concept of "nation" was unknown. After the *Rashidin* Caliphs, in the first Islamic century (seventh century AD) the Islamic State was led by the Caliphs who called themselves *Caliphs of Muslims* and governed the *Ummat*. After the death of Imam Ali, the fourth *Rashidin*, many Arab dynasties ruled the Islamic world until the emergence of the Ottoman Empire in the fourteenth century. After the disintegration of the Ottoman Empire, the last Islamic State, there were no powerful Islamic states to integrate all Islamic nations. Thus, from the beginning of the twentieth century, large Islamic countries occupied the centre stage becoming the core of the Islamic world. Saudi Arabia, as the land of Mecca and Medina (*Haramain-al-Sharifain,* the holy shrines); Iran as the land of the Shiites, who claim to be the direct descendants of Prophet Muhammad; and Turkey as the inherited land of the Ottoman Caliphs, the successors of Prophet Muhammad, would like to be recognised as the custodians of the core values of Islam.

Some of the real believers of Islam like to follow the same principles that were prevalent in the early years of Islam. However, it is believed that two main branches of Islamic thought emerged including one of moderate Islam which is being practised in Egypt by the *Ikhvan-ol-Muslemin* (Islamic Brotherhood) and in Turkey by the Justice and Development Party (AK Party), and the other of reactionary Islam, mainly practised by Salafi[1] thinkers who had within them the supporters of Talibanism. This apart, it is important to distinguish between the following groups, thought of as concentric circles. First, the "Jihadist Salafis" who are the followers of Al Qaeda and like-minded local groups; second, the "Salafis" who believe that the imitation of the behaviour of the Prophet's closest companions should be the basis for the social order; third, the "Islamists" who are a still broader category including anyone who thinks that the precepts of Islam, however interpreted, should be fundamental to the political and social order; and lastly the "Discontented Muslims" who identify themselves as Muslims, and who are unhappy with their life, with their societies, and/or with the state of the wider world. The Salafi jihadist movement has attracted rootless and/or committed international militants. They fight the jihad, seeking to recreate the Muslim *Ummah* and Shariat to build an Islamic community.[2]

Modern Islam which is practised in many Islamic countries such as Turkey, Malaysia [Sunni] and Iran [Shia], differs from region to region. In the Islamic World (comprising 54 countries), there are several different political, social and economic systems. Traditional Islamists are thinking about "Unity of Muslims" (*Itihad-al-Mislimin*) but in reality, Islamic territories are not integrated in any other way except by the religion Islam. Although, they have commonalities with respect to population (1.6 billion), natural resources (petroleum and natural gas) and cultural heritage—most of the Muslim scholars and thinkers who have tried across centuries to create a united Islamic state, have largely failed so far. For example, during the sixteenth century, till the collapse of the Ottoman Empire in the early twentieth century, there was no cooperation and integration between Sunni Ottomans and Shiite Iranians. Even political Islamic movements and scholars such as Hassan al-Banna, the founder of *Ikhvan-ol-Mulimin* in Egypt, and the Shiite movement led by Iranian Shiite leaders such as Jamal-od-Din Asad Abadi and Dr. Sharieti and Mehdi Bazargan, and recently Imam Khomeini, could not create their desired Islamic State. All Muslim communities (with the exception of Iran and Afghanistan, that follow the solar Islamic calendar) use the Christian calendar in which Sunday is the holiday, while among Muslims the last day of the week is Friday (*Jum'a*).

It is interesting to analyse why the Taliban leaders do not learn from these experiences and continue to support a reactionary political system financed by the drug mafia that has had and will continue to have a very negative effect on millions of Muslim *Ummah*. Unless Muslim Muftis approve a *Fatwa* that any income which comes from drugs is *Haram,* and giving up of their dealings in drugs should be obeyed as Muslims, and otherwise they are not Muslims—such practice cannot be stalled. Unfortunately, no Mufti or Taliban leader has undertaken this responsibility. In some weak countries such as Afghanistan, Pakistan and Central Asian Republics (CARs) like Tajikistan, that are designated as Islamic countries, there are some political parties, movements and even some people who would like to establish an Islamic government within their societies. But they are largely unsuccessful. In Iran, due to its political and economic conditions inherited from the Shah regime, an Islamic government was born through an Islamic Revolution in 1979 led by Ayatollah Khomeini, and supported by the Muslim population and very rich oil resources. The recent pro-democracy movements in North

Africa and the Middle East, which are commonly called the Arab Spring, are often evaluated as an "Islamic Awakening" in Iran and some other countries. Tunisia and Egypt were against the establishment of an Islamic State, but wanted a modern secular political system with Islam as the basis of civil law.

Afghanistan's entity is that of an Islamic and traditional country. Afghanistan, as many other developing countries, has to face the challenge of modernity versus tradition. It is actually a country steeped in tradition which since the beginning of the twentieth century has become partially modern, but it was a long and hard road to travel. Even now, there are differences between the various social strata. In rural areas and some small towns, the people live in societies based on tribal traditions. In some urban areas the tribal and traditional customs still endure. Sometimes the social structure itself creates obstacles for modern society, as is common with other countries of the world. Here, from the point of view of the Islamists and the traditionalists, women are in a situation supported by tradition which does not allow them to have social and economic rights. It means that half of Afghan society remains inactive. In some geographically isolated regions, girls are not allowed to go to school and traditional schools for boys are still functioning. Soviet occupation had only a marginal influence in the change from tribal to modern. The American occupation also could not change it successfully, because the system of production has not been changed and the relations between productive forces still remain traditional.

Furthermore, Afghanistan is a traditional Islamic community, which practises its own ways of governance. Many administrative units have been created keeping in mind its ethnicity; and one of the best examples of Afghanistan's traditional system of governance is the *Jirga.*[3] The *Jirga* as a council of elders is a unique forum in which tribal elders of each ethnic group convene to discuss and resolve issues related to polity and society. Even today in the Afghan government, they had to support the *Loya Jirga* to solve critical problems. The *Loya Jirga* is a centuries old tradition and a quintessential part of the Afghan government. As a decision-making assembly, the *Jirga* does not suffer from time limitations and continues until decisions are reached through consensus. The *Jirga* addresses a variety of issues, such as foreign policy, military action, or the introduction of new ideas and reforms. During the Karzai presidency, he and his government tried to engage the *Loya Jirga* to discuss some important national issues. Recently there was some debate between secular and traditionalist elements to employ the *Loya Jirga* to discuss the issue of whether or not to sign a strategic cooperation and giving its military base to the US. The secular and progressive forces believed that *Loya Jirga* is made up of tribal elders who have no knowledge and experience of modern governance and discussing new and modern national and international issues, as most of them are illiterate. Thus modern governance can only be successfully brought about in societies that have the potential to respond to it in a positive manner.

Entrenched Social Structure

Afghanistan is a poor country, with less than US $500 as per capita Gross Domestic Product (GDP). There is insufficient income generation because of weak economy, limitation of investment opportunities in the economic sector, lack of well-organised infrastructure, communication, transportation and lack of skilled manpower resulting in the continuation of a situation of underdevelopment. Economic data to explain the problem will be referred to later. The only economic sector which has potential and attraction for employment is agriculture and the main activity within it is opium cultivation. Those who belong to the traditional tribal culture are not able to break free from this system and have to coexist within the system. Some leaders of these traditional systems abuse their authority to gain the support of the community to maintain the status quo. One of the ways is production of drugs. Perhaps some tribals and their families work as a tool for drug mafias, but they are entrenched in the system to such an extent that they cannot break away from it. This is the reason why the system is still flourishing.

Government Effectiveness

The central government has minimal authority within the traditional system. A powerful modern government needs to be effective in order to be successful. The history of modern state formation in Afghanistan began in the early twentieth century under the reformist King Amanullah. Unlike other less developed countries, Afghanistan's late state-building exercise did not benefit from the political and economic resources of colonisation, as other countries in the region did, since Afghanistan was never fully colonised. Afghanistan's inexperience in building a new state was further undermined by Afghan conservatives and traditionalists, who reacted strongly to the austere modernisation reforms the reformist king introduced. This eventually led to the dethroning of the king, which effectively slowed down the process of state-building in Afghanistan in the following decades until the advent of the Cold War.

In the early decades of the Cold War, the Afghan monarchy pursued a neutral and non-aligned foreign policy, which isolated Afghanistan and thus affected its state formation efforts for some time. But it was soon realised that Afghanistan's severe underdevelopment needed long-term foreign aid, which would not be forthcoming unless the country changed its passive foreign policy. While the Soviet Union provided military and development assistance to Afghanistan in an effort to support the country's Marxist and Communist movements, Afghanistan was drawn into the Cold War. Therefore, during the last two decades of the Cold War, Afghanistan's young and weak state increasingly became dependent on Soviet aid, which meant that impartial Afghan technocrats lacked the freedom to pursue an effective state-building strategy. This led to an overly subsidised and centralised state, which was too ideologically inclined to be able to expand beyond urban areas with a small following.

The 1990s saw the complete destruction of state institutions that had been created till date. When the international community re-engaged in Afghanistan in 2001, they had to start building a state from ground up, and that process began with the Bonn Agreement of December 2001. Indeed, the shared goal of Afghanistan and the international community was to revive the Afghan state. However, many of the state institutions in Afghanistan continue to lack the basic capacity and resources to implement their mandates. One of the key factors contributing to the weakness of the state apparatus in Afghanistan is the emergence of a parallel aid bureaucracy operating alongside the Afghan state from which it is sapping the scarce aid resources provided by the donor. The donors strategically coordinate their aid efforts in Afghanistan and increasingly channel their assistance through Afghanistan's national budget or the Afghanistan National Development Strategy (ANDS) framework. The only way one can effectively measure success in Afghanistan is the extent to which the Afghan state has been collectively driven to take on the rebuilding task. If, for example, the army or the police is independently operational and can defend Afghanistan against terrorists, one can claim it as a success and be confident that when international forces exit the country, the Afghan state will be self-sustaining and will not collapse again.[4]

Rule of Law

Afghanistan needs a legal system which its people can trust. A reversion to the *Jirga* system would keep the country in the dark ages. But this issue has been persistently debated among the Afghan authorities. Traditionalists believe that age-old social customs are the only ways to promote security. The numerous meetings organised by the government and the international community in Kabul sought to legitimise and institutionalise traditional legal practices. But plans for rebuilding Afghanistan always seem to seek the shortest route and have repeatedly resulted in failure. The state structure in Afghanistan is such that makes the Taliban an intrinsic part of traditional Afghan society who also has an important role to play in the Islamic state. At the London conference in January 2010, there were talks regarding reconciliation or reintegration of the Taliban, but the Afghan government and its international allies failed to put a legitimate and functional judicial system in place. Reintegration of the Taliban should only be discussed when there is a proper judicial system in place. The London conference, for that matter, failed to consider how the judicial system could be strengthened and made more effective.

There are many problems with this short-cut approach. First, it will undermine the Constitution. Second, it will not allow the legal system to be implemented properly. Third, it will be an obstacle to legal practices based on international human rights. Fourth, and most importantly, it will keep Afghanistan away from progress and force it to stay in the dark ages. *Jirgas* are assemblies of men, organised by men for men. Women have never been involved in *Jirgas* in Afghanistan. Now there are talks about constituting a "women's Jirga," which, on the one hand, will satisfy our international allies, but, on the other, is likely to create more problems for the Afghan society. Afghanistan has many women as members of its parliament but very few of them are independent. The bottom line is that the decisions are made by men regardless of women's participation in the *Jirga*. Only through a proper legal system can we increase women's participation in the judicial system. In some of the distant villages a system of informal justice prevails. In most cases, the informal justice systems are not fair—they always benefit the party who is closer to the elders and decision-makers—and they are rarely in favour of women.[5]

Afghan people want and demand a legal system to fall back on and to trust. The only way to bring security back to Afghanistan, and therefore to the rest of the world, is through a legitimate legal system which protects the population. No matter how large the military or the police force becomes, if there is no legal system to shield the population from violations of human rights, we will not have the support of the Afghans, which is crucial to succeed in this fight. US efforts to promote the rule of law in Afghanistan are expanding and accelerating. Nearly a billion dollars has been spent in the past decade to strengthen Afghanistan's legal infrastructure, rising from $7 million in FY 2002 to an estimated $411 million in FY 2010. In July 2010, a new Ambassador-rank position was created to focus on justice-related issues in the country. Yet the effectiveness and even the feasibility of these efforts to establish the rule of law are in doubt.[6]

Control of Corruption

A recent survey by Integrity Watch Afghanistan (IWA) shows a sharp expansion in corruption in Afghan society. Most Afghans now see the payment of bribes as a routine part of obtaining government services. In the three years since IWA made public its previous corruption survey, the group found that the amount paid in bribes more than doubled. Afghans paid an estimated $1 billion in bribes in 2009, whereas IWA pegged the figure in its 2006 survey at $466 million. The so-called commission-kars, or fixers, are seen increasingly as a permanent part of the social landscape. These middlemen are believed to be involved in up to 40 per cent of bribery transactions. Though international attention has focused primarily on high-level corruption, it is the day-to-day graft involved in the provision of basic government services that impacts most Afghans. Overall, 28 per cent of the Afghan households had to pay a bribe to receive some sort of public service that, under different conditions, should have been easily accessible. One in seven Afghans was directly involved in a corrupt transaction in some manner, either paying or receiving, according to IWA. IWA's National Corruption Survey 2010 sampled 6,500 Afghans in 32 of the country's 34 provinces. The results were released on July 8, 2010.[7] Contrary to the image of the Afghan government and its institutions being inefficient and lacking capacity, 70 per cent of the respondents said they were certain they could get services if they paid a bribe.

The Economic Situation

With 80 per cent of the population living in the rural areas, the agricultural sector accounts for around one-third of Afghanistan's economy (excluding the illicit drug sector). Real GDP grew by around 8.5 per cent in 2010-11 (SY1389), down from 22.5 per cent the year before, which reflected recovery from the poor harvest in 2008-9 (SY1387). In 2010-11 (SY1389), per capita GDP reached $609. According to a report in the *Statistical Yearbook 2010-2011*, only 23 per cent of the Afghan population lives in urban areas. Approximately 70 per cent of the population is under the age of 30 years; 46 per cent of the population is under the age of 15 years. The same source shows that the agricultural sector accounts for 27-31 per cent of the GDP, while the share of industry is 20-25 per cent and that of services is 44-48 per cent. It is clear that the agricultural sector is not able to generate enough income for the rural population.

Education

Enrolment rates for primary school children (aged 6 to 9) increased nationwide by about 40 per cent between 2005 and 2007-8, but only 34.9

per cent of kids enrolled and attended school regularly. However, even with this improvement, only 37.6 per cent of the young adult population (aged 15 to 24) can read and write and the female literacy rate is less than half that of men, namely, 22 per cent for women against 51 percent for men.

Access to Electricity

The percentage of the population with access to electricity in Afghanistan is among the lowest in the world. The Ministry of Energy and Water estimates that about 30 per cent of Afghans have access to electricity from grid-based power, micro-hydro or solar panel stations. The situation has improved significantly in the major urban population centres along the critical northeast corridor between Mazar-e-Sharif and Kabul, following the import of power from Uzbekistan and the rehabilitation of three hydro plants (Mahipar and Sarobi completed, and Naghlu ongoing). Substantial parts of some urban centres, for example in Kabul, Herat, Mazar-e-Sharif and Pul-e-Khumri, now have 24-hour power supply for the first time in decades.[8]

Last year the international community allocated US $16.8 billion to help Afghanistan, out of which only 65 per cent was paid. Among Muslim countries, Iran paid $ 1 million and Turkey paid $ 38 million. China paid only $ 1 million, but India, the third largest Asian economy, paid $ 313 million. Russia paid only $ 5 million. It is interesting that Japan with $ 752 million, the US and the West with $ 13,069 million, Germany with $ 594 million, Great Britain with $ 383 million have totally paid 84 per cent of the donors' share to Afghanistan.

Conclusion

The hardline Islamic Taliban movement has proved to be a formidable fighting force in Afghanistan and a major threat to its government. The Taliban also threatens to destabilise Pakistan, where they control areas in the northwest and have been blamed for a wave of suicide bombings and other attacks.[9] Talibanism is a thought; it is not a political party. It is an ideology related to some kind of Islamic thought which may or may not be true. But it is a reality that it has thousands of believers who have accepted this ideology and obey it. How can we ignore it and its followers? They are Afghans and are citizens of Afghanistan and it is a fact that they established a government in Afghanistan and ruled between 1995 and 2000 until the US attacked the country. Would we be able to remove all of them from Afghanistan and Pakistan? This is an important question before the world community. In a decade of fighting with foreign troops, not only have they not been destroyed, but have also emerged stronger than before, with the result that they are able to threaten the capital city and indulge in terror activities like Burhan-ud-din Rabbani's assassination in Kabul. After a decade of fighting, the international coalition forces concluded that they have to negotiate with the Taliban. Many observers now believe that peace in Afghanistan can only be achieved if the government in Kabul negotiates with the Taliban. The announcement of the Taliban's plans to open an office in Qatar is seen as a positive step towards negotiations, but distrust on both sides remains. There are also unconfirmed reports stating that some of the Taliban-linked groups in Pakistan have held talks with the government in Islamabad.[10]

In recent times, some proposals of dealing with the Taliban including military operations and soft diplomacy have been discussed. In the 1980s Afghanistan was occupied by Soviet troops, but within 10 years of Soviet presence, there was instability in Afghanistan. By the end of the Cold War, the Soviets had to leave Afghanistan. After the withdrawal of Soviet troops, the Mujahideen appeared, and began governing the country. But due to clashes between different Jihadi groups, the Taliban occupied most of the country. Clashes between the Taliban and the Mujahideen continued. They ruled Afghanistan till September 11, 2001, by which time considerable damage had taken place in the country. The attacks on the US on September 11, signalled the arrival of Al Qaeda. All the tactics employed by the US and the North Atlantic Treaty Organisation (NATO) coalition forces with the help of UN Security Council resolutions, pushed the Al Qaeda back. But the problems of terrorism, drugs, arms trading, and the Taliban still remain.

While taking into account several models and methods practised in Afghanistan, it is clear that not even one of them has succeeded. The regional model comprising the Islamic countries and the Organisation of Islamic Cooperation (OIC) can be considered as an experimental model in this regard. Their efforts and resources towards social and economic development after taking care of security issues are susceptible to use by the warring groups to their advantage. To deal with such a situation, peacekeeping forces comprising troops from Islamic countries could replace the NATO coalition forces. The borders of Afghanistan and Pakistan (the Durand Line), are one of the most dangerous places in the world. The drugs, arms and human trafficking are being carried on from these borders. If these boundaries are controlled by military and police forces, it may reduce instability. To do so, more manpower and resources are needed. New technology can be used besides manpower. A coalition of armed forces must be created under the aegis of the UN, and the OIC comprising only Muslim countries. Neighbouring countries should be excluded, because all of them may develop economic, ethnic, political and cultural vested interests in

Afghanistan. The Taliban then will not be able to seek an excuse or pretext to be armed and fight with non-Muslim soldiers. In this regard the local tribes, institutions and individuals will not be forced to support the Taliban fighters on the basis of the pretext of fighting with non-Muslim forces that have captured and occupied their country or as a right to fight against them in a holy war (Jihad). Turkey, Egypt, Indonesia, Bangladesh and some other volunteer OIC member-countries, could participate in such peacekeeping operations.

As we know, Afghanistan is a landlocked country. Recently the Taliban reacted to the presence of the International Security Assistance Force (ISAF) and coalition forces, by closing the communication route and logistics for NATO from Pakistan. They blocked the Khyber Pass and burnt many fuel tankers and did not allow free movement for international forces. NATO requested Iran to provide a road from its territory, but due to friction in US-Iran relations the request was rejected. Support to the ISAF forces could have come from Russia and the CARs. This has its own problems and directly depends on Russia's relations with the West, mainly with the US, from time to time. In the case of the OIC forces there will be a chance of Iran providing a connecting route to the international forces and much more, because Iran's security is directly related to security in Afghanistan.

Afghanistan is suffering from the lack of a legitimate central government, drug trafficking, nomadic structure of society, an extreme form of Islam along with, more importantly, the rule of the mafias and the warlords. It has been repeatedly said that while the drug mafia is active, the situation will not improve. Money from drugs is considerable and it is an easily earned capital that has no substitute. While there are a few advantages for those who are dealing with agricultural activities and have an income from cultivation of poppy, the traders make a big profit. So it is beneficial to those who are on the other side and the conditions are stable for them. For fulfilling these aims, the farmers should be kept in a closed, traditional and tribal society. A closed society helps the drug mafia to carry on its activities undisturbed. One reason for the continuation of the present situation could be found here.

It is clear that in tribal society, the traditional hierarchical system is functioning. Nobody has rights to act independently. The leader and head decides on behalf of the others. So, when those leaders and heads of clans and tribes are ready to join the process of drug cultivation and trade, there will be no protest and obstacle and all members of society will obey. The reason is that agriculture alone, in the small plots that the peasants have, is not able to meet their livelihood costs. So, given the comparative weakness in relation to other economic sectors such as industry and trade, the best and easy source of money is drug cultivation and trafficking. But according to Islamic law any production, such as alcoholic drinks and materials which damage health, are "harăm," and those who engage in such activities, their incomes are defiled and the occupation should be given up. The "Mufti," a Sunni Islamic scholar who is an interpreter or expounder of Islamic law (Sharia) can issue *fetwă* (a holy commandment directed to Muslims). But the recent and contemporary history of Afghanistan does not highlight usage of this law. This procedure could be employed in an Islamic country such as Afghanistan where the faith and beliefs of rural societies are more powerful than urban areas.

Let us come back to the traditional means of Islamic society. In a traditional society like the one mentioned before it is possible to carry on these tasks. Many Afghan peasants and villagers are under the influence and authority of clerics. So in the framework that has been outlined, the social structure can prohibit the cultivation, trafficking and trading of drugs in the society. But there are no experiences of such a controlled influence. It should be practised at least once. When the production of drugs decreases, it means that the revenue of the drug mafia will reduce and they will not have enough funds to carry on. The Sunni Islamic leaders in Mecca, Medina, and Cairo, and Shiite centres such as Najaf and Ghom, could approve *fetwă* about prohibition of all processes of production of opium and heroin by any means and anywhere, and the *fetwă* should be implemented. It is natural that those persons who are engaged in drug trafficking and whose life depends on it, should be financially supported by rich Muslim countries till they find new sources of income. Investment in economic infrastructure to introduce new jobs is an important issue. In the years that have passed after the withdrawal of Soviet troops, we were witness to increasing drugs production by 8,000-9,000 tons annually.

In early Taliban rule the production of opium decreased. But it increased substantially after the attack of the coalition forces. It was clear that some groups could exploit the opportunities to their benefit. Their pretext was that an Islamic country was occupied by foreign and infidel forces, and they should protect the country's independence and rescue it from invaders. But, in fact, the coalition forces disturbed the autonomy leading to instability which continues to this day. The tribal system and traditions complemented the traditional way of life. It is hoped that after 2014, when the coalition forces leave Afghanistan, with simultaneous peace negotiations with the Taliban, the proposals enumerated above can be implemented.

Parallel to these initiatives, cultural activities should be carried on to prepare the much needed atmosphere for change which will take place in behaviour and habits. Mass media, especially radio and television, have an important role to introduce the initiatives to the masses. Local leaders should be well trained about the importance of changes, to influence the view of their people for change.

Notes

1. A Salafi is a follower of the Sunni Islamic movement, Salafiyyah, that is supposed to take the *Salaf* who lived during the patristic period of early Islam (c. 100-450) as model examples. The word *Salafi* should not be confused with the Arabic word *Salaf* ("predecessor" or "forefather"), and the first three Muslim generations are collectively referred to as *as-Salaf as-Saleh,* or The Pious Predecessors.
2. Salafi Islam, see http://www.globalsecurity.org/military/intro/islam-salafi.htm.
3. Historically a Pashto term, Loya Jirga, translates to "grand council."
4. "Building a New State in Afghanistan," Speech of Ashraf Haidari, Political Counsellor, at the School of Advanced International Studies (SAIS), Johns Hopkins University at http://www.embassyofafghanistan.org/07.20.2009ashraf.html.
5. "No short cuts to Afghan justice," February 10, 2010 at http://www.guardian.co.uk/commentisfree/2010/feb/10/short-cuts-wont-work-afghanistan.
6 Steven Aftergood, "Seeking the Rule of Law in Afghanistan," November 22, 2010 at http://www.fas.org/blog/secrecy/2010/11/afghanistan_rol.html.
7. Aunohita Mojumdar, "Corruption Expanding at Alarming Rate in Afghanistan—Survey," July 13, 2010 at http://www.eurasianet.org/node/61518.
8. "Afghanistan Country Overview 2011" at http://www.worldbank.org.af/website/external/countries/southasiaext/afganistanextn/
9. "Who Are Taliban?" *BBC*, January 3, 2012.
10. Ibid.

5. NATO's Withdrawal from Afghanistan: Post-2014 Scenarios

Maqsudul Hasan Nuri

Introduction

The fifth Afghan war seems to be winding down slowly but surely. In late 2009 President Barack Obama agreed to deploy 33,000 additional troops commonly termed as "surge" in Afghanistan in a bid to defeat the Taliban and start negotiations. This peaked to 100,000 in summer 2011 and since then the number is 91,000 troops with the remainder scheduled to withdraw by 2014. The United States (US)-led North Atlantic Treaty Organisation (NATO) forces have three broad options in Afghanistan: (a) To fight and destroy completely the Taliban insurgent forces; (b) To negotiate with the Taliban, and (c) To finally withdraw, leaving behind Afghan forces to deal with them. The chapter is premised on the assumption that barring any major untoward incident which could subvert the time table, total withdrawal of US-led forces shall be completed by the end of 2014 as planned. The National Intelligence Estimate (NIE) classified report[1] has outlined the differences that could jeopardise the Obama Administration's planned withdrawal of most of the US troops and oversee the smooth transfer of power to the Afghan government by 2014.

One view holds that the Taliban are gaining influence in eastern Afghanistan and a lot of territory is under their control. They are hence a force to be reckoned with. On the other hand, Pentagon and military commanders think that the above intelligence estimates may not be based on sound premises. Also, detractors hold that NIE estimates proved wrong in Iraq. The build-up of 400,000 Afghan troops and police will enable a phased withdrawal. The Obama Administration is positive of "substantial progress" in Afghanistan and their military commanders do not foresee post-2014 commitment to that country.[2] Moreover, the drone attacks were quite successful against militants and some sanctuaries on the Pakistani soil. Both views may border on the extreme, although the truth, to be sure, lies somewhere in-between. But the harsh fact is that the deteriorating US economy, the fatigue of a decade-long war, the stalemate in Afghanistan and the resulting public disenchantment together with coming US presidential elections, argue for a drawdown of forces.

Different scenarios are being conjured up after the US-led NATO forces withdraw from Afghanistan.[3] They range from the optimistic to the pessimistic and with a mixture of both. While it is always difficult to exactly prognosticate how the chain of events unfold and when intervening variables may suddenly appear to morph the scenarios, nevertheless, some broad generalisations based on existing trends and flow of events can be ventured.

Positive Scenarios

Peaceful Afghanistan

A peaceful Afghanistan is based on a pluralistic arrangement created after the exit of the NATO forces. There is a general tendency to coexist and share power by different ethnic groups. Some think that after the experience of thirty years of conflict, material and moral exhaustion, different parties will forge cooperation to rule together. Also, in a world where interdependence is the norm, no one group can dominate Afghanistan as did the Taliban from 1996 to 2001. The view is also supported by the fact that fast-track economic development should take place once a professional Afghan National Army (ANA) is operational. This could be an ideal dispensation in which the Taliban are delinked from Al Qaeda; a regional consensus of immediate neighbours emerges; a minimum protective security cover of foreign forces is available; and strong national and police forces are raised to maintain national integrity and sovereignty. In other words, an Afghanistan at peace with itself and with the outside world would be a boon for the region and the international community.

OIC-Sponsored Peacekeeping Forces

If the Organisation of Islamic Cooperation (OIC)-sponsored Muslim Peacekeeping Forces are deployed for a few years till the ANA and police are robust enough to undertake the burden, the scenario could be a positive one. Turkey has had a good track record of peacekeeping before and given its political and economic standing in the Islamic world, could be more acceptable than others. Albeit a good proposal, this is not very likely to happen as no country would easily volunteer to deploy forces in Afghanistan in present circumstances, given the traits of fierce independence, hostility and distrust of outside forces, history of violence and national hypersensitivities among Afghans.

Neutral Afghanistan[4]

A neutral Afghanistan is an excellent proposition. The ground reality is that neighbours could favour their own ethnic group(s) and proxies (Uzbeks, Tajiks). Iranians, Indians and Pakistanis have done so in providing weapons, training and logistics to their favoured groups. None of the big powers such as the US, China and Russia may tolerate a neutral Afghanistan. Each has a stake in that country. What incentives could all of these provide to keep Afghanistan neutral, it is often asked?

Negative Scenarios

Civil War-like Situation

A sordid scenario foresees eruption of an all-out civil war in Afghanistan once the NATO-led International Security Assistance Force (ISAF) forces leave, creating a vacuum of sorts. All regional players would like to protect their regional interests and support ethnic kinsmen/allies against the Taliban. This includes China, the Central Asian Republics (CARs), Iran, India and Russia. Some analysts think that setting a deadline for NATO forces' withdrawal is a mistake. This will result in internecine wars and the eruption of the prime sectarian and ethnic forces after the withdrawal.[5] The Taliban are the most aggrieved party and could make a bid for a war of vendetta and revenge against the Northern Alliance, now in power.

Takeover by the Taliban

The ANA comprising 300,000 troops is ill-equipped, ill-trained and not professionally competent to control the country, and there could be a replay of the 1992 scenario when the US departed in haste. This could lead to rise in militancy, influx of refugees in Pakistan and further souring of relations with Afghanistan. While the situation is qualitatively different from the 1990s when the Taliban ruled, they could still stage a comeback. Agreed that there is a state of exhaustion after decades of fighting, but new Taliban leadership has emerged, different from yesteryear and more pragmatic and aware of living in a globalised and interdependent world. Yet, their tribal culture of revenge and retribution and overvaulting ambition to control Afghanistan still exists. Moreover, if they are supported by external powers through ideological and financial props, they could go for capturing Kabul, the capital, in establishing an Islamic Emirate of Afghanistan.

Of course, this scenario will be anathema to all regional neighbours of Afghanistan as they do not want the Taliban to stage a comeback in any form and consequently infect adjoining borders by their radical ideology. That is one reason these countries shall exert to the hilt by arming their respective ethnic/ideological groups/proxies in resisting the menace of the Taliban.

US Residual Presence

There is a possibility that the withdrawal would not be completed unless some NATO residual forces are left to man some nodal installations and bases in Afghanistan. It is likely that the US may maintain its bases and station about 35,000 troops—the size of Korea or Japan—in Afghanistan. Perhaps this size may not be objected to by Russia and China and the CARs as a protective layer against Taliban influence. It is likely that Indian forces may be coopted. The US forces will include helicopter units for reconnaissance and possible military action in support of Afghan forces. Some contractors and intelligence personnel and American trainers may also be retained for the ANA and the police. These will follow a Status of Forces Agreement to protect the regime in Kabul. In case the US has plans of taking military action against Iran, then this plan may be delayed.

De Facto Partition

This option is neither liked by Pakistan nor any regional country as it could release dangerous forces and trends. This thesis has been propounded by former US Ambassador to India, Robert Blackwill, to break up the country on ethnic lines to stop internal fighting and make it manageable for the outside world. As ethnic identities of Tajiks, Hazaras and Uzbeks have become stronger over the years and the danger of civil war exists, the debate on limiting violence through separation of territorial units is in vogue in some quarters.

Break-up and disintegration of national units has taken opposing arguments. The disintegration of a nation is not liked by another or by its central leadership or the international community due to it setting a wrong precedent, and leading to emotional and physical suffering for that country's population. States do not like change in borders and birth of new units like Chechnya in Russia, Tibet in China. But in the last few years the break-up of Sudan, Kosovo and East Timor took place, and Somaliland, Palestine and Kurdistan are likely in the years to come. Chronic political instabilities in Africa, rise in ethnicities, high levels of poverty, crumbling infrastructures, ethnic and sectarian polarisation render many as "failing states" with added cartographic stresses.

Some observers foresee break-up of some nation states by 2030 and even recommend it.[6] Protagonists of the break-up theory argue that national integration can be promoted only on interconnectivity through infrastructure-building, end to violence (e.g., lingering or perpetual conflict or long civil wars) through speedy, quick divorce and sometimes fractionating the state for better integration with the world.[7] However, many countries have still not disintegrated despite these factors, namely, Congo, Yemen, Afghanistan and Iraq.

Pakistan's interest resides in a stable, sovereign and integral Afghanistan. But historical facts and current realities dictate that external interference in Afghanistan's polity is difficult to stop. In fact, Afghanistan as a state has always acted as a buffer with constant meddling from outside powers. It can only become a "roundabout" of commercial traffic when trade and commerce flourish with the cooperation of its neighbours.

Continuity-in-Change

An equally unwelcome scenario envisages that no major change would come about after US/NATO start exiting post-2014. Although the US has some plans of building and reviving the famous Silk Route, and craft integration plans in the region, this is going to take time and effort. Given the latest Doha initiative and US-Taliban talks, there is skepticism that prolonged negotiations and the "New Great Game" will persist in the foreseeable future—and could even flare up with intensity once the US forces leave.

Unlike the "Great Game" of former Great Britain and Russia in the early nineteenth century now it is not a bipolar competition of ISAF versus the Taliban only. A number of actors are vying for a greater share of the Afghan pie and old rivalries and animosities are surfacing, namely, China versus India, Saudi Arabia versus Iran, Pakistan versus India, China against Russia and the Taliban versus Non-Pushtuns.[8]

Pakistan-US relations have come under strain after the US attack on three check posts on November 26, 2012 killing and wounding many of its soldiers. Pakistan has stopped the passage of logistical supplies through Pakistan destined for US-ISAF forces in Afghanistan. This has sent a strong message of protest to the US and the international community about Pakistan's central role in any future settlement of Afghanistan.

Competing Perspectives and Interests

The Karzai Government

Notwithstanding the rhetoric, the Karzai government does not want an early exit of US-backed NATO troops unless the Afghan army and the police are ready to take their full responsibilities and unless foreign governments undertake to ensure the nation's security. Also, he is keen for a power-sharing agreement and on the US's token presence as residual forces like Iraq by signing the Status of Forces Agreement. Moreover, the Karzai government insists that there should be no reversal in the gains made under his administration: preservation of the Afghan Constitution, women's rights, education policies and parliamentary progress. Also some possible role for India should be earmarked once the US forces leave. It envisages that the ANA would be about 400,000 troops by 2014 against 25,000 Taliban forces but shall be hobbled by problems of adequate training, equipment, illiteracy, police and military desertions and drug issues. The Karzai government wants the international communities' continued stake in Afghanistan.

The Afghan Taliban Groups

The Afghan Taliban desire early repatriation of Taliban internees in Guantanamo Bay, an early ceasefire and complete withdrawal of ISAF forces. The start of US-Afghan Taliban negotiations in Doha, Qatar as a new place seems a welcome sign[9] but many observers still seem skeptical. While Germany, Turkey, Saudi Arabia and United Arab Emirates (UAE) were early meeting countries the new venue of Qatar is seen as promising. Some observers see the return of Taliban prisoners in camps as a confidence-building measure; the setting up of the Qatar office as a permanent address for engagement could provide the Taliban an opening to seek Qatar's economic largesse in rehabilitation and reconstruction of Afghanistan—should they come to power.

On the other hand, some opine that the choice of Qatar as a venue may not be auspicious, for Qatar is an ally of Saudi Arabia and the US and a centre of Sunni orthodoxy. The Saudis have already damaged the tribal structure of Afghanistan by fostering radicalism; secondly, Afghans should take ownership of their own security by induction of civil society members viz., intellectuals, moderate non-Pushtuns for settlement; thirdly, even if the "peace" agreement is struck with the Taliban, there are chances that the Afghan government and other ethnic groups will not accept this due to past experiences with repressive Taliban rule. Hence, the situation could easily spiral into renewed vendettas and violence.[10] Moreover, some doubt that the Taliban office in Qatar could be a "Taliban ploy" to gain time and seek political legitimacy at international levels, or to mark time till US/NATO withdrawal is completed, and then capture Kabul.

As far as the Northern Alliance is concerned, it is wary of any concessional deal with the US that could lead to the relapse of the system. Hence they remain dependent upon Russia, India and Iran for political and economic support.

Pakistan

Pakistan does not want the US forces to leave precipitately as they did in 1992, but would like a phased, planned withdrawal; this is, however, not officially stated but is the tacit view. There is a fear that more infighting after 2014 might add to Pakistan's travails, namely, influx of refugees and rise in terrorism. In turn, this could invite cross-border reprisals from US-Afghan troops. Also, there is a worry that the Afghan-Taliban may decide to join with Pakistani Taliban against the Pakistani state. As a last option, Pakistan relies on Pak-Taliban and their role in Afghanistan for some kind of say in Afghan affairs and a check against India. In addition, it desires Iran to remain quiescent and keep India and Russia out of the loop.[11]

Pakistan wants representation of Pushtun elements in any political dispensation in future Afghan governments. Based on geographical proximity, it has taken a large share of refugees (2.2 million still residing) and it has suffered a lot from the War on Terror. On a restart of US-Pak relations, Pakistan is about to set new terms of engagement including more fees and compensation for facilities used in transportation of supplies from Karachi to Afghanistan. Since carrying out many military actions against its own Taliban forces in the Federally Administered Tribal Areas (FATA) for the last seven years or so, Pakistan has realised that it cannot fight and crush them as the US in Afghanistan have experienced with Afghan Taliban. Therefore, it would like to coexist with them after US withdrawal. It has not welcomed the parleys by Qatar ostensibly thinking that it has been sidelined. It desires a leading role in parleys and would like to be a major component of any future political dispensation with a friendly Afghan government on its eastern borders. Whether they remain friendly or otherwise is a moot question. Later it hopes for a receptive Afghanistan for trade, investment and gas pipelines.

Pakistan's self-perception is that it occupies a central role in shaping events and future scenarios in post-2014 Afghanistan and hence sees a destabilising role by India and foresees that Indian-trained Afghan army personnel could turn out to be essentially anti-Pakistan. Pakistan also feels that given the tribal structure in Afghanistan, Afghans with Pushtun participation should be given their due share. As always there are policy ambiguities regarding the US's continued military presence or its complete withdrawal.

United States

The US is interested in a phased withdrawal and does not want to have a repeat of 1992 when it made a precipitate withdrawal which brought in Al Qaeda. It is wary of any comeback of Al Qaeda in the region and its linkages with the Taliban. There is a recent view that it wants to negotiate with the Taliban for an easy and planned withdrawal. In this regard, it is also banking on Pakistan for face-saving. Moreover, it is interested in protecting its gains made in Afghanistan, some of which are, protection of the Afghan Constitution, human rights, minorities and status of women. It does not want an overt influence of the Taliban in the region, destabilisation of Pakistan and any further deterioration in Pakistan-India relations. It wants to maintain liberal, friendly relations with Afghanistan as it is proximate to the Gulf. Also, it does not want open interference from China, Russia and Central Asia in that country and is keen to exploit mineral and other resources.

Ideally, it would desire a stable pro-US Afghanistan with a power-sharing government but without any preponderance of the Taliban, to keep China and Russia out but to bring India as a support to look after US interests. The US spent US$ 460 billion in Afghanistan whereas Pakistan has spent US$ 62 billion in Pakistan and 30,000 people have been killed so far.[12] The US has the biggest embassy in the world in Kabul—even surpassing Baghdad. This will help to maintain and control bases and facilities and safeguard its interests in Central Asia and the Gulf. In fact, Afghanistan is, in many ways, more important than Iraq, to keep away the terrorist elements from regrouping and from turning into a haven for them. Also, to keep surveillance over Pakistan's nuclear programme and use Pakistan as a cover for withdrawal which is not construed as a defeat.[13] Pakistan-US relations have got a rude shock after the US attack on three check posts on November 26, 2012, killing and wounding many soldiers. Ever since, the government in Pakistan has stopped the passage of log supplies via Pakistan to US-ISAF forces in Afghanistan.

India

The Northern Alliance government has been holding power since 2001. They are mortally apprehensive of the return to power of Pushtun Taliban elements, although all Pushtuns are not Taliban. Pakistan remains concerned about any rise in India's influence through the Northern Alliance which India has been supporting along with Russia and Iran since the Taliban rule. Also, disturbances in Balochistan are allegedly linked to Indian encouragement through its missions based in Afghanistan. Since the Karzai government came to power, India-Afghanistan relations have dramatically improved in all fields, from training of armed forces, albeit discreetly, to construction work, highways, construction of power lines, mining and dams—amounting in all to nearly US$ 2 billion of aid. The Afghans want to build a secular army on the Indian model drawn from all nationalities, which is presently dominated by Tajiks and Hazaras, while the Pushtuns, the majority, remain under-represented.[14] The US wants to give more responsibility to India in Afghanistan after its departure.[15]

Iran

Due to increasing pressure on Iran by the clamping of a fourth round of sanctions, European countries being barred from buying its oil and through continuous threats, Iran has adopted a two-pronged approach towards Afghanistan. It has signed a defence agreement in December 2011 with the Karzai government and is also making overtures to the Taliban. The Iranian government wants early departure of US-led NATO forces and the evacuation of all military bases. The US-Taliban talks are ongoing for the last few months ignoring Iran and Pakistan—two major players in the conflict. Observers feel that even if the US-Taliban talks succeed, can the process move ahead unless Pakistan, Iran and neighbouring regional powers are brought into the game?[16]

Post-2014 Outlook: More Bleak than Bright

The Soviet invasion of Afghanistan (December 1979) and then the US's in October 2001 unleashed many consequences. The first was popular in the West as it was waged against international communism; and the latter was based on a consensus—built by the 9/11 attacks on the US mainland—which included 50-plus countries. In both the cases jihad was waged; there was a long list of border casualties of the Soviets; the Afghan state survived for three years; and the Karzai regime also survived for 10 years or so; and in both cases there was a steady inflow and outflow of refugees. It is said that there were 12,200 full-time fighters, while under the Soviets, there were about 75,000; and another 25,000 were housed in eight training camps. The Soviet invasion was widely considered illegal and was condemned. But in the Afghan coalition of the willing, casualties were 13,310, while those of the US were about 4,000. The Mujahideen enjoyed global support but the Taliban from Pakistan and a few more countries. The Soviets instituted a "proxy government" under President Najibullah, who lasted from 1986 to 1992. The US has exceeded its stay compared to the Soviets. In fact, this is the longest war in post-World War history.[17]

Looking into the immediate and mid-term future, Afghanistan is likely to remain politically destabilised although with US/NATO forces' departure the anti-West, and especially anti-US sentiments, may lose their sheen.

However, there are lesser chances of reconciliation amongst the Afghans, as Afghan political traditions historically attest. It is thought that Al Qaeda may return and civil war could ensue as the Taliban would embark on a mission of vendetta in a bid to recapture total power. This fear may be somewhat exaggerated as Al Qaeda, after the killing of Osama bin Laden, has lost an icon of global Islamic resistance, although its ideology remains operative, however diffused or scattered. It is seen to be shifting its focus elsewhere in Yemen, Somalia and North Africa. Also, the so-called Arab Spring has dealt the radical Islamic movements a major dent, with the Islamic forces now following politics with a dose of pragmatic policies. Furthermore, Afghanistan's extreme poverty levels, corruption, poor infrastructure, and tribal culture remain the biggest obstacles. Its Gross National Product (GNP) is US$ 14 billion, per capita income US$ 1,000 per year, unemployment only 35 per cent with employment in industry 5.7 per cent and 78.6 per cent in agriculture. Nearly 5.1 million were unemployed youth in 2006 who are projected to increase to 90 million by 2017. Yet, the discovery of trillions of dollars' worth of different kinds of mineral resources evokes strong interest from outsiders.

A benign view about the future in Afghanistan is that, since the Taliban and their affiliates have exhausted themselves after decades of fighting, so, once in power, they would be more realistic and open to compromise and shall disassociate themselves from Al Qaeda, which, in any case, has grown weaker after the killing of Osama bin Laden on May 2, 2011. It has launched no major attack since 2001, suffers from problems of leadership and funding, has lost its public image and is on the run. Of course, it has cells which have reappeared but they are neither winning nor losing. There is a stalemate and the best time is now, to negotiate and reconcile, if the intent is to share power. However, this view is negated by the belief that the Taliban will race for controlling power and settling old scores with ethnic minorities once the US/ISAF troops leave. They happen to be the single largest group (Pushtuns)—43 per cent, though other ethnic groups (Tajiks, Hazaras, Uzbeks and Turkomen) together outnumber them. In the opinion of a seasoned observer, the violence is likely to grow due to developments in the Middle East, anti-US sentiments, departure of foreign forces due to fatigue, and reactivation of Al Qaeda cells because of factors within and outside Afghanistan.[18]

It is said that Afghanistan is a poor country and no government can make rapid progress unless a revolutionary ideological system is put in place. It suffers from a plethora of internal problems and would need retention of foreign troops for quite some time.[19] In the absence of this, the US forces might continue to launch drone attacks,[20] night raids, border transgressions and lightning attacks in Pakistan and occasionally support Afghan forces.[21] Russia, China, India and CARs may condone these acts—if not out rightly support them. Its army may also fragment under the influence of the warlords, drug mafias, and through renegade soldiers.[22] Refugees may start streaming in into neighbouring countries, especially Pakistan, after the fighting starts. This may pose fresh problems for neighbouring Pakistan. US-Pak relations are already strained after the November 26 military raid that killed 26 Pakistani soldiers. They could normalise after new rules of engagement are agreed upon. It is also being realised that no settlement can be made without Pakistan's participation. But, equally, Pakistan may come under increased pressures. Investment, trade and other assistance in the FATA region and the country as a whole could drastically drop. Pakistan faces a dilemma as to whether to go against the Haqqani network and risk alienation with other tribal groups that may retaliate, or stay with the US forces.

Conclusion

Afghans need to take up ownership of their own security. For too long, they have relied on foreign powers by playing one against the other. Post-2014, the US is likely to retain its advisors in Afghanistan for training and supporting Afghan operations and conducting special missions. Use of artillery, helicopter and other equipment will also form part of their forces. It does not however mean that the international community and regional neighbours should not help, but the Afghan civil society (if any) has to come forward to resist the warlords, the drug mafia, terrorists and criminal elements. At the same time, the US should not repeat the mistakes of the past. It should help in concert with the international community by pushing reforms in all domains of Afghan life—educational, legal, administrative, social and economic[23] and help the Afghan nation onto its feet. Nation-building was heretofore neglected and was on the backburner while counter-insurgency was the need of the hour. While Afghanistan—lying on the tri-junction of South, West, and Central Asia and China—offers possibilities in becoming an economic hub, a destabilised and volatile country will have a negative spillover on its neighbours—which, actually, is already happening. Hence the Afghan nation has to transform itself into a node of peace and development through cooperation with its neighbours[24] and the US[25] along with the wider international community.

Notes

1. NIE report is more than 100 pages long and represents the consensus view of CIA and 15 other intelligence agencies. Like previous ones it challenges the Pentagon's view of US/ ISAF military's stalemate in Afghanistan. It underlines rampant corruption, incompetence of Afghan national forces and the Taliban controlling southern Afghanistan. See, "US intelligence report on Afghanistan sees stalemate," *Los Angeles Times* (California), January 11, 2012. This is at odds with the Pentagon's assessment of progress being made by NATO forces in Afghanistan and recommends against any hasty withdrawal of troops.
2. For example, General John Allen, the commander of the US-led coalition, remarked: "What we don't want 31 December 2014 to become is the end of history. It isn't. In fact it's the beginning of history for Afghanistan." On another occasion, he remarked: "There will be US military presence [after 2014]. This is work in progress, we're not going to be done at the end of '14." As quoted in Kevon Baron, "US Military Wants Troops in Afghanistan Beyond 2014," at http:news//yahoo.com/u-military-wants-troops-afghanistan-beyond.../ (Accessed on December 20, 2011).
3. The writer is grateful to an insightful piece by Lt. General Kamal Matinuddin (Retd.), "Possible Post-Withdrawal Scenarios," Paper Presented at an International Conference on "Transition in Afghanistan: Post-Exit Scenarios," jointly hosted by IPRI and HSF, October 5-6, 2011, Islamabad.
4. This proposal is given by Ambassador Dennis Kux (Retd.), with Turkey as a likely choice. See Masroor Afzal Pasha, "Muslim forces should replace ISAF in Afghanistan: Former US envoy," *Daily Times*, November 22, 2011.
5. Cowper, *Daily Times* (Lahore), December 9, 2011.
6. Parag Khanna, "Breaking up is good to do," *Daily Times* (Lahore), January 15, 2011.
7. Ibid.
8. Brian M. Downing, "Negotiations and great games in Afghanistan," *Daily Times* (Lahore), January 14, 2012.
9. For a rather upbeat view see, "How to talk to the Taliban," *Foreign Affairs,* Snapshot View, January 9, 2012 at http://www.foreignaffairs.com/print/134283 (Accessed on January 10, 2012).
10. Michael Hughes, "Qatar dooms Afghans by opening tab office" at http://www.examinar.com/afghanistan-headlines-in-national/qatar-dooms-afghans-by-opening-taliban-office (Accessed on January 12, 2012).
11. Zafar Hilaly, "Power games in Afghanistan," *Daily Times* (Lahore), October 15, 2010.
12. Rehman Malik, talking to British Home Secretary Theresa May, "Pakistan, UK pledge to fight terrorism jointly," *Daily Times* (Lahore), November 25, 2011.
13. Some of these ideas are taken from Alexander Downer, former Foreign Minister of Australia, "The Way Forward in Afghanistan," *Daily Times* (Lahore), October 30, 2010.
14. Major General Ashok Mehta (Retd.), "With an eye on 2014, India steps up Afghanistan role," *Reuters,* November 9, 2011 at http://www.hindustantimes.com/world-news/SouthAsia/With-an-eye-on-2014-India-steps-up-Afghan-role/Article1-766676.aspx (Accessed on January 12, 2012).
15. On India's strengths, weaknesses and perspectives on Afghanistan, read Daniel Norfolk, "India's Engagement with Afghanistan: Developing a 'Durable Policy Architecture,'" ISAS Working Paper No. 138, National University of Singapore, ISAS, December 12, 2011, p. 21.
16. A. G. Noorani, "Obama and Iran," *Dawn* (Islamabad), January 14, 2012.

17. Patrick Cockburn, "US in Afghanistan longer than Soviets," *Daily Times* (Lahore), December 9, 2010.
18. Khalid Aziz, Former Chief Secretary, NWFP (now Khyber Pakhtunkhwa), "Back to square one," *Dawn* (Islamabad), March 18, 2011.
19. This is implicit in the Congressional Testimony before the House Foreign Affairs Committee—Subcommittee on the Middle East and South Asia, *2014 and Beyond: US Policy Towards Afghanistan and Pakistan*, Centre for New American Security, November 3, 2011.
20. Drone attacks, starting in 2004 and reaching their climax in 2010-11, have been criticised by the Pakistani public even if tacitly accepted by the Pakistan government. On the pros and cons, see Azizullah Khan Khetran, "In favour of drone attacks," *Daily Times* (Lahore), November 6, 2010.
21. Farhat Taj, "Now or perhaps never," *Daily Times* (Lahore), May 14, 2011.
22. See Interview with Bob Templer, "Afghanistan: After the Withdrawal," *International Crisis Group*, November 9, 2011 at http://www.crisisgroup.org/en/publication-type/podcasts/afghanistan-after-the-withdrawal. aspx (Accessed on January 20, 2012).
23. For suggested reforms, see Syed Iftikhar Ali Shah, "Prospects of Peace Talks in Afghanistan," FATA Research Centre, December 22, 2011 at http://www.frc.com.pk/linkc/articlecont/49 (Accessed on January 20, 2012).
24. On the need for regional cooperation, see Reza Sanati, "Transitioning Afghanistan in the Post-Withdrawal Era: Setting the stage for a Stable Political Order," *Alternatives: Turkish Journal of International Relations*, 10 (1), Spring 2011, pp. 93-114.
25. Joseph J. Collins, "Post-ISAF Afghanistan: The Need for a '15:20 Program,'" *Small Wars Journal,* January 8, 2012. Essentially, it calls for allied commitment *a la* South Korea in the 1950s, amounting to \$ 20 billion per year [\$ 6 billion to ANSF, and \$ 4 billion economic aid]. Also, by stationing 15,000 allied military personnel for ground assistance, air and logistical support and counterterrorist activities. With the strengthening of the Afghan government, rise in revenues and peaceful conditions, this manpower and funding can be reduced. See http://www.smallwarsjournal.com/jrnl/art/post-isaf-afghanistan-the-need-for-a-"15:20-program" (Accessed on January 20, 2012).

6. Where Is Afghanistan Headed?

Vishal Chandra

In 2014, Afghanistan witnessed a shaky transition of power amidst pull-out of thousands of Western troops. The presidential election proved to be a prolonged and messy affair beyond anticipation, calling into question the ability and credibility of the country's national institutions. Formation of the National Unity Government in September 2014, following allegations of massive fraud and irreconcilable differences between the two contending political camps, has led to speculations about the future prospects of the political system established after the overthrow of the Taliban regime. The terms and conditions of the American-brokered deal between Dr. Ashraf Ghani and Dr. Abdullah, the top two presidential contenders, involves change of political system by amending the Constitution in the next two years. This basically means that Afghanistan would remain in an extended state of transition.

Meanwhile, the United States (US) and the North Atlantic Treaty Organisation (NATO)-led forces are poised to end their combat mission in December 2014. The Western rush for exit from Afghanistan, even as the Pakistan-sponsored Haqqani-Taliban network remains resurgent, is said to threaten and possibly reverse the achievements of the last one decade. The Unity Government, which could also be regarded as the first post-ISAF government, therefore, will soon find itself up against growing security and economic challenges. Old political and social divides continue to intensify in anticipation of possible reordering of political and power structures in the coming years. The notably inclusive post-Taliban political system may not altogether wither away, but retaining its fundamental character will certainly be far more difficult in years to come.

The impending challenge and threat to the post-Taliban political system and the Constitution, is simply adding to the overall uncertainty about the political fate of the country. The political cost and consequences, both in the short and long-term, of withdrawing and letting Afghanistan slip into greater chaos and anarchy is something the West is unwilling to factor into its exit strategy. In fact, there is hardly any attempt to make a long-term assessment of how insecurity and instability in the Afghanistan-Pakistan region could be playing out after 2014. Not long ago, American

President Barack H. Obama had referred to the Afghan mission as a "war of necessity." The Afghan mission has since been reviewed several times by the Obama Administration, every time resulting in downsizing of the achievable objectives. Since the killing of Al Qaeda chief Osama bin Laden in May 2011, in a commando operation conducted by the US Special Forces deep inside Pakistan, the narrative of "Afghan good enough" has gained a certain traction in the Western thinking, long inclined at justifying quicker disengagement from the Afghan theatre.

However, it is still early to be decisively dismissive of the future Western role as both the US and NATO have entered into long-term partnership agreements with Kabul. The framework for a post-transition Western mission including the Bilateral Security Agreement (BSA) with the US and the Status of Force Agreement (SOFA) with NATO has already been endorsed by the new Afghan President Ashraf Ghani. Meanwhile, lack of policy direction and clarity of purpose in Western engagement continues to work to the advantage of a range of forces opposed to the current political structure and the Constitution of Afghanistan.

Though a vast and a diverse section of the Afghan population has benefited from the international engagement, it remains to be seen to what extent the momentum of the state-building process is sustained in post-ISAF Afghanistan. The political transition of 2014 certainly does not present a picture of great hope. The thirteen-year-long Western engagement and investment appears to have largely failed in establishing institutional structures strong enough to sustain the post-2001 political process, without financial and political support from outside.

Ensuring continued international engagement after the security transition in 2014, often referred to as the "Transformation Decade (2015-24)," is already proving to be a major challenge. As of now, the international commitment to post-2014 Afghanistan appears somewhat vague, though several international conferences have been held, beginning with the Bonn II Conference in December 2011, to build a general consensus on sustained long-term assistance to Afghanistan. The growing frustration and to an extent a sense of betrayal among sections of the Afghan population over the non-committal attitude of their Western partners, may manifest in strange ways in time to come. Though Kabul has entered into strategic partnerships with various countries—the US, India, China, and several European countries—and may enter into some more, but such partnerships are not irrespective of the final outcome of the political and security transition currently in progress. The various trilateral, and even a quadrilateral, dialogue mechanisms that have cropped up over the last few years, are often experimental, exploratory and symbolic in nature, driven by narrow short-term interests based on politics of exclusion. They are mostly working at cross-purposes and often result in reiteration or hardening of stated positions.

In the absence of a single dominant ideological discourse or a strong political consensus on the nature and authority of the Afghan state as well as the developmental vision for the future of the country, which could have reinforced an inclusive national identity transcending (not negating) multiple socio-ethnic identities, the old conflicting interests and factional divides are likely to exacerbate at sub-national levels after 2014. What happened to Afghanistan after the Soviet withdrawal in 1988-89, and the subsequent collapse of the Najibullah regime three years later in early 1992, should serve as a constant reminder, rather a key reference point, when working towards post-2014 Afghanistan. It remains to be seen if President Ghani and Chief Executive Abdullah would be able to reconcile the divergent political perceptions prevalent within their respective support groups and finally reach a consensus on how exactly the power is to be shared or divided.

Meanwhile, the two key components of the ongoing transition process in Afghanistan—building an effective national security force comprising both the national army and the police, and political reconciliation with the top Taliban leadership operating from Pakistan—are still way behind in terms of evolving as effective guarantors and instruments of stability in the country.

Priming the Afghan Army

The ongoing security transition process from the NATO-led International Security Assistance Force (ISAF) to the ANSF is in its fifth and final phase, which is supposed to conclude with the end of combat mission in December 2014. It was in June 2013 when President Karzai had announced the initiation of the final phase of the security transition.[1] Launched in July 2011, the security transition process continues despite deteriorating conditions on the ground in several parts of Afghanistan.

As far as the pace of withdrawal of the US troops (which had peaked to nearly 100,000 by June 2011) is concerned, nearly 68,000 troops (10,000 in 2011, 23,000 in 2012 and 34,000 in early 2014) have so far withdrawn. Another 20,000 are expected to withdraw by the end of the year. In May 2014, Obama had announced that there will be approximately 9,800 US troops at the beginning of 2015, which will be reduced roughly by half by the end of the same year. Thereafter, the number of troops will be further reduced to the embassy level presence by the end of 2016.[2]

However, more than the numbers, it is the long-term security agreement (BSA, part of the US-Afghanistan Enduring Strategic Partnership

Agreement of May 2012) which was considered as decisive in terms of defining the nature and level of the US-led Western political and military engagement in the post-transition period. Former President Hamid Karzai had repeatedly refused to sign the BSA, despite the same being endorsed by a Loya Jirga specially convened by him in November 2013, in view of growing differences with Washington over operational issues as well as the key objectives of the future Western mission in Afghanistan. By early 2014, at the height of ongoing tension between the two, Washington was alluding to the possibility of "zero-option" or leaving no troops at all if there was any further delay in the signing of BSA. However, Karzai, who had since long argued that the West needed to change its counterterrorism approach by way of re-strategising the war on terror, remained adamant on not signing the security agreement till his last day in office. The BSA along with SOFA was finally signed on September 30, 2014, a day after President Ghani was sworn in. Both agreements were soon ratified too by the Afghan Parliament in November 2014.

The Obama Administration, having shifted the focus of American commitment from Iraq to Afghanistan in 2009, had prioritised the rebuilding of the ANSF. However, with the endorsement of the roadmap for phased transition of security responsibilities at the November 2010 NATO Lisbon Summit, there has been a rush to meet the targeted numbers for both the Afghan army and police, all at the expense of quality training and soldiering. Developing logistics critical to sustaining a 352,000 strong force, including necessary air capability, is now proving to be difficult. The growing number of what is referred to as "green-on-blue" or "insider" attacks due to infiltration by insurgents and increased friction between Afghan recruits and their foreign trainers as the size of the army increases, has further complicated the task of rebuilding the army. Besides, the training and mentoring of the army remains bedevilled with various logistical limitations, shortcomings and socio-political challenges.[3]

According to the July 2014 report of the *US Congressional Research Service* on Afghanistan:

> Among the major concerns about the ANSF is that about 35% of the force does not re-enlist each year, meaning that about one-third of the force must be recruited to replenish its ranks. Many believe that the force has been expanded too quickly to allow for thorough vetting or for recruitment of the most qualified personnel. Many units also suffer from a deficiency of weaponry, spare parts, and fuel, although those shortfalls are ebbing, according to DOD.[4]

The uncertainty about sustained financial aid and logistical support for the ANSF after 2014 could well be gauged from the outcome of the NATO Summit held in Chicago in May 2012:

> The pace and the size of a gradual managed force reduction from the ANSF surge peak to a sustainable level will be conditions-based and decided by the Government of the Islamic Republic of Afghanistan in consultation with the International Community. The preliminary model for a future total ANSF size, defined by the International Community and the Government of Islamic Republic of Afghanistan, envisages a force of 228,500 with an estimated annual budget of US$ 4.1 billion, and will be reviewed regularly against the developing security environment.[5]

This means that the size of the ANSF would be pruned 2015 onwards from 352,000 to nearly 228,500, as stated above. Interestingly, nothing was said or plans were put forth for nearly 120,000 trained ANSF personnel who would have to be retrenched after 2014. The declaration further stated: "As the Afghan economy and the revenues of the Afghan government grow, Afghanistan's yearly share will increase progressively from at least US$ 500 million in 2015, with the aim that it can assume, no later than 2024, full financial responsibility for its own security forces."[6] However, during the NATO Defence Ministers meeting in Brussels on February 21-22, 2013, it was indicated that the current numerical strength of the ANSF, i.e., 352,000 might be retained through 2018.[7] To what extent the signing of BSA and SOFA would help in terms of sustaining financial aid and building logistics for the ANSF in the long run, is still far from certain. Nevertheless, the new Afghan National Army remains a source of hope even as political uncertainty grows.

Politics of Reconciliation

A multi-track highly competitive politics has evolved around the idea of negotiating "peace" by seeking "reconciliation" with the top Afghan Taliban leadership operating from Pakistan. It has acquired a dynamics of its own in the light of a supposedly "irreversible" security transition taking place in the country.[8] From the Western viewpoint, a political deal with the Taliban leadership was initially expected to facilitate a smooth transition of security from the Western to the Afghan forces, finally paving the way for a relatively peaceful withdrawal of the Western military. At the domestic level, it is considered critical for the survival and sustenance of the regime in Kabul after 2014.

However, the idea of reaching out to an exiled and inaccessible Taliban leadership has so far been a non-starter as Pakistan's powerful military establishment, which has long regarded armed Afghan insurgents as an asset against successive Afghan governments, is unlikely to facilitate direct talks between Kabul and the Taliban and particularly so when the Western forces are drawing down. Kabul, as was agreed during the London Conference on Afghanistan in January 2010, was never really the sole negotiating authority as several foreign entities competed to reach out to the Taliban leadership. In fact, in 2013, former President Karzai had to call off talks with the Taliban who had opened a political office in Doha in Qatar as the office complex displayed the flag as well as the plaque of the "Islamic Emirate of Afghanistan," symbolising Taliban rule from 1996-2001. Kabul has long been resentful of the independent initiatives often taken by Western entities to open direct channels of communication with Taliban representatives.

The High Peace Council, appointed by the Karzai Government in September 2010 to initiate talks with the Taliban, too could not make much headway. Its first Chairman and former Afghan president, Burhanuddin Rabbani, was killed in a suicide bombing in September 2011. Similarly, another senior member of the Council and a former Taliban deputy minister, Mullah Arsala Rahmani, was assassinated in Kabul in May 2012. Earlier, Mullah Abdul Ghani Baradar, a senior member of the Quetta-based Taliban Leadership Council or *Rahbari Shura*, was arrested from Karachi by Pakistan in January 2010 for reportedly trying to negotiate with the Afghan Government.[9] Again, in early April 2012, it was reported that Mohammad Ismail, chief of the Taliban military council, has been detained by Pakistan for reportedly conducting "unauthorised negotiations" with members of the Afghan High Peace Council during his visit to Dubai.[10]

Despite initiatives at various levels, both the US-led Western and the Afghan government-led local reconciliation efforts have yet to register any credible progress. The Haqqani-Taliban network and the Hizb-e Islami (Gulbuddin Hekmatyar) continue to publicly rebuff offers of a negotiated settlement of the conflict, and have instead been strengthening their position in anticipation of a "post-West" scenario. The hardcore segment of the Taliban leadership and their chief patron, the Pakistan military, have throughout been averse to engaging Kabul. In the rush to fill in the vacuum created by the pull-out of thousands of Western troops, Taliban and its various allies are rather engaged in strengthening their position vis-à-vis the Afghan army and police.

Even if some defections do take place from within the Taliban, it is least likely to help strengthen the current political system or pave the way for the resolution of the Afghan conflict. There might be differences within the Taliban rank-and-file on the issue of negotiating with the US or the Afghan Government or on relations with the Al Qaeda and its local affiliates; it is the hard core irreconcilable view which clearly seems to be prevailing at the moment. The hard core elements are simply convinced of their impending "victory" as the Western military prepares to end its combat mission, and sees no reason to negotiate with Kabul. One is inevitably reminded of similar perceptions prevailing among Afghan Islamist groups backed by Pakistan (the Peshawar Seven) against the then President Najibullah and his effort for national reconciliation in the wake of Soviet withdrawal. Though friction between sections of the older Taliban leadership and the Pakistani military too cannot be ruled out, they largely remain hostage to Pakistan's post-2014 agenda in Afghanistan.

The Taliban neither recognise the democratic political system nor the new Afghan Constitution currently in place. In fact, the current reconciliation process could hardly be regarded as "national" in character and orientation. A close scrutiny of the politics of reconciliation with the Taliban leadership suggests that it is more about striking short-term tactical deals, than working towards a sustainable, comprehensive and an inclusive nationwide peace process. Given the ambiguity about the whole process, it is difficult to ascertain the terms and conditions of talks with purported Taliban representatives. Often it is difficult to verify the identity of the Taliban negotiators/interlocutors and the level of their proximity to the senior leadership of the Afghan Taliban, which remains largely inaccessible. There is also an opinion that Mullah Omar may not even be alive. The political objectives of these talks too are far from clear. What exactly does/would reconciliation with the Taliban mean for the future of Afghanistan is open to several interpretations.

Perhaps, the following set of six questions assumes significance as politics over reconciliation with the Taliban leadership gains traction: (i) Is Taliban leadership at all interested or is in a position to negotiate with the government in Kabul? (ii) Does the government in Kabul have the institutional capacity/capability to survive the challenges of sharing power with a much stronger opponent? (iii) Is the current reconciliation process unifying or dividing the country, or to what extent the Taliban have reconciled to the social and political diversity of the country? (iv) Would it strengthen or weaken the political process that began after 2001 and help revive a functional modern Afghan state? (v) Would it help restore a sustainable internal balance of power whereby various Afghan factions, while reconciling to each other's political space, would work towards a unified Afghan state? (vi) Finally, who would ensure that parties to the "deal" stick to the terms and conditions of the agreement? Where are the enforcement mechanisms?

The answers to the above questions are too well understood to be elaborated here, but they are germane to the future of Afghanistan. The Taliban continue to stand for an *emirate* and thus far have not evinced any interest in the democratic political system. The current debate, especially among the factions from the north, about the nature of the Afghan State—whether to continue with a highly centralised presidential system or work towards a more decentralised/federalised structure with greater powers devolved to the provinces—is very much linked to the idea of reconciliation with the Taliban. It remains to be seen how the Unity Government would approach the idea of reconciliation with the Taliban leadership. President Ghani's visit to Beijing in October 2014, his first state visit coming within a month of taking over as president, immediately followed by a visit to Pakistan in November, suggests that transforming ties with both Pakistan and the Afghan Taliban with Beijing's support are high in the order of his priorities.

Meanwhile, there is no credible indication from the Taliban as to on what terms and conditions or under what kind of political arrangement would they be willing to share power with Kabul. Their *jihad* against the Afghan Government and the Western forces continues as before. They also continue to demand complete withdrawal of foreign forces and the establishment of a pure Islamic system based on their own interpretation of *Sharia*. However, it is quite clear from President Ghani's engagements with Beijing and particularly with the Pakistan Army that the peace process aimed at reconciliation with the Taliban is likely to gain further traction in the coming times.

Towards New (Dis)Order

Apart from establishing political legitimacy and credibility of the Unity Government, reconciling the varying perceptions about state and central authority prevalent among various political groups and ethnicities, could prove to be a far bigger challenge for President Ghani than it was for his predecessor. The end of the Western combat mission means that the Unity Government would soon be operating in a somewhat different security setting. Perhaps the following set of factors would be critical to defining and shaping the post-transition Afghanistan:

- The survivability and sustenance of the current Afghan political system and, more importantly, the 2004 Constitution, basically it is about the strength of the Afghan institutions to withstand the various implications of the Western drawdown;

- The nature and level of Western engagement and commitment in the post-transition period;
- The effectiveness of the extended US-led Western presence in restraining Pakistan's military establishment from supporting and sponsoring various militant religious and terrorist organisations; and, finally,
- The political perception, orientation and composition of the new political coalition or the Unity Government in Kabul.

Despite a substantive military drawdown and the end of the combat mission, the US is likely to remain a leading military and external force inside Afghanistan. Even a minimal Western military presence on Afghan soil has implications for the future course of Afghan war. The Obama Administration is likely to be more cautious, rather flexible, in timing the withdrawal of remaining troops. Withdrawal of thousands of troops and huge amounts of equipment would itself be a complex, costly and a long-drawn process. The American strategy towards countering unconventional threats posed by transnational non-state actors is rapidly changing. The growing emphasis on employing drones, increased reliance on quick surgical strikes and special operations as opposed to conventional fighting involving huge mobilisation of armed forces and military logistics, is quite in sync with their evolving counter-insurgency/terrorism strategy given the proliferation of radical groups opposed to the US interest and presence in various parts of the world. One would have to also closely watch the evolving US diplomacy not only in and around the Pakistan-Afghanistan region, but at the wider Asian level as well. The US would certainly not like Afghanistan to go the Iraq way. The rapidly deteriorating security situation in Iraq due to the emergence of "Islamic State" certainly has some valuable lessons to offer.

Though most of Afghanistan's neighbours remain opposed to a permanent Western military presence in the region, they at the same time seem to be acquiescent to a slightly extended but reduced US presence in view of a variety of threats posed by growing instability in Afghanistan. However, the nature and the level of their response to the Afghan challenge are more likely to be determined by their individual relationship with the new government in Kabul than their perception of the Western presence after 2014. Meanwhile, regional mechanisms and efforts are likely to remain fragmented and ineffective owing partly to the politics of exclusion and, more importantly, the general reluctance among most of the regional countries to clearly identify the key source of state-sponsored extremism and terrorism plaguing the entire south-central Asia region.

In view of the uncertainty building up over post-transition Afghanistan, the future prospect of the current political system appears somewhat bleak. It is likely to get diluted as various political stakeholders seek to preserve and expand their competing interests in a supposedly de-Westernised political (dis)order after 2014. The worrying aspect here is lack of sustainable consensus on an alternative but inclusive political framework that could help restore internal socio-political balance of power based on changing ground realities. The emerging internal political configuration suggests reopening of old fault lines as multiple centres of power jostle for space and clout at both national and local levels in view of a waning American intervention. It should not come as a surprise if post-transition Afghanistan simply drifts into another round of chaos and anarchy, or continues to experience alternating phases of limited stability and unabated turbulence.

The 2014 political transition is not merely about change in leadership; it is about ushering the country into a "Transformation Decade (2015-24)" by further institutionalising a relatively inclusive political culture. It is about building a political order which is in tune with the changing socio-political realities, mindful of the several challenges ahead, the most important being strengthening the national institutions. The challenges before the Unity Government are not any different from the previous government: managing divergent perceptions and factional interests, competing patronage networks and parallel power structures at the sub-national level, seemingly irreconcilable ideological positions of the Pakistan-sponsored Haqqani-Taliban network and, most critically, sustaining the current constitutional framework to the extent possible. The key question now is will President Ghani and Chief Executive Abdullah be able to meet the expectations of millions of Afghan voters who, defying all threats, voted them to power?

Notes

1. The first phase of security transition or *Inteqal* from the ISAF to ANSF was announced by the Afghan Government on March 22, 2011, covering between 20-25 per cent of the Afghan population; the second on November 27, 2011, covering more than 50 per cent of the population; the third on May 13, 2012, covering 75 per cent of the population; the fourth on December 31, 2012, covering areas where almost 87 per cent of the Afghan population lives; and the fifth and final phase was announced on June 18, 2013, covering the last 11 remaining provinces. See, "Inteqal: Transition to Afghan Lead," *North Atlantic Treaty Organisation*, January 7, 2015, at http://www.nato.int/cps/en/natohq/topics_87183.htm.

2. "Statement by the President on Afghanistan," The White House, May 27, 2014, at https://www.whitehouse.gov/photos-and-video/video/2014/05/27/president-obama-makes-statement-afghanistan#transcript.
3. For details, see Vishal Chandra, "Afghanistan's National Army: Expectations and Scepticism," in Vishal Chandra (ed.), *India's Neighbourhood: The Armies of South Asia* (New Delhi: Pentagon Press, 2013), pp. 1-26; and Vishal Chandra, "Making of the New Afghan National Army: Challenges and Prospects," *Strategic Analysis,* 33 (1), Routledge, London, January 2009, pp. 55-70.
4. Kenneth Katzman, "Afghanistan: Post-Taliban Governance, Security, and US Policy", *Congressional Research Service (CRS)*, July 11, 2014, p. 27, at http://fpc.state.gov/documents/organization/229889.pdf.
5. "Chicago Summit Declaration on Afghanistan," Issued by the Heads of State and Government of Afghanistan and Nations contributing to the NATO-led International Security Assistance Force (ISAF), May 21, 2012, at http://www.nato.int/cps/en/natolive/official_texts_87595.htm
6. Ibid.
7. Thom Shankar, "NATO Plan Tries to Avoid Sweeping Cuts in Afghan Troops," *The New York Times*, February 21, 2013, at http://www.nytimes.com/2013/02/22/us/philip-m-breedlove-is-likely-candidate-for-top-nato-post.html?ref=asia&_r=3&.
8. For a detailed analysis of the idea and politics of reconciliation with the Taliban, see Vishal Chandra, "The Evolving Politics of Taliban Reintegration and Reconciliation in Afghanistan," *Strategic Analysis* 35 (5), Routledge, London, September 2011, pp. 836-48; also see Vishal Chandra, "Negotiating with the Afghan Taliban: Paving the Way to Peace or Civil War?" in Arpita Basu Roy, Binoda Kumar Mishra and Aliva Mishra (eds.), *International Intervention in Afghanistan: Motives and Approaches* (New Delhi: Shipra Publications, 2012), pp. 235-45.
9. Dexter Filkins, "Pakistanis Tell of Motive in Taliban Leader's Arrest," *The New York Times*, August 22, 2010, at http://www.nytimes.com/2010/08/23/world/asia/23taliban.html?pagewanted=all.
10. Praveen Swami, "Taliban military chief held after secret talks with Afghan envoys," *The Hindu*, April 16, 2012, at http://www.thehindu.com/news/international/article3318142.ece.

7. Women and the Political Future of Afghanistan

C. Sheela Reddy

Introduction

There was much hope pinned on the Bonn 2011 Conference before the withdrawal of the North Atlantic Treaty Organisation (NATO) forces in 2014. Unfortunately, the main players responsible for the future of Afghanistan—Pakistan and the Taliban—seem to be least interested, as their absence indicates. On top of this, the terrorist attack in Kabul the very next day of the conference portrayed a picture of an insecure and uncertain future for the Afghan people. This chapter discusses the future of women in Afghanistan since the 2001 Bonn Conference and the development of women's issues in general. It also aims to understand the perception of the West on Afghan women's issues and also to analyse how Afghan women themselves perceive their status in the political, constitutional, legal, employment, health, and educational fields. It is an attempt to understand the "mind" and "heart" of the woman vis-a-vis the political future of Afghanistan. To gauge the role of women, a comprehensive understanding of the status and condition of women in Afghan society becomes imperative. This necessitates an understanding of culture, tradition and facilities available and their accessibility for Afghan women in different sectors and areas.

The World Bank Report on *National Reconstruction and Poverty Reduction—The Role of Women in Afghanistan's Future*, March 2005 presents the deplorable situation of Afghan women in health, education, and employment sectors between 2001 and 2003, which certainly has had its own repercussions in impacting women's role in the political future of Afghanistan.

Health

Women of reproductive age in Afghanistan suffer from many problems due to inadequate health facilities and the conservative attitude of Afghan society. Surveys conducted in 2002 by the United Nations International Children's Emergency Fund (UNICEF) and the United States Centre for Disease Control and Prevention (CDC) in four provinces of Afghanistan estimated a maternal mortality rate (MMR) of 1,600 per 100,000 live births. There are indications of large variations across geographical areas; Kabul, for example, had an estimated MMR of 400 per 100,000 while Badakhshan with 6,500 per 100,000 had the highest MMR ever reported globally. The proportion of deaths of women that were due to maternity related causes ranged from 16 per cent in Kabul, where at least one maternity hospital was functional at the time of the survey, to 64 per cent in Badakhshan, where health care access was severely limited. More than half of all the hospitals in Afghanistan are located in Kabul and therefore serve only about one-fifth of the entire population.

More than 80 per cent of functional health facilities have some form of involvement from non-governmental organisations (NGOs), but the coverage is far from even, with a concentration in the urban areas and areas near the Pakistan border. A study in Herat province concludes that the extraordinarily high number of deaths of women during pregnancy and childbirth are largely preventable. They are direct consequences of the very young marriageable age for women and girls—according to United Nations Development Fund for Women (UNIFEM), 54 per cent of girls under the age of 18 are married—their poor health and nutritional conditions, practice of frequent childbearing and virtual inaccessibility to gynaecological and obstetric services. More than 90 per cent of the women give birth at home and most of these births occur without the assistance of a trained health attendant. Even if a primary health care clinic is available, 70 per cent of these are unable to provide even basic prenatal and post-natal services, while 90 per cent of the hospitals do not have the complete equipment to perform C-sections. Furthermore, there is widespread reluctance to let women be treated by male health workers, particularly in the case of obstetric and gynaecological matters. Even with availability of female medical staff, pregnant women may not receive the necessary medical attention. In Ishkeshm it was reported that most problems during birth were taken care of by relatives or by a mullah, who would provide amulets or written verses from the Koran.[1]

Education

In terms of female education, there are huge regional disparities, as well as rural-urban disparities. A number of supply factors that affect children's and, in particular, girls' access to school are the lack of school facilities, lack of female teachers and insecurity. Several sociocultural and political factors are also identified as having a negative impact on girls' enrolment and school retention, such as poverty, targeting of girls' schools by opponents of the present government, and culturally determined notions of education as "unnecessary" or "harmful" for girls. Considerable regional and ethnic heterogeneities exist within Afghanistan—not only in the matter of constraints, but also in the matter of opportunities.

After the downfall of the Taliban, Afghanistan saw the highest school enrolment rates in its history, with more than 4.3 million children enrolled in primary and secondary school in 2003, of which one-third were girls. In the age group 7-12 years, 67 per cent of boys and 40.5 per cent of girls were enrolled, with such a high level of girls' enrolment in particular representing an impressive achievement. Likewise, the number of schools has increased from 3,800 in 2002 to 7,134 at present. The Asian Development Bank (ADB) reports that demand for girls' education is surging and that the girls' schools that opened for informal winter sessions in all parts of the country after the defeat of the Taliban were overflowing in 2003, even in traditional Pashtun areas like Griskh in Helmand Province, where 500 girls showed up on the first day. At Kabul University, more than 18,000 students took the admission examination at the beginning of 2002. Thus, demand for education is high, but there are also serious constraints. The spurt in enrolment still represents only a little more than half of school-age children and 40 per cent of the girls. Moreover, these figures hide dramatic regional and urban-rural disparities, with girls representing less than 15 per cent of total enrolment in nine provinces in the east and south. Girls' enrolment is determined by not only the availability of girls' schools but also whether there are female teachers. The urban-rural distribution of teachers was (and still is) highly uneven in favour of urban areas, particularly in the capital and other cities in the north and west of the country. Higher education experiences a similar gender disparity among its teaching staff. In 2003 around 12 per cent of professors were female, one-sixth of them with a Bachelors degree and only one out of thirteen professors with a Masters degree. Only two female professors had a PhD as compared to 130 male professors.[2]

Employment

The striking feature of Afghanistan's economic structure is the dominance of the informal sector. Although it is inherently difficult to estimate the size of the informal economy, it is clear that some 80-90 per cent of economic activity in Afghanistan occurs in the informal sector, which has been largely responsible for the recent economic recovery and dynamism. Exchange services between households are widespread, and women perform a major part of this non-monetary work. However, the traditional role of women in Afghanistan is a constraint to their more equitable participation in economic activities, which is especially hard on the large number of female-headed households, for whom eking out an existence without a male bread-winner is very difficult. In particular, female wage labour is still viewed as a last resort solution for households in dire straits, and their wage rates are normally only half the level of men or less.

In urban areas women's employment outside the domestic sphere has always been limited and subject to severe restrictions. When the Taliban assumed power and initially prohibited all female employment, it was estimated that in Kabul city there were some 40,000 women in public service. They accounted for 70 per cent of all the teachers in Kabul, about 50 per cent of civil servants and an estimated 40 per cent of medical doctors. Professions in the medical, academic, administrative or engineering fields were generally considered "appropriate" for women in the urban context and were seen as an extension of women's roles as mothers and caretakers at home. But the Taliban initiated wholesale dismissal of female government employees—resulting in international protests in 1996. As a result, a compromise was reached whereby women could draw their salaries without working. This clearly reflects the Taliban's conservative attitude of confining women to houses. In 1999, the Report of the United Nations (UN) Secretary General on the situation of women and girls in Afghanistan noted the widespread dismissal of female civil servants in a move to cut government spending. The Special Advisor on Gender Issues and Advancement noted that by mid-2000, there were a total of 5,874 Afghan women employed by the international assistance community in Afghanistan in different spheres. According to 2003 data from the Central Statistics Office, 21 per cent of all permanent government employees were women. The available evidence on educational qualifications suggests that these women are significantly less educated than male civil servants. Women were never encouraged to take up employment.[3]

Legal Protection and Judiciary

Women face many restrictions in accessing systems of justice. With women's chastity, modesty and overall behaviour seen as a reflection of family honour, most domestic problems and cases involving any perceived transgressions of women tend to be handled inside the family. Restrictions on women's mobility and the expectations that they be accompanied by a male relative when outside their home, limit their ability to access courts on their own. Furthermore, according to the Sharia, the testimony of a woman in court is worth half of that of a man, and female defendants thus may face difficulties in proving their innocence. Domestic abuse can be given as the basis for divorce, but there are no legal codes that criminalise domestic abuse or violence within the home, and the courts routinely send back women to abusive spouses telling them to "come to an agreement."

Afghanistan has signed a number of international gender-related conventions, including the Convention on the Political Rights of Women, the Convention Concerning the Equal Remuneration for Men and Women Workers for Work of Equal Value, and the Convention Concerning Discrimination in respect of Employment and Occupation. These international standards have apparently not affected domestic law. On March 5, 2003, Afghanistan ratified the UN Convention on the Elimination of all forms of Discrimination against Women (signed in 1980), which, like the other international ratified conventions, will require legislative and administrative measures, to give legal support to the nation's commitment to the advancement of its women. Until that happens, a large degree of confusion over the exact rights of women and their legal status will continue to exist. Widespread violations of the most basic rights of women and girls, including physical abuse, underage marriage, exchange of girls to settle feuds, have been reported by Amnesty International during recent visits.

The personnel of the Afghan judiciary have a wide range of educational and training backgrounds. Most are graduates from religious schools, with a small number from the Sharia School or the Law School at Kabul University. Indeed, according to the study by the Tufts University team, many lack training in both Islamic and statutory law. The Law School and Sharia School differ significantly in the training they provide. Currently, however, graduates from the Sharia School form a majority in the judicial leadership, which presumably affects the judicial reform process, as they represent the conservative camp in Afghan law. The Judiciary has been an exclusively male domain, which is still largely the case. Of a total of 2,006 sitting judges, only around 27 are female. With the exception of the heads of the juvenile and family courts in Kabul, women are not found in key positions within the judiciary. Where women do serve as judges, reports indicate that they do not perform the same functions as their male counterparts. Female judges tend to act in the capacity of judicial clerks and are rarely involved in the adjudication of cases. In general, there seems to be considerable resistance in the judiciary against greater inclusion of women in the judiciary. However, approximately 25 per cent of law students at the Universities of Balkh and Kabul are women, so the potential for achieving a better gender balance exists.

There is heavy reliance on informal justice mechanisms in Afghanistan. The Jirga (among Pashtuns) and Shura (among Dari-speakers), comprising elders, resolve community problems, including those related to land, property, family and crime. Since the Jirga and Shura throughout Afghanistan are exclusively male-dominated, women are unable to approach these informal mechanisms without the support and assistance of a male family member. In the process of decision-making the Jirga and Shura apply different sources of law, including Sharia law, tribal law and other customary law. The predominance of customary law in the Jirga/Shura decisions is by and large to the disadvantage of women, as customary law throughout Afghanistan tends to grant fewer rights to women than Islamic law or civil law in matters relating to inheritance, property and marriage. The inaccessibility of the Jirga and Shura to women also exacerbates the problem of impunity in relation to crimes against women; for example, in cases of so-called "honour killings" for which the perpetrators are generally not punished. Rather than being sent to prison for a wrong committed, a criminal offender will be required to pay compensation to the victim and ask forgiveness.[4]

Political Participation

During Taliban's rule, women were banned from working outside the home. They were forced to wear the *burqa* and had to be escorted by a *muharam* (a male relative). Girls' schools were closed down all over the country. Despite facing enormous challenges under the Taliban, women were still active, organising underground schools and community-based health work. After the Taliban were ousted in 2001, a number of important steps were taken to restore and promote women's rights, with the support of Western leaders, including US President Bush and then US Senator Hillary Clinton.

The Bonn Agreement (2001) led to the establishment of the first Ministry of Women's Affairs (MoWA) and the Afghan Independent Human Rights Commission. In 2003, Afghanistan acceded to the Convention on the Elimination of all Forms of Discrimination against Women (CEDAW) without reservations. Largely thanks to campaigning by Afghan women, supported by international allies, the country's 2004 Constitution guaranteed a number of important rights for women, including the right to equality before the law (Article 22), the right to an education (Articles 43 and 44), and the right to work (Article 48). The government also developed a ten-year National Action Plan for Women of Afghanistan (NAPWA), launched in 2008, which outlined plans to realise women's rights under the twin goals of "women's empowerment" and "gender equality."

Before 2001, women were kept hidden at home. Just ten years later, Afghanistan has 69 female MPs, which, at 28 per cent of the total, is one of the highest rates of female representation in the world. This is the result of a quota system which guarantees women 25 per cent of seats at the district, provincial, and national level. In 2005, Habiba Sarabi was appointed Afghanistan's first female governor for Bamiyan province, and in 2008, Azra Jafari became the first woman mayor in Nili, Daikundi province. In addition, about 30,000 women are members of mixed Community Development Councils (CDCs) established since 2003 under the state-run National Solidarity Programme (NSP), giving women a formal voice at the community level for the first time. The NSP experiment grants Afghan women their first opportunity to participate in local level politics—and it has been met with scepticism and resistance in a number of places, including the suspicion that the NSP is a "foreign" and anti-Islamic programme which aims at religious conversion and abolition of traditional Afghan values, especially concerning women and family.

The government has pledged to "increase female participation in elected bodies at all levels of governance to 30 per cent by 2020" under the Afghan Millennium Development Goals. It has also set a target of 30 per cent of all government employees to be women by 2013 and, in 2009, established the Gender Directorate within the Civil Service Commission to help achieve this. All ministries have been tasked with establishing gender units.[5]

The Real Scenario

In Afghanistan the international community has pushed strongly for the inclusion of women in all spheres of life. However, female networking and the building of a broad platform of women are essential in the struggle for women's emancipation in Afghanistan. Historically, there has never been an organised bottom-up women's movement. Most women's rights in Afghan history were granted from the top. That is why many activists today stress that women need to fight for their rights rather than rights being granted to them due to international pressure. Women's chances to build up common networks and institutions were curtailed by restrictions on their movement in public under Mujahideen and Taliban rule.[6] Unfortunately, the position and hardship of women in Afghanistan, even after the fall of the Taliban and 10 years of international help, did not seem to alter much. The following Table is just a glimpse of their position in society.

Table 1: Female/Male Participation in the Public Sector (2010)

	Men (%)	Women (%)
Population	51.2	48.8
Judges	95.3	4.7
Prosecutors	93.6	6.4
Attorneys	93.9	6.1
Police	99.5	0.5
Army	99.4	0.6
Parliamentarians	72.7	27.3
School teachers	71.5	28.5
University teachers	84.8	15.2
Civil servants	81.5	18.5
Agricultural workers	56	44

The Role of the International Community

Publicly, Western politicians still back Afghan women. In July 2011, US Secretary of State Hillary Clinton reiterated her commitment to women, saying: "Any potential for peace will be subverted if women and ethnic minorities are marginalised or silenced ... And so when we look at what will happen in Afghanistan, the United States will not abandon our values or support a political process that undoes the progress that has been made in the past decade."

But behind the scenes it is less clear what will happen if the Taliban make demands that require compromise on women's rights, as the US government prepares to withdraw the majority of its troops by the end of 2014 and seeks a political settlement to bring an end to the fighting. In July 2011, a *Washington Post* article reported one United States Agency for International Development (USAID) official as saying, "gender issues are going to have to take a back seat to other priorities." This reflects "growing realism" tempering expectations of what they can achieve on the ground after ten years. As one analysis puts it, "on this list of priorities, 'gender' is generally seen as a luxury to be left aside until the supposedly gender-neutral objectives in the domains of security and governance has been achieved."

Western leaders have a responsibility towards Afghan women, not least because protection of women's rights was sold as a positive outcome of the international intervention in October 2001. In the report, *A Place at the Table: Safeguarding Women's Rights in Afghanistan*, written by Oxfam together with well-known Afghan academic Orzala Ashraf Nemat, in 2011, he warns that women's hard-won gains are fragile and could slip away. It stresses that women could face a dangerous future after 2014, if the US, the United Kingdom (UK) and the Afghan government sideline them in the search for peace. At the 10th anniversary of the intervention, Oxfam calls on world leaders not to sacrifice the hard-won gains that Afghan women have made. Madeleine Bunting remarks that, "a war of revenge was reframed as a war for human rights in Afghanistan and in particular the rights of women." Laura Bush, the then First Lady, on a radio talk the week before thanksgiving in 2001, banged the drums of war. She conflated the battle for women's rights and the war on terror by claiming that "the brutal oppression of women is the central goal of the terrorists." She said the "civilised people" had an "obligation to speak out" across the world against what was happening to Afghan women and the "world that the terrorists would like to impose on the rest of us." She concluded with "the fight against terrorism is about the fight for the rights and dignity of women." Cherie Booth Blair echoed her sentiments.[7]

The issue of women's rights opened up divides between the urban and rural populations and between different ethnic groups in an already fragmented country. The position of women has been deeply politicised in this war-torn country. What has also been ignored is any understanding of how Afghanistan's long history of conflict affected gender roles. The women experience violence from both enemies and friends. "The common pattern is that conflict polarises gender roles: masculinity becomes more aggressive and women are idealised as "the bearers of a cultural identity," in the words of the World Health Organisation. Importantly, Madeleine Bunting says, "I'm sceptical as to whether foreign powers are in a position to impose negotiating terms. A degree of security in Afghanistan—it hardly merits the word peace—may cost women's rights as it did in the 1990s, and many Afghan women may regard that as tragic but necessary."[8] Similar views are expressed by Praveen Swami, when he brought to light the opinion of Leon Panetta, former Director of the Central Intelligence Agency (CIA): "who bluntly asserted last summer that he had 'seen no evidence that they [Taliban] are truly interested in reconciliation where they would surrender their arms, where they would denounce the Al Qaeda, where they would really try to become part of that society.'"[9]

The sad truth is that the images of carnage from Kabul, where dozens of Shia worshippers were killed in a sectarian attack on the eve of the Bonn Conference, are a more likely image of Afghanistan's future than the sight of diplomats in elegantly tailored suits signing on to high-minded declarations. From Farhat Taj's book, *Taliban and Anti-Taliban*, we know just what an Islamic Emirate looks like. Her work shows how Taliban jihadists massacred

Shias in Orakzai; how traditional tribal leaders were eliminated; how human rights were degraded—all in pursuit of something packaged, virtuously, as a negotiated peace. Bonn's outcome has been marketed as a roadmap to peace. Its words are, in fact, magnificent mainly in their sheer banality. This is the sad reality of the future of Afghanistan even after the Bonn 2011 Conference.

Fears and Aspirations

Some blogs below clearly depict the fears and aspirations of Afghan women. "I have been working on Afghanistan since 2006, and living there for most of the last three years. For the past year much of my focus has been on women's rights—including authoring a report, *We Have the Promises of the World: Women's Rights in Afghanistan* published in December 2009. The report details emblematic cases of ongoing rights' violations in five areas—attacks on women in public life; violence against women; child and forced marriage; access to justice; and girls' access to secondary education. I've just flown in from Kabul, where for the past few weeks I've been asking women leaders about the prospect of the Taliban's reintegration and reconciliation with the government. Most women I've spoken to say they want *peace with justice, transparency and inclusion, no illusions about 'moderate Taliban.'*"

While the oppression of women and girls under the Taliban was cited as a justification for the 2001 invasion, the Afghan government and its international supporters have not always treated women's rights as a high priority. The role of the US in helping to ensure the long-term promotion and protection of women's rights in Afghanistan is crucial. The gains made over the past eight years are being threatened daily. US development and military assistance, political support, and reintegration and reconciliation efforts all need to be conducted giving full consideration to their impact on the women and girls of Afghanistan.[10]

As momentum gathers towards a troop withdrawal, *Christian Aid* journalist Johanna Rogers went to hear the voices of women who fear that the clock could be turned back when the international forces pull out.

> I do not want to lose what we have achieved so far, and I do not want to go back to my previous life. A peace process should not come at any cost. I worry other countries may compromise to achieve a very superficial peace; they may make a mistake and ignore Afghan women and all Afghan citizens.

Afghan MP Shinkai Kharokail voices the concerns of many throughout Afghanistan, that women's rights are being overlooked by the international community as it plans its withdrawal. They fear that the fragile progress towards greater equality could be reversed. "In 10 years we have achieved a lot, especially after five years of Taliban, when women were absolutely excluded from social, economic and political life. Now women are everywhere, women are part of the decision-making process, part of development in this country," says Shinkai, founder-director of Christian Aid, a partner of the Afghan Women's Education Centre (AWEC), and renowned women's rights activist, who has successfully lobbied for laws to protect women, including banning child marriage. However, as international forces start to pull out, Shinkai, and many like her, fear the implications of a possible resurgence of the Taliban.

Fawzia Koofi, the first female elected as second deputy speaker of Parliament, explains that

> there are three angles to the Afghan triangle: the government and international community, the Taliban, and the people. Unfortunately, the angle of the people is being ignored. How can we share power with the Taliban if they do not accept the Afghan constitution? How can we share power if they are unhappy with seeing a woman like me in Parliament?

Under the Taliban, human rights groups were not even allowed to exist. In the past 10 years groups such as the *Christian Aid*-funded AWEC have been able to establish a strong network to protect women's rights and provide education to the poorest. But, for all of these achievements, Afghanistan is still a country with some of the worst social indicators in the world. Ninety per cent of Afghan women face some form of domestic violence. Afghanistan is the most dangerous place to live as a woman and a mother, according to a recent poll by Thomson Reuters. It cited a "near-total lack of economic rights" as the main reason for this. Most Afghan women are not economically strong enough to protect themselves, as all property almost always belongs to the male members of the family.[11]

If peace is anything, it is surely far more than just an absence of war. A return to a situation where women are prisoners in their homes, without the enjoyment of the most basic rights, would be no peace at all. Let us remember that the position of women was cited as one of the reasons for the military intervention by everyone, from Laura Bush to Tony Blair, Hillary Clinton and Mark Malloch Brown. After the invasion, the US State Department even produced a dossier chronicling the Taliban's "war against women." What

Afghan President Hamid Karzai's announcement of an end to negotiations with the Taliban actually meant in practice was extremely unclear. The US is known to be in negotiations with the Taliban, and it was recently reported that the Taliban may open an "embassy" in Qatar to make negotiations easier. The fog surrounding the negotiations makes Afghan women feel that they are in the dark about what the future will hold. The High Peace Council has nine female members out of 79, but they often do not take part in the proceedings. In the words of Dr. Soraya Sobhrang, Commissioner of the Afghanistan Independent Human Rights Commission, "There are negotiations going on with the Taliban, but no one knows in reality what is going on. It is an underground process. Women are the victims and everyone is playing with their future."

The Afghan women have fought tooth and nail for a better future. Many have put themselves and their families at risk and some have paid with their lives. The governments of the US and the UK encouraged them all the way, and to abandon them now would be a cowardly betrayal. Those who have put their heads above the parapet have good reason to fear the return of the Taliban and their sympathisers, which would be a real danger of violent retribution. So the Afghan government must ensure that they are protected as part of any reconciliation. Furthermore, they must force all signatories to a peace deal to guarantee that women's rights are sacrosanct. As Homa, a 50-year-old teacher from Mazar-e-Sharif, told us, without this, "women are the most vulnerable if the Taliban comes back. Women will be back in their homes like prisoners."[12] Deputy Speaker Fawzia Koofi says "during the Taliban [era] and the civil war, everything was taken from women." It would be terrible if Afghanistan saw a repeat of this. The ability of women to fully exercise their rights is, however, still marred by social constraints. Forced marriages, child marriages and domestic abuse are still very common and security concerns remain a constant fear for both men and women. According to a UN report from 2009, the lack of female electoral staff made families reluctant to allow women to go to the voting booths. "I know it's a traditional society and things will not just change overnight," says Koofi. If the country wants to progress, politically and economically, she argues, the new Afghan government cannot continue to ignore 50 per cent of the population.[13]

Even before the Bonn 2011 Conference took place, scholars like Dr. Massouda Jalal, founder and head of Jalal Foundation (foremost advocacy organisation working in the field of women's and girl's rights in Afghanistan) took a two-week advocacy tour of two European cities and emphatically said that "excluding the voice of women and girls from the forthcoming

Bonn Conference on the future of Afghanistan will embolden the Taliban and create untold problems for the country's future."[14] As a prelude to the Conference, on November 23, 2011, the Afghan Women's Network (AWN) posted in its website a document entitled *Afghan Women's Declaration: International Conference on Afghanistan in Bonn*, consulting 500 women leaders representing 20 provinces of Afghanistan. Though the document noted some positive outcomes since 2001, it clearly expressed not only the aims, aspirations and dreams of Afghan women but also the fears relating to political representation, good governance, peace and reintegration. What is notable in this document is that the women seem to be more dependent on the international commitment to Afghanistan with respect to women and their security.[15]

Several organisations, intellectuals and the lay women in Afghanistan are highly insecure about NATO withdrawal. The international community should understand the bitter truth that, after the NATO withdrawal of 2014, there will be no matching military force to control the Taliban and the traditional Jihadi forces in Afghanistan, making women's rights in Afghanistan a serious calamity. Unless there is an international military force, perhaps under the UN, which can offer security in Afghanistan, women will go back to their position of 2000. Therefore, an international force is compulsory for the women in Afghanistan. The traditional religious and cultural realities are to be accepted and dealt with suitably. Probably, some progressive Islamic preachers from countries like Turkey may be engaged to teach and train the mullahs and leaders of Afghan society with regard to women's rights in Islam. Almost 80 per cent of women in Afghanistan live in the rural areas. The international community should change its policy of Kabul-centric and urban-centric development activities and should diversify and relocate schools and hospitals to the rural areas. Though education for the girls and women in the traditional Afghan style is important, the international community should establish Western-style education in all sectors—primary, secondary, technical and so on. Particular attention should be paid to the training of teachers, midwives and nurses, doctors and the like. For the political participation of women based on the Constitution and international conventions, an overarching body governed by the UN should supervise their representation in politics, employment, business, etc.

In October 2011, three major reports (the Oxfam report, *A Place at the Table: Safeguarding Women's Rights in Afghanistan*, the Action Aid report, *A Just Peace? A Legacy of War for the Women of Afghanistan* and the published results of AWN based on consultation with women from all over

Afghanistan) about women's participation in a possible peace process and their stake in the future of Afghanistan were released. The hook for all three reports is transition and reconciliation, but what they catch is much broader, it is the day-to-day struggles of women to advance their rights in a context that is conservative, violent and unpredictable. The reports portray as to how little control women feel they have over their own lives and key decisions relating to the future of their country. Many of the individual women interviewed in especially the Action Aid report express frustration of having little control over their own lives. As one of the women interviewed noted: "I'm not sure that my daughters' lives will be better than mine. I would rather have been born a man." Another woman, currently in prison, noted that "life in prison is better for women in Afghanistan than life outside." The AWN report focuses on how women's experiences of transition are not taken into account, as women were not consulted about transition and as they are not enabled to monitor transition. Consequently, there are no formal avenues for making women's voices heard.[16]

On January 6-10, 2011, there were reports that the Taliban kidnapped about 15 Pakistani paramilitary soldiers, held them captive for two months and threw their nude bullet ridden bodies near the Pakistani border. Likewise, the bodies of 10 Pakistani paramilitary personnel were reported missing after a clash with militants who were found in the lawless tribal belt of north-west Pakistan. The Taliban claimed the responsibility for both these atrocities. This shows the lack of security for Afghans in general amidst the Taliban's persisting prowess.[17] In addition, the Americans are also trying to accommodate the Taliban in the political structure of Afghanistan as clearly indicated by the American-supported emissaries in Qatar. The Afghan endgame has got off to an exciting start. The great reconciliation with the Taliban is all set to begin. Through sustained diplomatic efforts, Washington has gained acceptance—within the domestic opinion in the US as well as internationally—of the idea that durable peace in Afghanistan can be reached only through an inclusive settlement involving the reconciliation of the Taliban.[18] This clearly proves that even America is unable to ignore or bypass the Taliban. In such a scenario, after the withdrawal of the International Security Assistance Force (ISAF), one can easily imagine the plight of women with or without the Taliban in the political structure of Afghanistan. With the Taliban, women will have problems. Without the Taliban, they will face more problems. So it would be in the interest of Afghan women that after the withdrawal of the ISAF in 2014, the UN should supervise all the development-related activities such as education, health, employment and political participation of women. It is also necessary to have UN-supervised security forces to protect women in Afghanistan.

Afghanistan is a country that has known little else than war for more than 30 years and faces Taliban-led insurgency. For years, even the nightwatchman did not dare enter Kabul's Ghazi stadium afraid that the dead would haunt them. Many Afghans were convinced that grass did not grow in sports complexes because its pitch had been soaked in blood. Afghan film-maker Sedigh Barmak remembers not only those who were executed, stoned and mutilated by the Taliban, but also the 2,500 films they burnt in the stadium.[19] This speaks volumes about the ruthless acts of Taliban rule.

The Bonn 2011 Conference was supposed to be an assessment of developments that took place since 2001. But, unfortunately, in one day, with 80 countries participating, it is impossible to discuss any matter except to issue a joint statement. Women were eager to have an assurance from the Bonn 2011 Conference about their security and political future. It is disheartening that no meaningful deliberations on issues related to women took place, and there was no notable Afghan women participation in the conference. Surprisingly, even South Asian women politicians, intellectuals or even NGOs did not seem to raise their voice in support of Afghan women.

With the imminent withdrawal of international forces, there is a risk that the government may sacrifice women's rights in order to secure a political deal with the Taliban and other armed opposition groups. The women in Afghanistan are scared about their future after the withdrawal of the International security forces in 2014, and the actions of the US, the main international player in Afghanistan, are only making those fears real. According to Praveen Swami, the people of Afghanistan will pay the price for the West's looming deal with the Islamic Emirates it destroyed after 9/11. "The US is spreading an effort to make peace with the Islamists it promised to free Afghanistan from. The part of the story that is strangely absent from history-telling today is this: until the events of 9/11, the US was engaged in precisely the same process of reconciliation that is being marked today." Commenting on the West's recent effort to reconcile the Taliban in Qatar, Praveen Swami says "Afghanistan's political parties and political representatives aren't the ones, notably, who will be doing the deal. The Taliban isn't being asked to agree to terms acceptable to other Afghans. Afghanistan's women's organisations or ethnic minorities aren't at the table in Doha." We can imagine what will be the position of Afghan women if the West reconciles with the Taliban.[20]

Unfortunately, even in the Bonn 2011 Conference the voice of the women of Afghanistan was not heard. Paradoxically, the willingness of

Afghans to leave for Europe is fuelling a lucrative business in fake passports and Taliban death threats. The Afghan government reported that as many as 50,000 Afghans cross illegally to Greece each year spending US$ 20,000 each. Other popular destinations are the UK and Australia. Even in this illegal migration business the fake documents are for "mostly young, unaccompanied Afghan males overseas." No one cares for women. One Mohammed, pointing to the mountain peaks surrounding the Afghan capital, says "The Taliban are behind those mountains; they can come tomorrow or the day after."[21] If Afghan men are so scared about the "return of [the] Taliban," who will protect women?

Conclusion

The government and its international partners must do much more to support Afghan women's efforts and uphold their rights while ensuring that women have a strong voice in any future negotiations and political settlements. Afghan women want peace, but not at the expense of their hard-won rights. Life has improved for many Afghan women, who have fought for their rights over the last decade, often with the support of international donors, Afghan officials, Afghan activists, and NGOs. But this is not yet enough. There is a long way to go and many women have yet to benefit from the changes in Afghanistan since 2001.

In this context, while addressing women's rights, international players often ignore the specific Afghan culture in a unique religious situation and try to impose the so-called "Western" concept of women's rights. Afghanistan is somewhat different from the other countries in South Asia. Countries like India, Pakistan, Bangladesh and Sri Lanka had evolved strong political structures and broad political representations encompassing the general populace since the 1980s. But Afghanistan had to face a unique situation since the Soviet occupation and the subsequent American-assisted, Jihad-inspired, liberation struggle. Finally, the dominance of the Taliban and Talibanisation is too well known to be quoted in detail. One important aspect that is generally ignored by the international community is the unique religious situation in which the communist/Soviet occupation occurred. As that regime was anti-religious, those sentiments were used by the CIA to topple the Communist regime. Importantly, the women in Afghanistan also wholeheartedly supported the Jihad-inspired struggle by religious fundamentalists like the Taliban. It is important to note that in Afghan culture, we cannot separate women from men. They follow the same religion, the same Shariat, the same family values and traditions. Therefore, it is not only very complex but also very difficult to address women's rights in Afghanistan without the approval of men.

Afghanistan is also unique in the sense that it consists of different sects and ethnicities. It is neither like an Arab state nor like any other South Asian state like India or Pakistan in terms of composition of its population, language and customs. It is very difficult to understand why Afghanistan's political culture or even Islam is not influenced much by other South Asian countries. However, it needs to be emphasised that even the continuous occupation by both the Soviets and the Taliban have not altered much of Afghanistan's religious beliefs, its culture, family traditions or family honour. Any attempt by the experts, planners, or the international community at transition and reconciliation must take into account this unique situation in Afghanistan.

Notes

1. "World Bank Report on Afghanistan's National Reconstruction and Poverty Reduction," *The Role of Women in Afghanistan's Future*, March 2005, pp. 34-35.
2. Ibid., pp. 50-58.
3. Ibid., pp. 82-85.
4. Ibid., pp. 96-98.
5. "A Place at the Table: Safeguarding Women's Rights in Afghanistan," Oxfam Briefing Paper, no. 153, October 3, 2011.
6. Friederike Böge, *Women and Politics in Afghanistan: How to Use the Chance of the 25 per cent quota for women?* Friedrich-Ebert-Stiftung, Kabul, September 2004 at http://library.fes.de/pdf-files/iez/02536.pdf.
7. Madeleine Bunting, "The Afghan war and the myth of women's rights," *The Hindu*, October 5, 2011.
8. Ibid.
9. Praveen Swami, "Sound and fury signifying nothing," *The Hindu*, December 10, 2011.
10. "Afghan Women and Girls: Building the Future of Afghanistan," Testimony of Rachel Reid to the Senate Foreign Relations Committee at http://www.hrw.org/news/2010/02/24/testimony-rachel-reid-senate-foreign-relations-committee (Accessed on February 24, 2010).
11. "Afghan women: Hopes and fears for the future," at http://www.trust.org/alertnet/news/afghan-women-hopes-and-fears-for-the-future/ (Accessed on November 9, 2011).
12. "Return of the Taliban? Afghan Women Speak of Their Fear for the Future," at http://www.huffingtonpost.co.uk/melanie-ward/return-of-the-taliban-afg_b_990936.html (Accessed on October 4, 2011).
13. Sella Oneko, "What next for the women of Afghanistan?" at http://www.newstatesman.com/blogs/the-staggers/2011/10/women-rights-afghanistan-koofi (Accessed on October 7, 2011).
14. See www.prnewswire.com.
15. See www.afghanwomennetworkof/latest%20updates/AFGH.
16. "Women and Reconciliation (3): One Step Forward and a Running Match Backwards," at http://aan-afghanistan.com/index.asp?id=2132.

17. *The Hindu,* January 10, 2012.
18. M. K. Bhadrakumar, "US trump card in the Afghan endgame," *The Hindu*, January 9, 2012.
19. James M. Dorsey, "Kabul's stadium of horrors," *The Hindu*, January 14, 2012.
20. Praveen Swami, "West's romancing of the Taliban," *The Hindu*, January 18, 2012.
21. John Boone, "It's boom time for people smugglers," *The Hindu*, January 20, 2012.

8. Music as a Factor in the Political Stabilisation of Afghanistan

Diloram Karomat

> *The powerful appeal of music—its engagement with human emotions—is the reason it serves effectively as an instrument of politics and a medium of power.*[1]

For centuries, Afghanistan has been at the crossroads of civilisations, peoples and societies, a land "in-between" the East and the West and a territory contested by political powers. Moreover, as a part of the ancient "Great Silk Road" it has played an important role in transportation of not only merchandise, but more significantly, of various artistic and cultural products, the different kinds of musical genres (forms) and musical instruments. The uniqueness of Afghan music interconnects the musical culture of more than twenty ethnic groups and local nationalities like the Pashtuns, Tajiks, Uzbeks, Turkmens, Baluchis as well as the Indians, Iranians and Central Asians through the ages.[2] One of the modern Afghan activists in the field of musical education, Dr. Ahmad Sarmast[3] states:

> Historically, music has been a vibrant and important part of Afghan culture, but war and neglect has left students without teachers, teachers without resources, and professional musicians without a context for their art.[4]

The history of the region shows that Afghan culture, like any other Central Asian culture, has been destroyed many times and rebuilt again. The so-called post-Taliban period starts with intensified efforts by the Afghan government and its international allies to bring the conflict to an end and help in the social and cultural reconstruction of Afghan society. The Afghan government has to decide on bringing the inter-ethnic conflicts to an end by promoting education and cultural collaboration. Some of the Afghan officials like Minister of Information and Culture, Sayeed Makhdum Raheem,[5] believed that Sufism can act as a tool to stop political Islam and the Taliban,[6] while others stressed that musicians are central to social reconstruction.[7] Moreover, according to well-known ethnomusicologist John Baily, "Music, was a key part of the cultural identity of Afghanistan."[8] In fact, both Sufism and music have played a very important role in Afghanistan through the ages, not only as necessary components of communal life, but also as factors which bring all Afghans together. So, in the post-Taliban period, music of all kinds became a space for promoting particular ideologies and positions of authorities for stabilising the situation in Afghanistan. This article aims to briefly look at the achievements in this direction and the potency of music as a powerful agent for political stability of the country.

In the global information age, the term "Silk Road" evokes expressions like multiculturalism, cross-culturalism, and transnationalism as well as globalisation.[9] It is a well-known fact that in contemporary music the boundaries are blurring—between tonal music and atonal contemporary music, classical versus popular forms of music, traditional ethnic music versus world music, and Western music versus Eastern music—as global culture and economies are encouraging new artistic identities and the questions of authenticity and individuality are becoming significant. One cannot possibly celebrate diversity without knowing oneself.[10] Moreover, for contemporary Afghanistan, diversity becomes the challenge for peace and a brighter future and the interest for promoting the concept of multiple identities and a common heritage of the country. The new issues concerning assimilation of regional traditions into modern, and the activities of fusion musicians try to bring a new and free lease of life into the development of musical culture. On the one hand, this is the result of post-Taliban times; while, on the other hand, this is a continuation of the processes which began in the mid-twentieth century.

Since the late 1970s, constant war, conflict and displacement in Afghanistan was hard on everyone, and particularly musicians. Many of the traditional musicians were broke under such circumstances and were forced to go on exile. This had a profound impact on traditional music which underwent deep change. In every period one can recognise the importance of music in relation to political power.[11] John Baily in his article "Music and Censorship in Afghanistan, 1973-2003" described the two-sided attitude to music:

> At various points ... we see that music is the focus for the exercise of political power. During the jihad period, the Mujahideen ban music in the refugee camps, but use it for their own entertainment in the war zone. In Herat, musicians are under extreme pressure, but are occasionally summoned by the local authorities to entertain visiting dignitaries or sent abroad as cultural ambassadors. In Badakhshan, a local commander displays his authority by organising an evening of music in his house, with

a display of "naughty dancing." In Paghman, people complain that the gunmen have music for themselves but prevent others from having access to it. After the passing of a new constitution, the Afghan Government reinstates women singers on state television; the Supreme Court tries to intervene in order to reinstate the ban, but is unsuccessful.[12]

Actually, the case of Islam and music is dual in its essence.[13] Through the ages Islam does not ban music, but considerably limits and regulates its sphere of influence and its application. So, the al-Qur'an does not directly condemn or ban music.[14] All bans on music came out of a desire to maintain the purity of Islam. The history of Islam, for example, in the case of music, has shown that a negative attitude towards music could be felt in definite historical periods and mainly was a result of the prevailing political situation and change in cultural orientation, also related to the attitude of ruling dynasties. One can assert that the complete ban on music strictly enforced by the Taliban was imposed for political rather than religious reasons.[15]

It is true that the Afghan concept of music is closely associated with instruments, and thus unaccompanied religious singing is not considered music. The Taliban followed this tradition and the attention given to national musical instruments, the instrumental musical tradition, and all other genres where musical instruments were used, steadily dwindled. The Taliban even tried to destroy records of Kabul Radio. It is commonly believed that Sufi shrines were a place where music was followed and protected through the ages.[16] But even here, musical instruments were not safe. Sayeed Makhdoom Raheem, Minister of Information and Culture, who has a Sufi background himself, said in one of his interviews:

> The Taliban invaded Sufi gatherings, humiliated and beat up many of them and their musical instruments were smashed.[17]

Some Sufis, especially members of the *Chishtiyya* Sufi Order which considers music to be an effective route to reach Allah, were prosecuted. Only the frame drum,[18] a musical instrument used by women and one which was accepted by Prophet Muhammad, was allowed to survive.[19] Aziz Ghaznavi, the enterprising music director of Afghan television, himself a popular singer of the pre-Mujahideen period, has stressed:

> Of course, practice makes perfect and during the Taliban period none of us could practise. We lost so much. After five years of not singing at all, I was afraid to hear my own voice, and it was a very scary moment, to sing

> again for the first time ... In recent months, we have been starting over with these warped, broken instruments ... There is only one instrument maker in Afghanistan, and he is now fixing all the broken instruments; he has no time yet for new ones.[20]

After the foundation of the Afghanistan National Institute of Music (ANIM)[21] under the direction of Dr. Ahmad Sarmast, the Afghan government and its international allies helped to bring Western musical instruments into the country for young musicians. At ANIM[22] students learn how to play traditional and Western instruments as a part of the government's initiative to relieve the pains of decades of war through music. Prominent Afghan musicians, such as Gholam Hossein, Ustad Amruddin, Abdul Latif, Mohammed Murad[23] and Mohammed Jawid Mahmood, teach students to play traditional Afghan instruments. Western and traditional musical instruments were also brought by foreign and Afghan professional musicians who came for rebuilding the musical culture of the country.

Preachers, renowned Qawwali singers and prominent politicians all flock to Kabul's Karte-Seh district's garden to sample Sufi music.[24] The tradition entails 24 to 48 hours of non-stop music, played by musicians alternately. Promoted for several years now by local and foreign authorities,[25] a Sufi-based approach arguably enjoys an advantage over other more political or economic strategies because it offers a faith-based answer that comes from within Islam itself. Moreover, Sufis have considerable influence in both rural and urban settings—they are an effective popular force to bring change into society—and people consider them as disinterested mediators in disputes.[26] Sufi saints continue to keep the countries united even in the worst of times.[27]

Almost every book (treatise) on Sufism has a special chapter which is dedicated to *Sama'* (musical audition) and their rules. It is not surprising that Sufis place so much emphasis on music and especially poetry in their teachings and their understanding of the way to salvation or reunion with the Divine. Sufi poetry delivered the message of love, tolerance and harmony in lyrical form and through the tunes of local folk music. Moreover, poetry plays an important role in the cultural heritage of Afghanistan. In Sufi medieval manuscripts, in chapters about *Sama'*, it is often mentioned that music and sound besides their spiritual importance have the power to heal body, mind and spirit. This is due to Qawwali being an important form of healing within Afghan culture. The Taliban banned Qawwali music along with all other music,[28] during their rule and Qawwali music was the first to return after their expulsion. One of the most famous Qawwali groups in Afghanistan is the Ahmad Sham's Sufi Qawwali group,[29] which has performed not only in Afghanistan, but all over the world.

"We are committed to build ruined lives through music, given its healing power," Dr. Ahmad Sarmast said in an interview to Reuters. In another interview he stressed:

> Music can greatly contribute to the rehabilitation or healing process of the nation, which is badly traumatised because of 30 years of war. Music has a very strong power for social change. Music has the ability and the force to overcome social, economic, ethnic, and religious barriers and to unite the Afghan people.[30]

It is true that music is much more than a series of notes and rhythm, it is a universal language. Our auditory systems, our nervous systems, are tuned for music. Perhaps we are a musical species no less than a linguistic one. Moreover, in all societies, a primary function of music is collective and communal,[31] to bring and bind people together.[32] John Baily has stressed:

> Music is bound up with identity and memory in a special way ... it has potent *emotional* connotations and can be used to assert and negotiate identity in a particularly powerful manner.[33]

Indeed, music helps when all else fails. But still, for many people the question is whether those who are in conflict will ever listen to music and even if they do, would it change them? One can only hope for the better. Musicians in Afghanistan continue to face several security problems. Nowadays, these problems are not only related to the Taliban, but also to the warlords and traditional cultural norms. During the two workshops of the World Forum on music and censorship (Freemuse) funded by the Swedish Special Initiative for Democratisation and Freedom of Expression, which were held in Kabul and Islamabad during November 12-21, 2011 participants from all over the country identified some of the key problems faced by the Afghan musicians and composers. During these workshops the two local support networks for musicians at risk were established. According to Freemuse's report:

> The workshop identified weak legislations, lack of organisational structures and general lack of knowledge of the rights of musicians to be among the key problems. The workshop, which included civil society organisations, media, music institutions and musicians, noted that although music life

in general had improved since the Taliban were ousted from Kabul there are still several types of music which can put musicians at risk. Songs criticising warlords are considered very dangerous and most dangerous of all are songs that question religion, and heavy metal music.[34]

Australian guitarist Travis Beard, one of the musicians of *White City* rock group based in Kabul and organiser of rock festival Sound Central, in one of his interviews has stated:

> … all the Afghans that we know and we work with and we play with, they know the risks. It's a calculated risk. I think a lot of them would prefer to take that risk so they can have the freedom of expressions through the music rather than be silenced by peer pressure from their community or from certain elements, like the Taliban. They ask me these questions all the time, "Can we do this? Can we do that?" And I always answer them saying, "Well you know your country better than me, you make the final decision." We are not trying to control these kids or influence these kids. We're just giving them an opportunity." "There are classic stories, like Jalalabad, a city south of Kabul had numerous music shops where they sell CDs and music being burned down. There have been stories of wedding musicians tied up in trees overnight and their instruments being snatched. It does exist but Kabul is a bit of an island, a bit of an oasis where as an Afghan you can live a westernised lifestyle and not have so much pressure from your community as in some of the other regional capitals around the country.

John Baily in his articles[35] has written about difficulties faced by women musicians in the last 20 years. Ustad Farida Mahwash[36] is one of the famous and best-loved female singers who gained the title of *Ustad* (Master) in Afghanistan. After relocating to the West she has joined internationally renowned composer and *rubâb* (Afghan lute) virtuoso, Homayoun Sakhi, in a celebration of their country's diverse musical heritage. She as the singer of *Voices of Afghanistan* has triumphed over censorship and the prohibition of women singing in public.[37]

There are several difficulties and dangers which female musicians still face in present-day Afghanistan. They must practise music under cover and be protected,[38] like Sosan Firooz,[39] the first Afghan female rapper, by their families.[40] Dr. A. Sarmast faced related problems in the process of teaching girls in ANIM, where a third of the seats were reserved for girls. He found ways to solve problems [41] and nowadays one can see a girl student practising music. The ANIM is committed to providing a dynamic, challenging and safe learning environment for all students regardless of gender, ethnicity or social circumstances. One of the teachers, Mashal Arman, daughter of famed Afghan musician Hossein, stated:

> They are so thirsty for music and art, it is fabulous to see the country finally changing.

At ANIM, equal time is given to restoring the Afghan musical tradition and teaching Western music. The school is trying to follow tradition and at the same time trying to westernise their students to bring about a change in society. There are 16 foreign instructors at the school including an Indian teacher of classical music. Some of the main goals of ANIM declared by Dr. A. Sarmast are establishing music schools throughout Afghanistan, creating a strong curriculum for all classes, and creating the first symphony orchestra in the nation's history. It took several years for Dr. Sarmast's Institute to achieve success. Under the vision, "Establish Intercultural Dialogue," students and the faculty of ANIM were involved in the International Music Festival Sharq Taronalari Uzbekistan (2011),[42] the Golden Key International Piano Competition (2012), Glomus Camp Tanzania (2013),[43] and the Safar Germany.[44] One of the last reports about the school is that its students were part of the "First Afghan Youth Orchestra to perform in the United States."[45] The report by Mirwis Adeel highlighted the way ANIM reflects a modern Afghanistan, in which the musical traditions of the East and West come together through gifted teachers and students.[46]

It is true that all educational and cultural infrastructure in Afghanistan right now is still dependent on the support of the international community and international donor organisations. Besides the political support of the Afghan government, what is important is the financial, academic, and professional support of the international community.[47] Many of the charity organisations which are supporting education and cultural development of the country are realising that—for educating the next generation of musicians (in our case) and providing them with an opportunity to experience and express themselves through music irrespective of ethnicity or background—ANIM is a project with better prospects for a brighter future. The aims of the Institute were described by Dr. A. Sarmast in one of his interviews:

> From the very beginning, my intention was to establish a dedicated school of music to rebuild the ruined lives of the most disadvantaged class of Afghan kids, the street children and orphans, through music education

> and training. If we can save fifteen lives, it is a great achievement. It is a human achievement, and it is an educational achievement. Beyond that, I discovered that the music education was never set up properly in this country, even in better times when music had a lot of support; especially in the '80s … Establishing a music school with all the prerequisites and necessities of a music education is not a cheap exercise. You need millions of dollars, and there are also other priorities in Afghanistan. At the very beginning, the idea was to establish a music school only for orphans and street-working kids.[48] But then, we decided to compromise with the Minister of Education, not shutting the gates of ANIM to other talented kids of Afghanistan.[49]

Dr. Sarmast recalls the musical cultural programmes of the former Soviet Union, where as a student in Moscow he acquired the best musical education from Russians and integrated it with American-European traditions. Actually Soviet ideologues, at the beginning of the formation of the Soviet culture, supported the traditional national culture and started to teach Western music by establishing institutes, musical schools and Conservatories (for example, in Tajikistan and Uzbekistan). So, when the Soviets came to Afghanistan they already had the experience of using the power of music in Oriental societies. This experience was borrowed from the past and the same format was used in Afghanistan and in many ways it has worked. Not only did the musical culture of neighbouring Uzbekistan and Tajikistan influence the same in Afghanistan, but the historical and cultural cross-relations between the countries of Central Asia also had a role in this regard. During the 1980s, under Soviet influence, popular music in Kabul became increasingly westernised and modernised. John Baily in his book "Music and Censorship in Afghanistan, 1973-2003," emphasised:

> The successions of communist governments supported music, which they saw as indicative of the type of secular society they believed they had established ... Television was a powerful way through which to present music to the general public.[50]

For modernisation and liberalisation of society a significant role was played by Radio Kabul which was established in 1940. Radio not only transported its listeners to the modern world, but also helped change traditional values. A number of women, mostly from educated middle-class families, became radio stars. However, Westernisation of Afghan society started much before the 1980s. The 1970s were the golden age of

Afghanistan's music industry when the new style of popular music was personified by Ahmad Zahir,[51] the "Afghan Elvis," Ustad Farida Mahwash among others and Western Jazz music enjoyed a certain degree of exposure. The thousands of Afghans, men and women, who returned from abroad carried with them expectations that broadened conflicts over values.

In 2001, the ban on Western music and films was lifted. Nowadays, there are a dozen independent radio and TV channels in the country. Many of them are sponsored by foreign investors. Radio and TV programmes are not only dedicated to world news and analysis, but also to international music. It seems that popular music in Kabul continued the gradual process of Westernisation manifest in Kabul's rock groups. The students and recent graduates of ANIM also have formed a rock band named *White Page*, which plays a mix of their own music and songs from other groups.

"Sun, peace, and amplifiers," was a kind of slogan for Afghanistan's first rock music festival[52] named *Sound Central*—The Central Asian Modern Music Festival.[53] This was the first rock festival in the country since Ahmad Zahir's show in 1975. The Festival was organised by Travis Beard, the Australian photographer and guitarist of *White City*, who after many years' stay in Afghanistan felt that such a festival is necessary not only for bringing together all like-minded people of the region, but also for encouraging youngsters[54] to listen to the latest in modern music in addition to traditional.[55] *White City,* a multinational band, featuring English singer and bass guitarist Ruth Owen, Australian guitarist Travis Beard, and Swedish drummer Andreas Stefansson, wanted to highlight the fact that today's Afghanistan has a place for rock music, even though they are not allowed to perform in public,[56] and there are armed security personnel checking their instrument cases and the audience, at every concert.[57] *White City* conducted a tour in the Central Asian Republics, where they performed in clubs, concert halls, and theatres and sometimes even outdoors in Kazakhstan, Kyrgyzstan, Tajikistan and Uzbekistan in May 2011. The band met a number of groups during this tour who expressed a desire to come to Kabul and share their art. There were rock groups from Australia (*White City*), Uzbekistan (*Tears of the Sun*), Kazakhstan (*Eklektika*)[58] and Afghanistan (*District Unknown, Kabul Dreams* and others).[59] A festival of this kind remains a gathering for music and for dialogue between different types of cultures, religions and thought. Music is coercive if it is excessive, or has an overwhelming beat at rock concerts where thousands of people, as one, may be taken over, engulfed or entranced by the music.

Rock and Afghan hip hop[60] are the types of music which are very popular nowadays among Afghanistan's youngsters and its immigrant community.

For instance, *White City* which is promoting the popularity of rock music, rap (Afg. *guftor*) and hip-hop, there are also upcoming genres of music in Afghanistan that are emerging as alternatives to traditional music. Rap is a radical way of musical expression and one that is used as a symbol of protest against injustice in society. Several modern Afghan singers find this genre the most comprehensible form for expression of their ideas. Afghan singer and composer, Fared Rastagar, who recently returned from Germany and has a recording studio in Kabul, said:

> Rap is needed here. We need to bring changes in all parts of life including music.[61]

The name of Sosan Firooz has already been mentioned.[62] She is the first Afghan female rapper.[63] Firooz is not yet widely known among Afghans, but she is breaking tradition for women.[64] In an interview to Associated Press, 23-year-old Sosan Firooz spoke about her debut track, *Our Neighbours*,[65] which describes life as a refugee in Iran and Pakistan. With lyrics such as, "Listen to my story! Listen to my pain and suffering!" Firooz sings about repression of women and her hopes for a peaceful Afghanistan. The *Tribune* reported:

> Her song's message to Afghans: "Stay in your homeland." "Those who leave," she sings, "will only get jobs washing dishes or working at a car wash." "They will miss their homeland," she raps in a staccato style, part rap and part hip-hop. "They will want to kiss the dust of their homeland." "What is the result of Afghans being refugees in Iran and Pakistan?" she raps in Dari, one of Afghanistan's two main languages. "Half of them are addicts and the other half are terrorists!"[66]

Most of the music is aimed at helping the people of Afghanistan and bringing unity to her native country. On the street one suddenly can listen to the sound of looped drums and a thudding bass-line topped by the machine-gun delivery of a man rapping in the style of America's gangsta rap stars. This is singing of the first internationally known formal Afghan Hip Hop artist, Bejan Zafarmal (nicknamed DJ Besho).[67] In the beginning, many people find this very irritating. They say this is not a song because this man is not singing, he is talking. Rap and Hip-hop in Afghanistan are filled with local traditional values and intonations along with American. DJ Besho has Rap songs, where he is using quotations from the Qur'an, and in others he uses popular local folk melodies.[68] He reached the top of popularity with the

Rap song named *Gap*.[69] Farhad Darya is credited for the music and lyrics of the song.[70] For many years, Farhad Darya has been supporting young Afghan musicians and composing songs for newcomers along with his team. His music is a result of changes in the popular musical culture of Afghanistan. Farhad Darya stated:

> By supporting the young generations, I am paving the way towards a different level of Afghan music benefiting from world class standards. While most of the work is being produced inside of Afghanistan, my team and I are dedicated to a challenging and inspiring long-term commitment to help the desperate Music scene in Afghanistan and achieve what Afghanistan really deserves.

The future of Afghanistan very much depends upon the ability of its national and local leaders to create favourable conditions for cultural development. Most of the educated Afghan people understand that without cultural development the country cannot have economic development and cannot get political stability. In this process music has played a great political role for the propagation of the key ideas of the establishment. The *Gap* is one of such songs, where singer DJ Besho, in very simple language, raps in a staccato hip-hop style and delivers the message with lyrics such as:

Bagu ey, Vatana ki Obod mekuna, o jonon?
Amriko? Pokiston? Urusiya ya Arabiston?
... Khud mo Obod me kunem Vatana
Khudi mo parvarish metyem Chamana
Moh nakunem tu nakuni o nakuna.... Khay ki mekunah,hah?
Gorbachyov? Usomo? Obama? Sarkozi?/Ne ... ne...
... Megam Mo chu hamaki Afghon astem.../Shukur Musulmon astem
... Yaki rah Pushtun gufta/Digah ro Tojik megan,
Yaki ra Hazarah gi/Digah ra Ouzbek megan[71]

In these kinds of songs we can see how musicians try to use the power of music and lyrics to inspire, touch, influence, uplift, heal and transform society. By using the peculiarities of musical language in a special way, the actual messages have a deep impact on the listeners. This example shows that music can play a significant role in Afghanistan, bringing peace and stability and development to the country. Many years ago, California's Afghan leader, Sher Ahmad (Director of International Immigrant Services), in an interview to John Baily said:

> Music brings unity to the people, old and young together, and helps us not to lose our identity. We Afghans have some differences, but the concerts are the only times when we forget about everything, all people from different parts, different sects, come and buy our tickets and go to the concerts.[72]

Since the beginning of the twenty-first century, musicians from Afghanistan have been organising concerts in different parts of the world that showcase cultural developments in the post-Taliban period. Moreover, interviews and dozens of clips of modern Afghan singers based in Afghanistan and abroad, can be viewed on the social media and news channels like the BBC and Al-Jazeera and so on. All this reflects the support for Afghan musical culture in America and Europe.

The people and the government of Afghanistan are very appreciative of India's cultural efforts in the country. It would be impossible to talk of India or Central Asia building equities in Afghanistan without acknowledging how popular the influence of music is. There was a large musicians quarter (the *Kucheh Kharabat)*,[73] in the old city of Kabul. Some of the musicians here were descendants of court musicians from the Indian subcontinent brought to Kabul in the 1860s. The musicians quarter was badly damaged by the Taliban and musicians were forced to live in exile. Recently, some of them came back to Kabul's music quarter, helping to train a new generation of musicians. One of them is tabla player Ustad Asif Mahmoud.[74] Borzou Daragahi in *Los Angeles Times's* article "Afghan musician returns to keep a tradition alive" has reported:

> The master sits in a newly painted house on Kharabat Street, in the oldest quarter of this ancient city in the mountains. He plies his craft with his fingers, palms and wrists, beating, tapping and scraping the oiled surface of his drums as if he were listening to the secret pulse of the universe. *Daw-tiki-tak, tiki-tiki, daw-tiki-tak, tiki-tiki* ... the beat goes. "Tabla has its own notes," Asif Mahmoud says. "It speaks to us. It speaks from my heart. When I play tabla, I open my heart to listeners. Music is the language that speaks for the heart, for the soul." The 63-year-old Mahmoud keeps alive an ancient flame, an authentic Afghan culture that has managed to survive decades of war ...[75]

Many *Ustad*s, or professional musicians, have learned North Indian classical music in India. The late Ustad Mohammad Hussain Sarahang (1924-1983), was one of the master singers of Patiala Gharana in North Indian classical music. His composition *Pai Ashk* was used as the theme song of the Hindi film *Mera Saya.* The Art music (*Musiqi-ye klasik)* of Afghanistan refers to Hindustani vocal music of the khayal and tarana genres, ragas and taal. The development of Afghan popular music took place with the assistance of the above-mentioned descendants of Indian court musicians and songs from Indian films.[76] Even now, the Afghan version of the popular TV reality show, American Idol, has Afghan participants singing Hindi songs. Bollywood broke new ground in Afghanistan in 2006 with the release of *Kabul Express*, the first international movie filmed in post-Taliban Afghanistan. The Indian Cultural Centre in Kabul, which was formally inaugurated in September 2007 by the Afghan Minister of Culture and Information, Mr. Abdul Karim Khurram, and the Vice-President of Indian Council for Cultural Relations (ICCR), Mr. Sayed Shahid Mahdi, became one of the main places for learning Indian music (classical and popular) and practising musical instruments.[77] Moreover, it became a place where people of all backgrounds came together in the spirit of mutual bonding. India has played an active role in the development of Afghanistan based on the understanding that social and economic development is key to the country's stability in the region. Musical collaborations are significant in this context, which reflects the close cultural links between the two countries. In her book, *Soundscapes: Exploring Music in a Changing World,* Kay Kaufman Shelemay has stressed:

> … as an important "medium for the negotiation and communication of power" (Averill, 1997: 210), music can itself perhaps contribute to a greater understanding of the nature of power. Since power is always relational and all social relations involve power, and since music serves as an important forum for playing out social relations, music may be "crucial in helping us to understand and interpret how power is enforced as well as how it is challenged.[78]

Through a variety of its musicians Afghan music serves effectively as an instrument of politics and a medium of power and negotiation. Afghans from all backgrounds come together to bring stability to the country. Moreover, the engagement and involvement of youngsters has contributed to poverty reduction. As Dr. Sarmast stressed:

> I can tell you that since the establishment of ANIM, we have already contributed to poverty reduction. Now we have several kids who used to work on the street as street vendors or other jobs, selling plastic bags or boiled eggs on the streets of Kabul, but they are not doing these low-

> paying jobs anymore. They get to have sponsorship here: they have access to general education and to a vocation that really provides them with a sustainable economic future.

And in the home page of the Institute one can read:

> Through the provision of an internationally-accredited curriculum our graduates will have the skills, creative vision and confidence to contribute to the artistic, social and cultural life of Afghanistan, and the rebuilding and revival of Afghan music traditions.

The process of rebuilding and revival of Afghan musical traditions is becoming stronger. Music is also doing its best to be a factor of political stability in the country. There is hope for no more bans for music, no more exile for musicians and less government control ushering a brighter and stable future.

Notes

1. Gage Averill, *A Day for the Hunter, A Day for the Prey: Popular Music and Power in Haiti* (Chicago: Chicago University Press, 1997), p. 19.
2. See the ethnomusicological research works by Mark Slobin, *Music in the Culture of Northern Afghanistan* (Tucson: University of Arizona Press, 1976); Hiromi Lorraine Sakata, *Music in the Mind: The Concepts of Music and Musician in Afghanistan* (Kent and Ohio: Kent State University Press, 1983); John Baily and John Blacking, *Music of Afghanistan: Professional Musicians in the City of Heart* (Cambridge: Cambridge University Press, 1988); Ahmad Sarmast, *A Survey of the History of Music in Afghanistan: Special Reference to Art Music from c. 1000 AD* (Saarbrücken, Germany: VDM Verlag Dr. Müller, 2009).
3. Dr. Ahmad Naser Sarmast is a native of Afghanistan and a son of well-known Afghan composer, conductor, and musician, the late Ustad Sarmast. He received his PhD in music from Monash University, Australia in 2005 and became the first native of Afghanistan ever to receive that degree. He has a Masters Degree in musicology/ethnomusicology, from the Moscow State Conservatorium in 1993 and a Bachelors Degree in performance and music education from the same school. Dr. Sarmast is founder-director of the Afghanistan National Institute of Music (ANIM) in Kabul. An expert in the music of Afghanistan, Dr. Sarmast is a Research Fellow of the School of Music-Conservatorium and Monash Asia Institute of Monash University, an Honorary Fellow of the National College of Music, London, and the author of the book, *A Survey of the History of Music in Afghanistan.* In 2006, Dr. Sarmast founded the Revival of Afghan Music Program (ROAM), and in 2009, with the assistance of Afghanistan's Ministry of Education, founded the Afghanistan National Institute of Music (ANIM) in Kabul. The ANIM was formally inaugurated on June 20, 2010. See Kimball Gallaghe, *The Interview Magazine for Creative Professionals,* at http://notesontheroad.com/dr-ahmad-sarmast.html; and "Dr. Ahmad Sarmast on the Afghanistan National Institute of Music" at http://notesontheroad.com/dr-ahmad-sarmast.html.

4. "Afghanistan National Institute of Music Hopes to Bring Comfort in Time of War," at http://www.huffingtonpost.com/2012/01/13/afghanistan-national-institute-of-music_n_1204054.html (Accessed on January 13, 2012).
5. Sayeed Makhdum Raheem (Raheen) is ethnic Tajik and attached to Karzai's cabinet as Information and Culture Minister from 2002. See Current Government Officials: Afghanistan—Infoplease.com at http://www.infoplease.com/world/leaders/afghanistan.html#ixzz2JROoW7TY.
6. "Raheem is reviving Sufism and restoring khaneqahs [lodges] that encourage mysticism exactly because he believes that it can act as a tool to stop political Islam and the Taliban," said Nasir Farahmand, a Kabul-based professor of philosophy who is an avowed secularist. Sufism also promoted for several years now by U.S.-based think tanks such as RAND and the Heritage Institute, a Sufi-based approach arguably enjoys an advantage over other more politically or economically based strategies because it offers a faith-based answer that comes from within Islam itself. See Dawood Azami (BBC World Service Bureau Editor, Kabul) "Sufism returns to Afghanistan after years of repression" at http://www.bbc.co.uk/news/world-south-asia-12539409; Iason Athanasiadis, "Afghanistan: Sufi Mysticism Makes a Comeback in Kabul," August 26, 2011, at http://www.eurasianet.org/node/64095; "Sufism returns to Afghanistan after years of repression," at http://www.defence.pk/forums/world-affairs/95186-sufism-returns-afghanistan-after-years-repression.html#ixzz2ItLjCxYm.
7. "Pakistan: Focus on Afghan musicians in Peshawar" at http://www.irinnews.org/Report/17806/PAKISTAN-Focus-on-Afghan-musicians-in-Peshawar.
8. Stephen Moss, "The hills are alive," *The Guardian*, November 15, 2001, at http://www.guardian.co.uk/world/2001/nov/15/afghanistan.terrorism3.
9. In "Prelude: Power and the Play of Music" on page 13 of the book, *Music and the Play of Power in the Middle East, North Africa and Central Asia*, Dr. Laudan Nooshin has stressed: " … dimensions of power which have been of interest to ethnomusicologists in recent years include the intersection between music, power and place …, particularly in relation to concepts of 'globality' and the growing economic power of transnational capital. … More broadly, global interconnectedness and the collapsing of time and space facilitated primarily by electronic communications is impacting on notions of belonging, of 'self' and 'other,' all of which have far-reaching implications for power relations … shared cultural space no longer depends upon shared geographical place … ."
10. From the talk of Jinmi Huh Davidson (University of North Carolina at Chapel Hill), "A contemporary Implication of the Silk Road: Globalisation of Arts," delivered in the 8th Conference of Asia Pacific Society for Ethnomusicology, September 28, 2003-October 2, 2003.
11. As Marie Korpe, Executive Director of the anti-censorship organisation, Freemuse, says in a 2001 report on the banning of instrumental music in Afghanistan: "Censorship of music has existed ever since the time of ancient Greece. Plato distinguished between 'good music' and 'bad music'—suggesting that 'bad' music had to be controlled or banned, as it had the potential to divert people away from the 'good life.'" (Stephen Moss, no. 8). During 14 years of communist rule, music in Afghanistan was heavily controlled by the Ministry for Information and Culture, while in the refugee camps in Pakistan and Iran all music was prohibited in order to maintain a continual state of mourning. The roots of the Taliban ban on music lie in the way these camps were run. In the Coalition Period (1992-96) there were severe restrictions on music. Professional musicians had

to apply for a licence which specified that they could only perform songs in praise of the Mujahideen or songs with texts drawn from the mystical Sufi poetry of the region. Professional women musicians were forbidden to perform. The Taliban Period (1996-2001) imposed an extreme form of music censorship, including banning the making, owning and playing of all types of musical instruments. The Taliban allowed various types of unaccompanied religious singing, and created a new genre, the Taliban Tarana (lit., "song"). Since the 2001 International intervention led by US in Afghanistan and the removal of the Taliban, the music scene has begun to re-emerge. John Baily, "Music and Censorship in Afghanistan, 1973-2003," in Laudan Nooshin (ed.), *Music and the Play of Power in the Middle East, North Africa and Central Asia*, SOAS musicological Series, Ashgate, 2009.

12. John Baily, ibid., p. 163.
13. Related duality, but in modern sense was marked by one of the members of *White City,* Ruth Owen: "There's sort of a dual attitude here. If you look at some of the Afghan bands' videos on YouTube, for example, Kabul Dreams, and you'll get comments like, 'This is just an example of America's westernisation as Afghanistan's stringed instruments are banned under Islam.' But there are dichotomies and contradictions in every single Islamic country around the world. I think, much like we found in Central Asia, people associate rock music with the West. They don't really understand what it is and what it can do and how they can make it. But what we found is a lot of young Afghans are listening to Western rock music but not necessarily making Western rock music. They're interpreting it in their own way and they're making it their own." See "They play rock music in Afghanistan—and get away with it," *Hello Magazine*, May 4, 2011 at http://www.freemuse.org/sw43379.asp.
14. The *Hadith* became the main source for development of legal regulations.
15. "Pakistan: Focus on Afghan musicians in Peshawar" at http://www.irinnews.org/Report/17806/PAKISTAN-Focus-on-Afghan-musicians-in-Peshawar.
16. Sufis seek to achieve communion with God by Zikr (reciting the names of God and other sacred phrases), dancing, hymn singing, music and physical gyrations. The intensely personal poetry of Sufis has been expressed in Dari, Persian and Pashto, the main languages spoken in Afghanistan. Like in India, the Chishti Sufi sect of Kabul use instruments like the *rubab, tabla* and *harmonium* in their worship; this music is called tatti ("food for the soul").
17. Dawood Azami, "Sufism returns to Afghanistan after years of repression," *BBC World Service*, Kabul at http://www.bbc.co.uk/news/world-south-asia-12539409.
18. Many researchers have written eloquently of the power of drumming in cultures all over the world, and here it is especially the dynamic power of rhythm that is pre-eminent. This motor power of rhythm may be especially strong in various forms of motor and impulse disorder—and music can indeed be therapeutic here.
19. Veronica Doubleday, "The Frame Drum in the Middle East: Women, Musical Instruments and Power," *Ethnomusicology*, 43 (1), Winter 1999, pp. 101-34.
20. Andrew Solomon, "An Awakening from the Nightmare of the Taliban," March 10, 2002 at http://www.nytimes.com/2002/03/10/arts/an-awakening-from-the-nightmare-of-the-taliban.html?pagewanted=all&src=pm.
21. See http://www.afghanistannationalinstituteofmusic.org/.
22. "Afghanistan National Institute of Music Hopes to Bring Comfort in Time of War," January 13, 2012 at http://www.huffingtonpost.com/2012/01/13/afghanistan-national-institute-of-

music_n_1204054.html; "Rediscovering Afghan music" at http://afghanistan.blogs.cnn.com/2011/02/11/rediscovering-afghan-music/; and Zia Ur Rehman, "Afghanistan revives music culture," July 2, 2012 at http://centralasiaonline.com/en_GB/articles/caii/features/pakistan/main/2012/07/02/feature-01.

23. Ghichak teacher Mohammed Murad founded and directs this group of young students playing traditional instruments such as dilruba, ghichak, rubab, sitar, tabla, tambur, and dohl with astonishing precision and precocious virtuosity. They have become one of the most beloved ensembles in the country and are in high demand for their wonderful performances.
24. This twice-weekly meeting is held at the home of a member of the ancient Chishti Sufi order who gathers together an all-male *crème de la crème* of Kabul's Sufi society. See Iason Athanasiadis, "Afghanistan: Sufi Mysticism Makes a Comeback in Kabul," August 26, 2011 at http://www.eurasianet.org/node/64095.
25. Tom Heneghan, "Sufi card very hard to play against Pakistani Taliban," June 26, 2009 at http://blogs.reuters.com/faithworld/2009/06/26/sufi-card-very-hard-to-play-against-pakistani-taliban/.
26. "The influence of Sufis will be very significant in bringing peace and tranquillity," says Sayed Mahmood Gailani, a Sufi master. See Dawood Azami, "Sufism returns to Afghanistan after years of repression" at http://www.bbc.co.uk/news/world-south-asia-12539409.
27. Sufi bondage between Afghanistan, Pakistan and India is worth recognition by the foreign policymakers of these countries.
28. The Taliban also react to Pakistan's Mystic Sufi Music by bombing Sufi shrines in Swat, Lahore, Karachi and Pakpattan. For example, a Sufi musician was killed by bomb in the middle of annual festival of Sufi shrine on August 16, 2010.
29. The Sham Qawwali group has been playing for over 30 years and is one of the most highly regarded Qawwali groups of Afghanistan. It has toured India, Russia, Tajikistan, all over Afghanistan and last year went to London and Scotland, brought over by Reel Festivals during the first Afghan Festival in the UK. See "Afghan Sufi Qawwali coming soon!" at http://www.reelfestivals.org/afghan-sufi-qawali-coming-soon/.
30. Frud Bezhan, "Music School Looks to 'Heal' War-Weary Afghans," May 23, 2012 at http://www.rferl.org/content/afghanistan-music-school-looks-to-heal-war-weary-country/24590493.html.
31. Anthony Storr, *Music and the Mind* (New York: Ballantine Books, 1992).
32. Music in Afghanistan is varied and has always been associated with joyous occasions, such as wedding festivities and country fairs held over a period of 40 days in the Spring.
33. John Baily, "So near, so Far: Kabul's Music in Exile," *Ethnomusicology Forum*, 14 (2); *Music and Identity in Central Asia* (Taylor & Francis Ltd. and the British Forum for Ethnomusicology, 2005), pp. 216-33.
34. "Freemuse workshop in Kabul," November 25, 2011 at http://www.freemuse.org/sw45436.asp.
35. John Baily, "Cross-Cultural Perspectives in Popular Music: The Case of Afghanistan," *Popular Music*, 1, Cambridge University Press, 1981, pp. 105-22; "The naghma-ye kashâl of Afghanistan," *British Journal of Ethnomusicology*, 6, 1997, pp. 117-63; John Baily, no. 33, pp. 213-33; John Baily, no. 11.
36. She had a major hit with "O bacheh" in 1977.

37. *Voices of Afghanistan* is a traditional Afghan musical ensemble showcasing some of the finest musicians from Central Asia and Afghanistan. Singing in Pashto and Dari (a dialect of modern Persian), the ensemble offers an acoustically rich experience filled with poetic *ghazals* (songs of love and longing), Sufi songs of devotion, and traditional folk melodies. A performance by *Voices of Afghanistan* is a journey through time and space, reprising the glories of the Afghan past and reaching all the way to its increasingly global contemporary life and expression. One of the members of the musicians of the ensemble is Abbos Kosimov from Uzbekistan. He is considered one the most entertaining and explosive players of the Central Asian frame drum called *doyra*. Uzbekistan and Afghanistan share a great deal of history and culture, including the doyra. Ultimately, they explore the interconnectedness of the seeker and sought, the sacred and secular, and the traditional and contemporary. See *Voices of Afghanistan* at http://oneworld.syr.edu/artists/voices.html; *Voices of Afghanistan* at http://asiasociety.org/texas/events/voices-afghanistan.
38. A report about Nazir Khara's music school in Kabul (supported by the Americans), was published in the *San Francisco Chronicle*. According to the report, Nazir Khara is well aware that teaching women music could mean a death sentence for them or himself, since "many Afghan men believe a woman's voice should not be heard by men, and some conservative clerics believe it is a crime against Islam for women to sing or perform music." Nazir Khara's music school is partly funded by the "Afghan Music Project," which was developed by students as their brainchild as their final Masters of Business Administration assignment. Chris Becherer, 31, of San Francisco and Adam Gouttierre, 36, of Seattle, were studying business at University of California Berkeley in 2005 when they developed a "social entrepreneurship" project for Afghanistan. The idea was simple: record an album of traditional music featuring a female vocalist, and sell it and an accompanying video on the Internet to pay for musical instructions for young Afghans yearning to play their own music. See http://www.freemuse.org/sw24048.asp (Accessed on January 15, 2008).
39. "Sosan Firooz: First Afghan Female Rapper," October 10, 2012 at http://tribune.com.pk/story/449452/sosan-firooz-first-afghan-female-rapper/; Her song on YouTube at http://youtu.be/1Gwi7SNiTx0.
40. Firooz's father Abdul Ghafar Firooz says he has quit his job at the government-run electronics department to accompany her whenever she leaves the house and protect her as she pursues her acting and music career. "I am her secretary, answering her phones. I am her bodyguard, protecting her. When she's out, I must be with her. Every parent must support their daughters and sons to help them progress." Firooz's mother, who does humanitarian work, is very careful not to mention her daughter's budding career. See "Sosan Firooz: First Afghan Female Rapper," at http://tribune.com.pk/story/449452/sosan-firooz-first-afghan-female-rapper/.
41. See YouTube's interview: "Reviving Afghan music", *Al Jazeera English* at http://youtu.be/AbISkMNiUvY; "Afghanistan's Music School," *natochannel 123* at http://youtu.be/26Hc7BTBzok.
42. In Samarqand, Uzbekistan, the ANIM faculty of Afghan Traditional Instruments participated in the 8th International Music Festival of Sharq Taranolari (Competition) held in 2011. The ANIM faculty ensemble of traditional instruments has been acknowledged by the Special Prize of UNESCO, the Public & Audience Award. ANIM participants of the 8th International Music Festival of Sharq Taranolari are: Abdul Latif (dohl and

tula), Jawed Mahmood (tabla), Ustad Ehsan Irfan (tanbur and sitar), Ustad Ghulam Hussain (rubab), Mohammad Murad (ghichak), and Dr. Ahmad Sarmast the Head of ANIM team. See http://www.afghanistannationalinstituteofmusic.org; http://kultura.uz/concerthall/1417-2011-09-02-awards-sharq-taronalari.html.

43. See http://www.afghanistannationalinstituteofmusic.org/tanzania-tour.
44. See http://www.afghanistannationalinstituteofmusic.org/safar-germany.
45. Mirwais Adeel, "First Afghan Youth Orchestra to Perform in United States," Khaama Press, January 31, 2013 at http://www.khaama.com/first-afghan-youth-orchestra-to-perform-in-united-states-1314; Frud Bezhan, "Music School Looks To 'Heal' War-Weary Afghans," May 23, 2012, at http://www.rferl.org/content/afghanistan-music-school-looks-to-heal-war-weary-country/24590493.html.
46. Ibid.
47. Dr. Sarmast stated: "We have the support of the World Bank, the German foreign office, the government of India—there is a long list of our sponsors ... to get the support of the government of Afghanistan; that was significant and important because to establish a music school here, if you do not have the support of the authorities—if you do not have the support of the Minister of Education or other related organisations—all of the hard work would be a waste." See Kimball Gallagher, "Dr. Ahmad Sarmast on the Afghanistan National Institute of Music," *The Interview Magazine for Creative Professionals* at http://notesontheroad.com/dr-ahmad-sarmast.html.
48. Fifty per cent of the school's spots are reserved for underprivileged children, whose families receive a monthly stipend of about US$ 30, so the children can attend the school instead of working.
49. Kimball Gallagher, no. 47.
50. John Baily, no. 11, p. 148.
51. Ahmad Zahir (June 14, 1946-June 14, 1979) was a singer, songwriter, and composer. He is widely considered an icon of Afghan music and is sometimes called the "King of Afghan music." The peculiarity of his songs is the synthesis of Persian, Indian and Western music in new setting. His songs are based on Persian poetry of Hafiz, Saadi, Bedil, Rumi, Hiloli, but his favourite poet was Sufi mystic Jalaluddin Rumi. Today, he is regarded as one of the greatest persons in Afghan culture and history. In the 1970s, Ahmad Zahir was one of the most popular singers in Iran, India, Tajikistan and Uzbekistan. He is a celebrity of enduring popularity almost three decades after his death. He remains a source of inspiration for new and aspiring artists and has rightfully earned the title of Afghanistan's Nightingale. His legacy as the most celebrated musical phenomenon in Afghanistan and the embodiment of modern Afghan music goes on. One of the sources is Ahmad Zahir's official website http://www.ahmadzahir.com/sub/biography.html.
52. See more in "First rock music festival," August 15, 2011 at http://www.freemuse.org/sw44060.asp; "They play rock music in Afghanistan—and get away with it" at http://www.freemuse.org/sw43379.asp; "Soundscapes | Rock Band White City Wakes Up Afghanistan and Central Asia," *Hello Magazine,* May 4, 2011 at http://hellomagazine.org/soundscapes/; "Kabul rockers promote peace in Central Asia," *Central Asia Online,* May 21, 2011, at http://centralasiaonline.com/en_GB/articles/caii/features/main/2011/05/21/feature-01; Rock Central Asia Festival profile on *Facebook*: "Rock Central Asia | For Freedom of Expression in Afghanistan"; White City's tour blog: biginthestans.com; White City's social media profiles: facebook.com/whitecitykabul; twitter.com/whitecitykabul; myspace.com/whitecitykabul.

53. "Sound Central" was created by Travis Beard, a Kabul-based journalist and guitarist for the expert band White City. It is being produced by Daniel Gerstle, a former humanitarian aid worker who now runs Hello Media in Brooklyn. The festival is sponsored by groups from the US Embassy, the Institute Francais Afghanistan and Paiste percussion. On the first day the festival is held at Bunker club, on the second day at Babur Park and on the third day in the villa of one of the organisers. See www.soundcentralfestival.com; http://www.youtube.com/watch?v=Dr2piObWxm0;http://www.facebook.com/pages/Rock-Central...148745891875322.
54. Sixty per cent of the population is young people, aged up to 20 years old. They are quickly adapted to new conditions of life and changes.
55. At the time of the Central Asian tour the group is shooting a video of all the countries it has visited. To the Central Asia Online the musicians said: "This is a film that will help tell about the culture, music, and individual traits of these countries."
56. Travis Beard explained in an interview with *Hello Magazine*: "In Afghanistan it's forbidden or it's not part of their normal culture to play music in public. You can play a cassette or CD through your stereo but live performances are only done behind closed doors and in private compounds."
57. Swedish Andreas Stefansson arrived in Kabul the first time in 2000 and worked there for three years. He returned in the end of 2006, working for a Swedish NGO, and was keen on playing music because he used to play music in the past, so he looked around to see if he could find musicians to play with. Travis and Ruth Owen turned up in Kabul in 2008 and 2009, and then they formed the three-piece band. Australian guitarist Travis Beard started "The House of Rock" in Kabul with some Afghan friends in 2009: "We were just playing loud music and having fun and we built a studio and we had our band practice there, and then some other bands were practising in our studio. We talk about music, we do some mentoring and it's just a place where people can come with their interest in music," he told *Hello Magazine.*
58. Afghanistan. "АФГАНИСТАН. Отчет о поездке Эклектики в Кабул на рок-фестиваль Sound Central 2011," at http://310.kz/bb/lofiversion/index.php/t13713.html.
59. Two videos came out to promote the festival and freedom of expression, which also can be seen in the Facebook page of White City. Moreover, recently the *Sound Central Radio Hour* was started. Now every Afghan can tune into it in Kabul: 98.1FM and listen to their choice of alternative music live on Arman FM with RJ Pedram.
60. Afghan hip-hop is mostly sung in Dari (Persian), Pashto, and English.
61. No. 39
62. Ibid. She can be watched on http://youtu.be/1Gwi7SNiTx0.
63. "The first Afghan female rapper" (*BB* in Dari), YouTube at https://www.youtube.com/watch?v=qJ3eG8xUByk; "Dari Afghan Female Rap Singer" (*News.com* in Dari), posted in YouTube, at https://www.youtube.com/watch?v=dNcghoFrLUk; "Afghan Female Rapper" (*News.com* in Pashtu), YouTube, at https://www.youtube.com/watch?v=-XW9b4amCXo.
64. Artists in Afghanistan do not enjoy the same perks and privileges as their peers do elsewhere in the world. Firooz lives with her family in a mud brick house in a poor neighbourhood in north Kabul. She uses an old desktop computer to write her music and recently received an electronic keyboard as a gift from one of her supporters. She does not even have the money to make CDs or a more elaborate music video. See No. 39.
65. See https://www.youtube.com/watch?v=1Gwi7SNiTx0.

66. No. 39.
67. DJ Besho grew up in Kabul in the communist era, but in the 1990s his family shifted to Germany. There he has a group of 18 musicians in Wiesbaden, not far from Frankfurt am Main. Besho can freely speak in American slang. For more information, see http://www.facebook.com/pages/farhad-darya/64705581122?v=info#!/pages/Dj-besho/306525046059756?fref=ts.
68. Afghan rap DJ Besho, Youtube link, http://youtu.be/UKHpLdRvmTI.
69. GAP. Composer, Lyricist: Farhad Darya, Artist: DJ Besho, Produced by: Darya Management, Haroon Kargha, to see the lyrics: http://www.darya-management.net/besho/index.htm; YouTube link http://youtu.be/DtOqS8IPLeI.
70. Farhad "Darya" Nasher (b. September 22, 1962, at Kunduz, Afghanistan) is an Afghan singer and composer, as well as a highly acclaimed music producer, and Good Will and Peace Ambassador for Afghanistan to the United Nations. Widely popular, he has earned affection for not only his music but also patriotism. He has a fan base that stretches from his native Afghanistan to Central Asia, Pakistan and extending to the West among the Afghans. Farhad sings in various languages including: Pashto, Dari Persian, Uzbek, English and Urdu. For more information see http://en.wikipedia.org/wiki/Farhad_Nasher; www.farhaddarya.info; www.daryasworld.com; www.farhaddarya.info/bio.html; www.facebook.com/pages/farhad-darya/64705581122?v=info etc.; *BBC Studio 7* with Farhad Darya and Haroon Yousufi, AfghanMusicChannel 1 at http://youtu.be/lSIqGNrOdok.
71. The English translation (done by author): "Tell me who will care for Motherland?/America? Pakistan? Russia or Arabiya? ... We ourselves will care for Motherland/We ourselves will care for Flower-garden, If we don't do it, you don't, he don't .... Then who will, hah?/Gorbachyov? Osama? Obama? Sarkozy? No ... No ... I tell that we all are Afghans ... Thanks to God are Muslims ... One of [us] are named Pashtun, other one calls Tajik/one more Hazara, other one named Uzbek ..."
72. John Baily, "Music and refugee lives: Afghans in eastern Iran and California," *Forced Migration Review*, 12 (6), 1999, pp. 10-13.
73. More than a century and a half ago, the Afghan monarch, Emir Sher Ali Khan established Kharabat Street as Kabul's music quarter, where those who entertained at the castle on the mountain ridge would live.
74. Mahmoud fled to India, where he stayed for two years before heading to Britain, where he lived for 18 years. In London, he performed concerts and was celebrated in newspapers such as *The Guardian* or *The Evening Standard.* He finally returned to Kharabat Street in Kabul in 2003.
75. "Afghan musician returns to keep a tradition alive" at http://articles.latimes.com/2011/jan/30/world/la-fg-afghanistan-music-20110130.
76. "Hindustan, Bollywood Popular in War-Torn Afghanistan" at http://news.outlookindia.com/items.aspx?artid=688457.
77. See http://www.iccrindia.net/kabul.html.
78. Kay Kaufman Shelemay, *Soundscapes: Exploring Music in a Changing World* (New York: Norton, 2001), p. 283.

9. US Policy towards Afghanistan and Options for India

Venkat Lokanathan

In response to the September 2001 terror attacks, the American decision to use force by launching the Global War on Terror with the support of a coalition of willing countries has had a significant impact on the international security environment over the next decade. This chapter will make a modest attempt to analyse the evolving responses to nine pertinent questions. First, what was the basis on which the United States (US) decided to go to war in Afghanistan? Second, was the American strategy during the initial war effective? Third, what were the influential factors behind the American decision to continue its presence in Afghanistan after displacing the Taliban from power? Fourth, what was the US strategy on governance building? Fifth, why and how did the Taliban re-emerge? Sixth, what were the challenges to the American strategy to build effective governance? Seventh, how did the US respond to these challenges? Eighth, why is Afghanistan of strategic importance to India? Ninth, can India play a role in bringing stability in Afghanistan, and if so how?

War on Afghanistan

The primary basis on which the US decided to launch a war on Afghanistan was the Taliban's refusal to a final offer to extradite Osama bin Laden, the perpetrator of the September 2001 attacks, in order to avoid military action. President George W. Bush went on to articulate a policy that equated those who harbour terrorists with terrorists themselves, and issued a global warning that: "You are either with us or with the terrorists." The Bush Administration decided that a friendly regime in Kabul was needed to enable US forces to search and hunt down Al Qaeda members. By doing so, the US had, ironically, opted for an extreme response to an act of extremism. Subsequently, it sought and obtained the backing of the United Nations (UN) through the United Nations Security Council (UNSC) Resolution 1368 of September 12, 2001, which stated that the Council "expresses its readiness to take all necessary steps to respond (implying force) to the September 11 attacks." Interestingly, this was widely interpreted as a UN authorisation for military action in response to the attacks, but crucially it did not explicitly authorise Operation Enduring Freedom (OEF) to oust the Taliban. Nor did the Resolution specifically refer to Article 51 in Chapter VII of the UN Charter, which allows for responses to threats to international peace and security. It was only the congressional resolution riding on the wave of anger and frustration within the US, that explicitly authorised the use of necessary and appropriate forces against those nations, organisations, or persons that the US considered to have determined, planned, authorised, committed, or aided the terrorist attacks that occurred on September 11, 2001, or even harboured such organisations or persons.[1] In hindsight, the American response revealed a serious error in judgement which severely underestimated the Taliban's capability, preparation and strategy, and a lack of understanding of the topography of Afghanistan.

US Strategy during the War in its Initial Phase

When major combat in Afghanistan began in October 2001, the American strategy comprised air strikes on the Taliban and Al Qaeda forces facilitated by the US Special Operations Forces (SOF) and Central Intelligence Agency (CIA) operatives. The purpose of these operations was to provide information to direct air strikes against Taliban positions and to help the Northern Alliance and Pashtun anti-Taliban forces on the ground. In part, the US forces and operatives worked with Northern Alliance contacts such as Amrollah Saleh, who served as Afghanistan's intelligence director during November 2001 to June 2010, to weaken Taliban defences. The Taliban regime disintegrated rapidly after it lost Mazar-e-Sharif on November 9, 2001. Other, mainly Tajik, Northern Alliance forces entered Kabul in November 2001, in popular jubilation. The Taliban subsequently lost the South and East to US-supported Pashtun leaders, including Hamid Karzai. The end of the Taliban regime occurred in December 2001, when the Taliban surrendered Kandahar and Mullah Umar fled the city, leaving it under tribal law administered by Pashtun leaders such as the Noorzai clan. On May 1, 2003, Secretary of Defence Donald Rumsfeld announced an end to "major combat."[2] Crucially, during 2001 to mid-2006, American forces and Afghan troops fought relatively low levels of insurgent violence with focused combat operations against Taliban concentrations in the South and East. For example, the US and its partner forces conducted "Operation Mountain Viper" (August 2003); "Operation Avalanche" (December 2003); "Operation Mountain Storm" (March-July 2004); "Operation Lightning Freedom" (December 2004-February 2005); and "Operation Pil" (Elephant, October 2005). Some US combat units (about 1,300 Marines) moved into Afghanistan to pressure the Taliban around Kandahar at the height of the fighting (October-December 2001), but critically there were few pitched battles between US and Taliban soldiers.[3]

The Taliban had smartly realised that it was no match to the technical superiority and military might of the US-led forces. The American strategy to avoid direct confrontation on the ground allowed and enabled the Taliban to quickly disappear into the rugged terrains of the Afghanistan-Pakistan border to fight a guerrilla style war. Additionally, the lack of hot pursuit and intent to finish the job meant that the pressure on the Taliban was released quickly. There were some low-level operations conducted like "Operation Anaconda" in the Shah-i-Kot Valley against 800 Al Qaeda and Taliban fighters in March 2002, and "Operation Valiant Strike" against suspected Taliban or Al Qaeda fighters in villages around Kandahar in March 2003. However, these operations did not continue with the same degree of intensity, as by late 2005, the US and its partner commanders appeared to believe that the combat, coupled with overall political and economic reconstruction, had virtually ended any insurgency.[4]

The American Presence (Post-2001)

With the ceasing of major hostilities, the attention of the international community turned towards the extent of American commitment towards Afghanistan. The Bush Administration decided to confront the arduous challenge of building a relatively strong central government and economy. This was supported by the UN, international institutions, and US partners in several post-Taliban international meetings. The basic pillars of US and North Atlantic Treaty Organisation (NATO) security strategy post-2001 included combat operations by US forces and a NATO-led International Security Assistance Force (ISAF) to "provide space" for the expansion of Afghan governance, security leadership, and economic development; US and NATO operation of "provincial reconstruction teams" (PRTs) to serve as enclaves to facilitate the strategy; and the equipping, training, and expansion of Afghanistan National Security Forces (ANSF).[5]

More importantly, the American decision to continue its presence was also heavily influenced by its capitalist decision-making system primarily focused on profit-making and reaping economic benefits. Traditionally, a Republican government has always been domestically backed by a strong military-industrial complex in the US. Hence, the numerous opportunities in the field of energy and security for American private firms presented a perfect playground for new investments. Additionally, the Bush Administration was also looking forward to establishing a presence in the neighbourhood, in proximity to its rivals—Iran and Iraq. Subsequently, after attacking Iraq and dethroning Saddam Hussein from power in 2003, the US succeeded in establishing an overwhelming presence and influence around Iran. Another important factor was the threat of terror attacks emanating from the region targeting the American homeland. The Bush Administration realised that the US decision of leaving the region after the 1989 Soviet pull-out had created a power vacuum that allowed Afghanistan to degenerate into chaos and become a breeding ground for terrorists who were ultimately responsible for the September 11 attacks.[6]

The American Strategy for Democracy Promotion

The US made efforts to introduce an American style of democracy by creating an inclusive structure that represented the various ethnic groups and tribes in Afghanistan. The interim administration, formed by the Bonn Agreement in 2001, was headed by Hamid Karzai, an ethnic Pashtun, but key security positions were entrusted mostly to the members of the minority group named "Northern Alliance." Ahmad Zia Masud, a Tajik was appointed the first Vice-President and Karim Khalili, a Hazara was made the second Vice-President. Similarly, Mohammad Fahim, an ethnic Tajik, was appointed the Defence Minister; Dr. Sima Samar, a Hazara, was appointed Deputy Prime Minister and in charge of women's affairs; and Mohammad Mohaqiq, an ethnic Hazara, was appointed the planning minister. Additionally, many important portfolios like water and electricity, mines and industries, communications, education, labour and social affairs, rural development, transport and justice were given to either Tajiks or Hazaras.[7]

However, this attempt did not take into account two very important characteristics of Afghan society. First, the Pashtuns, who are ethnic Afghans, constituted the majority with 42 per cent of the 31 million population of Afghanistan. Second, the Tajiks, closely related to the Persians of Iran, and the Hazaras—Persian-speaking people, residing mainly in the Hazarajat region—were far behind with 27 per cent and 9 per cent respectively. Thus, any attempt by the US to build stable governance without majority representation in proportion to the Pashtun population was unpopular within the community.

The Afghan society was also filled with warring tribes that had fought for power and honour over many years. It was only the strong who survived that were respected and heard. Hence, the imposition of an American style of democracy was alien to these tribes as it required for them to share democratic space with each other and solve issues by sitting across the table in a non-violent manner. This brought a lot of discontent and frustration among the warlords who were looking for an opportunity to break the shackles imposed.

Additionally, the US also made a fundamental error by allowing a coterie to be formed around President Karzai. Essentially, this coterie consisting of a few powerful advisors usurped the decision-making authority from a larger body thereby creating disillusionment among members of the interim administration.

Re-emergence of the Taliban

There was a strong perception within the Bush Administration that the US had won the war convincingly and Afghanistan was increasingly stabilising, especially from early 2003 to about mid-2006, when it announced the ceasing of major hostilities. However, contrary to such expectations, violence increased significantly in mid-2006, particularly in the East and the South, where ethnic Pashtuns predominated. Hence, the key theatre of implementation of US strategy was concentrated in eastern and southern Afghanistan, especially Helmand and Kandahar provinces, since 2006. Crucially, even though NATO counter-offensives during 2006-2008, such as Operation Mountain Lion, Operation Mountain Thrust, and Operation Medusa (August-September 2006, in Panjwai district of Kandahar Province) cleared key districts, it did not prevent subsequent reinfiltration because Afghan governance was not established in cleared areas. As a further response, NATO and OEF forces tried to apply a more integrated strategy involving pre-emptive combat and increased development work. Major combat operations in 2007 included the US's and NATO's efforts to pre-empt an anticipated Taliban "spring offensive" ("Operation Achilles," March 2007) in the Sangin district of Helmand Province, around the Kajaki dam; and Operation Silicon (May 2007), also in Helmand.[8]

Challenges for Stable Governance in Afghanistan

The rampant corruption at all levels of the Afghan government, in the initial years, undermined domestic support in the US for its mission in Afghanistan, and also caused the Afghan population to turn pessimistic towards the Karzai government. In choosing to press the Karzai government to initiate investigations against senior Afghans or Afghans close to President Karzai, the Bush Administration created tension in relations. A major corruption-related issue was the scandal surrounding concessionary lending to allies of senior government figures by the Kabul Bank, an issue that led to the suspension of the International Monetary Fund (IMF) aid programme and related withholding of some donor funds. It was the Obama Administration's decision in late 2010 to shift focus to lower level corruption which reduced tensions with the Karzai government. Subsequently, the Afghan government after a lengthy delay approved of a process to recapitalise the Kabul Bank, recover a portion of the money lost, and prosecute figures responsible for the fraud at the bank in September 2011.

Since the process of building the central government had been tardy and official corruption was widespread, there was also a shift in American strategy, predating the Obama Administration, towards promoting governance at lower levels of the society. The Bush Administration felt that in addition to offering the advantage of bypassing an often corrupt central government, focusing on local governance was more compatible with Afghan traditions of local autonomy. Interestingly, the US Department of Defence report on stability in Afghanistan, covering late 2010 and early 2011, reported that governance was emerging or taking root in large portions of the districts that had been the focus of US and NATO stability operations in 2010. However, efforts towards building local governance continue to suffer from a deficit of trained and respected Afghan administrators ready or willing to serve, particularly where hostilities continue. One thing that emerges clearly though is that the slow progress accounts for many of the uncertainties clouding the prospects for transition to Afghan leadership by the end of 2014.[9]

Another area of concern was the progress in building a democratic Afghanistan that adheres to international standards of human rights practices. There was no doubt that Afghans were freer than they were under the Taliban. Women enjoyed legal protection and played public roles unheard of during the Taliban era, although conservative attitudes prevail and often undermine the intentions of formal laws and regulations.[10] However, the State Department report on human rights practices for 2010 as well as the reports on religious freedom and on human trafficking, have presented a substantial list of human rights deficiencies in Afghanistan, including extra-judiciary killings, torture, arbitrary arrest and detention, restriction on freedom of the press, limits on freedom of assembly, official corruption, violence against women, sexual abuse of children, child labour, and abuse of workers' rights. The reports have attributed many of the shortfalls to the overall state of continued conflict as well as conservative attitudes mainly in the rural areas. It will also be interesting to note whether gains made by women since the fall of the Taliban can be sustained as the US-led coalition transitions to Afghan leadership, particularly if there is an overall political settlement between the government and insurgent leaders.[11]

Narcotics trafficking also emerged as a major impediment by undermining rule of law and providing funds to the insurgency. Although there has been progress in recent years, its sustenance is questionable. The poppy crop acreage had shot up from 20,000 acres in 2001 to over 4,77,000 acres in 2007. The Taliban had ensured that Afghanistan was producing 82 per cent of the world's poppy and 93 per cent of its heroin to provide some US$ 4 billion each year to fund its insurgency against the Karzai government. Until July 2009, the US focused on eradication of poppy fields from Afghanistan by conducting aerial spraying. However this strategy backfired as it drove Afghans into the arms of the Taliban as protectors of their ability to earn a living. Surprisingly, cultivation flourished in provinces under Northern Alliance control, such as Badakhshan.[12] The Obama Administration has focused on promoting legitimate agricultural alternatives to poppy growing in line with Afghan government preferences. The de-emphasis on eradication also put aside the long-standing differences with Karzai over whether to conduct aerial spraying of fields. Siding with the Karzai government, the US Congress has also passed successive annual appropriations laws since FY 2008 that have prohibited US counter-narcotics funding from being used for aerial spraying on Afghanistan poppy fields without Afghan concurrence. Other policies, such as "good governance" US funded bonuses, give an incentive to provinces to actively work against cultivation. In support of the effort after initial reluctance, the US military is flying Afghan and US counter-narcotics agents like Drug Enforcement Agency (DEA) on missions and identifying targets. To help break up narcotics trafficking networks, the DEA presence in Afghanistan has expanded from 13 agents in 2008 to over 80 by the start of 2011. One bright spot was that the area under poppy cultivation in Helmand province, the main opium producing centre of Afghanistan, fell by about 3 per cent from the prior year. A UN Office on Drugs and Crime (UNODC) report noted that 17 provinces out of 34 provinces fall into the "poppy free" category, down from 20 provinces in the previous year's UNODC report, and warned that there could be a sharp rise in the price of opium crops in the near future.[13] The Obama Administration has also placed additional focus on the other sources of Taliban funding, including continued donations from wealthy residents of the Persian Gulf. It has established a multinational task force to combat Taliban financing generally, not limited to narcotics, and US officials are emphasising with Persian Gulf counterparts the need for cooperation.[14]

As far as threats to security, US commanders have, prior to mid-2011, worried most about insurgent use of Improvised Explosive Devices (IEDs), including roadside bombs. IEDs are the leading cause of US combat deaths, although the Joint Improvised Explosive Device Defeat Organisation, a part of Department of Defence (DOD), reported in February 2011 substantial progress in finding IEDs before they explode. In January 2010, President Karzai issued a decree banning import of fertiliser chemicals (ammonium nitrate) commonly used for making roadside bombs, but there is, reportedly, informal circumvention of the ban for certain civilian uses, and it is believed that the material still comes into Afghanistan from at least two major production plants in Pakistan. Throughout 2011, insurgents appear to have made increasing use of infiltrators within the Afghan security forces, persons impersonating Afghan security personnel, or recruits to their ranks from amongst aides trusted by Afghan leaders. Afghan officials have tried to increase monitoring over the sale of military-style clothing that might be used for such attacks. Other insurgents appear to be making increasing use of bombs hidden in turbans, which have, until October 2011, generally not been searched out of respect for Afghan religious traditions. Such a bomb killed former President Barhanuddin Rabbani on September 20, 2011.

Security in Afghanistan is also being challenged by a confluence of armed groups whose tactics continue to evolve based on experiences from previous fighting. The core of the insurgency remains the "Quetta Shura Taliban" movement, to varying degrees loyal to Mullah Umar, who led the Taliban regime during 1996-2001. It is reported to have a relatively safe haven in Pakistan around the city of Quetta. For now still committed to insurgent action, Umar has been making appointments to replenish the leadership ranks. The Taliban operates a clandestine radio station, "Voice of Shariat" and publishes videos. American officials argued that the successes produced by the US "surge" in Afghanistan were causing some Taliban leaders to mull the concept of a political settlement. Interestingly, Mullah Umar released a statement on the tenth anniversary of the September 11 attacks on the US, acknowledging there have been some talks, although only over prisoner exchanges.

Al Qaeda has been long considered by the US to have been largely expelled from Afghanistan itself. American commanders have for several years characterised any Al Qaeda militants in Afghanistan as facilitators of militant incursions into Afghanistan rather than active fighters in the Afghan insurgency. However, it is generally accepted by the US and NATO leadership that at present there are approximately 50-100 Al Qaeda fighters in Afghanistan. US efforts in the region have killed numerous senior operatives other than bin Laden. A January 2008 strike near Damadola killed Abu Laith al-Libi, who purportedly masterminded, among other operations, the bombing at Bagram Air Base in February 2007 when the then Vice-

President, Dick Cheney was visiting. In August 2008, it was confirmed that an airstrike had killed Al Qaeda chemical weapons expert, Abu Khabab al-Masri. Two senior operatives allegedly involved in the 1998 embassy bombings in Africa reportedly were killed by an unmanned aerial vehicle (Predator) strike in January 2009.[15] Following the killing of bin Laden, another top Al Qaeda leader, Ilyas Kashmiri, was reportedly killed by an armed drone strike in June 2011. Such aerial-based strikes have become more frequent under President Obama, indicating that the administration sees the tactic as effective in preventing attacks. US efforts to find Al Qaeda leaders are expected to now focus on his close ally, Ayman al-Zawahiri, who is also presumed to be on the Pakistani side of the border and who was named new leader of Al Qaeda in June 2011. Other senior Al Qaeda leaders are either in or are allowed to transit or reside in Iran. Among them are Al Qaeda's former spokesman, Kuwait-born Sulayman Abu Ghaith, as well as Sayf al Adl. The US has no diplomatic relations with Iran, and has urged it to arrest and submit any Al Qaeda operatives to international authorities for trial.

Another "high value target" identified by US commanders is the faction of former Mujahideen party leader, Gulbuddin Hikmatyar (Hizb-e-Islami Gulbuddin, HIG) allied with Al Qaeda and Taliban insurgents. Hikmatyar's faction is now active against US and Afghan forces in Kunar, Nuristan, Kapisa, and Nangarhar provinces, north and east of Kabul. In February 2003, the US government formally designated Hikmatyar as a "Specially Designated Global Terrorist," subjecting him to financial and other US sanctions. Hikmatyar has expressed a willingness to discuss a ceasefire with the Karzai government since 2007, and several of Karzai's key allies in the National Assembly, including the Speaker of the lower house, Abdul Raouf Ibrahimi, are members of a moderate wing of Hikmatyar's party. While US commanders continue to battle Hikmatyar's militia, there have been reports of conciliatory talks between the Afghan government, US representatives and the faction.[16]

Another militant faction, cited by US officials as perhaps the most potent threat to Afghan security, is the "Haqqani Network" led overall by Jalaludin Haqqani but made operational by his sons Sirajjudin and Badruddin. Since the ousting of the Taliban regime in 2001, he has been a staunch opponent of the Karzai government and his faction is believed to be closer to Al Qaeda than to the ousted Taliban leadership. Press reports indicate that the few Al Qaeda fighters that are in Afghanistan are mostly embedded with Haqqani fighters. The faction is believed to be primarily interested in earning illicit monies and in controlling parts of Khost Province. It is estimated that there may be as many as 3,000 Haqqani fighters. Suggesting it may act as a tool of Pakistani interests, the Haqqani network has primarily targeted Indian interests. That the faction is tolerated or protected in the North Waziristan area of Pakistan and its purported ties to Pakistan's Inter-Services Intelligence Directorate (ISI) are causes of sharp US criticism of Pakistan. The ISI is believed to see the Haqqanis as a potential ally in any new Afghan political structure that might be produced by a political settlement in Afghanistan. In addition to pressing Pakistan to deny the group a safe haven, the US is increasingly pressuring the Haqqani network with military action in Afghanistan and air strikes on the Pakistani side of the border, as well as with direct ground action, such as a raid in late July 2011 that reportedly killed over 80 Haqqani network militants. However, the faction is viewed as resilient and able to tap a seemingly infinite pool of recruits. The faction has generally been considered least amenable to a political settlement with the Afghan government, but it is possible that the May 1, 2011 raid that killed Osama bin Laden will reinforce those within the faction who might want to reassess that stance. In May 2011, there were reports that ISI is pushing the Haqqani network to join nascent settlement talks under way between the Afghan government and other insurgent factions. It has also been reported in the media that US officials met with Haqqani representatives over the summer of 2011, in meetings facilitated by the ISI. The faction's calculations could be affected by how the US characterises the group. In July 2010, General Petraeus advocated that the Haqqani network be named as a Foreign Terrorist Organisation (FTO) under the Immigration and Naturalisation Act (INA). Such a move is intended to signal Pakistan that it should not continue to support the Haqqani network. Till date, seven Haqqani leaders have been sanctioned as Specially Designated Global Terrorists (SDGT). However, such designations could make it difficult to conduct further contacts with the faction, if the Haqqani network is amenable.[17]

The Taliban of Afghanistan is increasingly linked politically and operationally to Pakistani Taliban militants. The Pakistani groups might see a Taliban recapture of Afghanistan's government as helpful to the prospects for these groups inside Pakistan or in their Kashmir struggle. A major Pakistani Taliban group, namely, Tehrik-e-Taliban Pakistan (TTP), is primarily seeking to challenge the government of Pakistan, but they facilitate the transiting of Afghan Taliban into Afghanistan and support the Afghan Taliban goals of recapturing Afghanistan. The TTP may also be seeking to target the US, an assessment based on a failed bombing in New York City in May 2010. The State Department designated the TTP as an FTO under the INA in September 2010, allegedly for having close connections with the Al Qaeda. Another Pakistani group said to be increasingly active inside Afghanistan is Lashkar-e-Taiyyiba (LeT), an Islamist militant group that has previously focused on operations against India in Kashmir.[18]

US Responses to Growing Challenges

Throughout 2008, growing concern over the deteriorating security situation in Afghanistan took hold within the Bush Administration. In September 2008, Admiral Mike Mullen, the Chairman of Joint Chiefs of Staff (CJCS), commented pessimistically that "I'm not sure we're winning" in Afghanistan. Several major incidents supported that assessment, including the expanding Taliban operations in provinces where it had not previously been active, particularly Lowgar, Wardak, and Kapisa, close to Kabul; high-profile attacks in Kabul, such as the attack on the Serena Hotel in Kabul in January 2008, and the suicide bombing at the Indian Embassy in Kabul in July 2008; the assassination attempt on Karzai during a military parade celebrating the ouster of the Soviet Union in April 2008; and a Sarposa prison break in Kandahar, in which several hundred Taliban captives were freed in June 2008.

To prevent further deterioration, the US and its partners decided to increase force levels by partly fulfilling a mid-2008 request by General McKiernan, Commander, US Forces Afghanistan (USFOR-A) and ISAF, for 30,000 additional American troops. Troop levels started at 30,000 in 2006, which increased slightly to 32,000 by December 2008 and reached 39,000 by April 2009 (shortly after President Obama took office). Partner forces were also increased by about 6,000 during this time to a total of 39,000 by the end of 2009.[19]

A significant challenge to the American strategy was the change in leadership from Bush to Obama Administration. Hence, in September 2008, the US military and NATO began to review their strategies. The primary American review was headed by Lieutenant General Douglas Lute, the senior adviser on Iraq and Afghanistan (who also became a part of the Obama National Security Council with responsibility for Afghanistan) during the Bush Administration. These reviews were briefed to the incoming Obama Administration. The Obama Administration maintained that Afghanistan needed to be given a higher priority than it was given during the Bush Administration, but also asserted that the US mission in Afghanistan will not be indefinite.[20] The new Administration integrated the reviews under way at the end of the Bush Administration, into an overarching 60-day inter-agency "strategy review." Following its initial review, President Obama announced a "comprehensive" strategy in March 2009 where he underlined the deployment of an additional 21,000 American forces, of which about 4,000 would be trainers.[21]

Shortly after Obama's announcement in March 2009, the Administration decided that US military leadership in Afghanistan needed to be replaced. After succeeding General McKiernan, General Stanley McChrystal assessed the security situation in August 2009 and suggested that the goal of the US military should be to protect the population and to help the Afghan government take steps to earn the trust of the population, rather than to focus on searching out and combating Taliban concentrations. Hence, indicators of success such as ease of road travel, participation in local shuras, and normal life for families was more significant than counts of enemy fighters killed. Further, he warned that there is potential for "mission failure" unless a fully resourced, comprehensive counterinsurgency strategy was pursued which reversed Taliban momentum within 12-18 months. About 44,000 additional US combat troops (beyond those approved by the Obama Administration's strategy review in March 2009) would be needed to ensure the strategy's success.

The McChrystal assessment set off a debate that also revealed deep-rooted divisions within the Administration over its Afghan strategy. Some senior US officials, such as then Secretary of Defence Gates, were concerned that adding more US forces could create among the Afghan people a sense of "occupation" that could prove counterproductive. The high-level review including at least nine high-level meetings, chaired by President Obama, led to the decision in December 2009 that 30,000 additional US forces would be sent (bringing US levels close to 100,000) to reverse the Taliban's momentum and strengthen the capacity of Afghanistan's security forces and government. More importantly, it announced that there would be a transition, beginning in July 2011, to Afghan leadership of the stabilisation effort and a corresponding beginning of a drawdown of US force levels. Why did the US make public its decision to drawdown troops in Afghanistan? The Administration explained the time frame as a means of demonstrating to a war-weary public back home that military involvement in Afghanistan was not open-ended, and it was to compel the Afghan government to assume greater ownership and responsibility for the mission.[22] Subsequently, Leon Panetta, the Defence Secretary announced that US military troops will transition from combat to a role of providing training and advising safety and ultimately withdraw by the end of 2013.

However, this strategy received a further setback in June 2010, when President Obama accepted the resignation of General McChrystal, who had served for less than a year, following his comments to *Rolling Stone* magazine that disparaged several civilian figures involved in the Afghanistan policy and announced General Petraeus as his successor. Additionally, the 2011 deadline was interpreted by some critics of administration and by some Afghan and regional leaders as laying the groundwork for a rapid winding down of US involvement. Perhaps to address perceived criticism of such a deadline in the upper ranks of the US military, in an August 2010 statement the President asserted that the pace and scope of any drawdown would be subject to conditions on the ground. Subsequently, the debate over the July 2011 drawdown abated substantially with an agreement between the US and NATO partner forces to focus on allowing a longer time frame for transition to Afghan leadership. At the November 2010 NATO summit in Lisbon, it was agreed that the transition to Afghan leadership would begin in 2011 and would be completed by the end of 2014. Interestingly, President Karzai had articulated in 2009 that Afghan forces would be able to secure Afghanistan by 2014.[23]

Although the formal Obama Administration policy goal was to prevent Afghanistan from becoming a safe haven for global terrorism once again since 2002, the American criteria for judging achievement of that goal have been the degrees to which the Afghan government and security forces can defend itself, govern effectively, and develop economically. The President's June 2011 speech on Afghanistan announcing a US troop drawdown outlined that the Afghan government was to progressively assume the lead on security as the US reduced its level of military effort over the next several years.[24] Hence the transition phase from the 2011 announcement to the 2014 deadline is a crucial phase for Afghanistan.

India's Role and Options in Afghanistan

In this complex environment, if India harbours serious intentions of becoming an active global player, its strategic vision has to unfold on a three-pronged strategy. First, India must seek to be a dominant player, both diplomatically and politically, in its immediate neighbourhood. Second, it has to play a significant role in Asia, by constantly engaging with countries in West, Central, South East and Far East Asia. Third, in the long term, it must increase its role in world affairs by playing a constructive role that seeks solutions to global problems. However, to achieve these objectives, India will have to display consistent intent, clarity in thought, strong resilience under pressure and the ability to lead other countries towards seeking solutions to global problems. In this context, Afghanistan has always remained a country of geopolitical importance. Post-9/11, India has looked to constantly engage with Afghanistan in order to gain a significant presence in the north-west border of its traditional arch rivals, Pakistan. A significant manoeuvring space for India would, in turn, restrict Pakistan's role in Afghanistan. With demands for energy growing worldwide, access to energy markets becomes critical. Hence, if bilateral relations between Afghanistan and Pakistan become stronger, it would be detrimental to India's larger interests in the region, especially in gaining access to natural gas in Afghanistan and the lucrative markets of Central Asia such as Iran, Turkmenistan and Kazakhstan. Additionally, over the years, India has realised that the threat from cross-border terrorism has its roots in Afghanistan. Indian intelligence has painstakingly unearthed camps where terrorists of all the major terrorist groups targeting India like Harkat-ul-Jihad-al-Islami (HUJI), Lakshar-e-Taiyyiba (LeT), Harkat-Ul-Mujahideen (HuM) and Harkat-Ul-Ansar (HuA) have trained. A significant concern that has emerged recently is the role of these camps in ideologically indoctrinating dissatisfied sections of the Indian population, including the Indian Mujahideen, to engage in Jihad against the state. Finally, India is also concerned over the increasing role played by the other major Asian power, China, in the region.[25]

Indian Role in Afghanistan: Possibilities

India has moved quickly to assist in reconstruction by focusing on development projects, humanitarian assistance and providing financial aid. The then Indian Prime Minister, Atal Behari Vajpayee announced a US$ 100 million line of credit with one million tonnes of wheat and a team of doctors and technicians for fixing artificial limbs for amputees of war. Since then, India has committed an additional US$ 750 million and again another US$ 450 million over the last decade. Significantly, Indian Prime Minister Manmohan Singh raised the overall financial aid to Afghanistan to US$ 2 billion in July 2011. India has also increased its role in strategic infrastructural projects in recent years. It has built a transmission line for power to Kabul and completed construction of the Zaranj-Delaram highway in Southwest Afghanistan near the Iranian border in January 2009. It is constructing a new parliament building and is also constructing the Salma Dam power project in Herat Province. It has also assisted in training Afghan police officers, diplomats and civil servants. The Indian Council for Cultural Relations (ICCR) has offered 500 scholarships a year to Afghan students. India is also hoping that its investment in the Iranian port at Chabahar will allow it to gain trading access to Afghanistan, bypassing Pakistan.[26] It is also apprehended that Pakistan's relative lack of risk aversion will enable it to pursue dangerous policies to minimise India's presence in Afghanistan, including continued support of groups such as the Haqqani network, LeT, and the Afghan Taliban, among others. There are currently about four thousand Indian workers and security personnel working on different relief and reconstruction projects in Afghanistan. Unfortunately, since 2006, they have come under increased violence including the two attacks on the Indian embassy in Kabul and assaults on consulates in Herat and Jalalabad. This has raised serious concerns over the deterioriating security environment in Afghanistan. In response, India has sent the Indo-Tibetan Police Force (ITPF) and additional army commandos to protect its civilians and workers of the Border Roads Organisation (BRO). It has, on numerous occasions, brought up the unworthiness of Pakistan as an ally to the US operations in Afghanistan. It has consistently highlighted that US funds to Pakistan for fighting the Taliban have been diverted towards cross-border terrorism against India.[27]

India is increasingly concerned over its future in Afghanistan both leading to and after the US exit in 2014. It has attempted to convince the US to avoid making a hurried departure from Afghanistan. It will have three clear options to choose from in pursuit of its Afghan policy. First, India can continue to enhance its presence in close coordination with the US and then withdraw its presence simultaneously with American forces and make a quiet exit from Afghanistan, thereby assuaging all concerns emanating from Pakistan. A positive scenario that will emerge is that it can avoid being exposed to terror attacks on its citizens in Afghanistan which can turn domestic public opinion critical. However, a drawback will be that India will have to undo all the good work it has done in reconstruction and development over the last decade. It will also create a vacuum for Pakistan and China to step in, which will be detrimental to India's national security. Second, India can choose to drawback its numbers in Afghanistan significantly along with the US but yet leave a minimal presence to keep Pakistan guessing about its real intentions. This might ensure that Pakistan is distracted by the Indian presence on both sides of the border. However, this option might work in the short and medium term as the vacuum created by the drawdown of Western and Indian presence will be eventually filled by other players such as Pakistan and China in the long run, which in turn will provide the realistic picture of India's influence and presence. Third, the most compelling option will be for India to increase its role in the reconstruction and development sector in Afghanistan by assisting in completion of more projects. This will also provide more jobs to domestic Indians and increase India's ability to leverage, both diplomatically and politically, in Afghanistan. It will also indicate to the US that India is willing and capable of playing a global role.

Significant presence would in turn require an increase in Indian troops. However, the political mandate for military presence needs to be clearly restricted to protecting civilians and workers in Afghanistan. At no time should Indian troops appear to replace the US and NATO troops by engaging in protecting the Afghan government or peacekeeping which can be best left, if absolutely necessary, to the local Afghan security forces and a UN peacekeeping force or a regional security force respectively. India will need to engage with Iran consistently in order to keep alternative options to intervene in Afghanistan should Pakistan intervene directly. However, any engagement with Iran will have to be carefully managed keeping the US in mind.

One factor that might assist India in pursuing its Afghan engagement is its greatest asset of soft power. Indian television soaps and Bollywood films are very popular in Afghanistan which will assist the local populace to see Indians in a more positive light. This, in turn, will hopefully convert into locals providing intelligence inputs of impending attacks on Indian establishments. If India wants to pursue its three-pronged strategy vigorously, it will have to indicate a strong political will to engage actively, resist insurgent attacks and stay in the background as much as possible in Afghanistan. Ultimately, what option India chooses to go with in Afghanistan might well provide an insight into its ability to play a prominent global role in the future.

If it envisions creating stability in Afghanistan in the near future, the US will find it increasingly difficult to keep engagements with India and Pakistan separate on matters related to Afghanistan. It is becoming more and more evident that the US cannot realise its goals for India, Pakistan and Afghanistan simultaneously without taking all these players on board collectively.

Notes

1. Kenneth Katzman, "Afghanistan: Post-Taliban Governance, Security, and US Policy," CRS Report for Congress, October 21, 2011.
2. Ashley J. Tellis, "The Decade That Took Us from Peace to War," Carnegie Endowment for International Peace, September 16, 2011 at http://www.carnegieendowment.org/2011/09/16/decade-that-took-us-from-peace-to-war/8kxy (Accessed on December 24, 2011).
3. Alexander Thier, "The Future of Afghanistan," United States Institute of Peace, January 2009 at http://www.usip.org/peaceops/afghanistan/book.html (Accessed on January 23, 2012).
4. Frederick Starr, "US Afghanistan Policy: It's Working," Policy Paper, Central Asia-Caucasus Institute, Paul H. Nitze School of Advanced International Studies, Johns Hopkins University, October 2004.

5. Kenneth Katzman, no. 1.
6. Ashley J. Tellis, "Gambling on Reconciliation to Save a Transition: Perils and Possibilities in Afghanistan," Carnegie Endowment for International Peace, December 2011 at http://www.carnegieendowment.org/2011/12/02/gambling-on-reconciliation-to-save-transition-perils-and-possibilities-in-afghanistan/8khg (Accessed on January 2, 2012).
7. Kenneth Katzman, "Afghanistan: Current Issues and US Policy," CRS Report for Congress, August 27, 2003.
8. US Department of State, "Background Note on Afghanistan" at http://www.state.gov/p/sca/ci/af/ (Accessed on January 5, 2012).
9. Ashley J. Tellis, "Negotiations Cannot Solve Afghanistan's Problems," Carnegie Endowment for International Peace, November 3, 2011 at http://www.carnegieendowment.org/2011/11/03/negotiations-cannot-solve-afghanistan-s-problems/8khk (Accessed on January 11, 2012).
10. Human Rights Watch, "Afghanistan: New US Policy Should Stress Human Rights," March 26, 2009 at http://www.hrw.org/news/2009/03/26/afghanistan-new-us-policy-should-stress-human-rights (Accessed on January 12, 2012).
11. United States Department of State, "2010 Country Reports on Human Rights Practices—Afghanistan," April 8, 2011 at http://www.unhcr.org/refworld/docid/4da56defa3.html (Accessed on January 20, 2012).
12. Cato Policy Report, "Should the United States Withdraw from Afghanistan?" November/December 2009 at http://www.cato.org/pubs/policy_report/v31n6/cpr31n6-3.html (Accessed on January 7, 2012).
13. United Nations Office on Drugs and Crime, "Opium production in Afghanistan shows increase, prices set to rise," October 2011 at http://www.unodc.org/afghanistan/en/october/2011/opium-production-in-afghanistan-shows-increase.html (Accessed on January 16, 2012).
14. Derek Reveron, "Afghanistan and the Future of US Foreign Policy," *Foreign Policy,* October 6, 2011 at http://afpak.foreignpolicy.com/posts/2011/10/06/afghanistan_and_the_future_of_us_foreign_policy (Accessed on January 15, 2012).
15. David Aaron, Brian Michael Jenkins, Terrence K. Kelly, James Dobbins and Zalmay Khalilzad, "US Policy in Afghanistan: Basic Questions—Strategic Choices," RAND Conference Proceedings, CF-274 at http://www.rand.org/pubs/conf_proceedings/CF274.html#welcome (Accessed on January 25, 2012).
16. Richard C. Holbrooke, "US Policy in Afghanistan," Council on Foreign Relations, December 15 2009 at http://www.cfr.org/pakistan/us-policy-afghanistan/p21000 (Accessed on January 17, 2012).
17. Stephen Tankel, "The Haqqani Network and Pakistani Intelligence," *C-SPAN's Washington Journal,* Carnegie Endowment for International Peace, October 4, 2011 at http://www.carnegieendowment.org/2011/10/04/haqqani-network-and-pakistani-intelligence/8khi (Accessed on December 29, 2011).
18. Gilles Dorronsoro, "Afghanistan: The Impossible Transition," Carnegie Endowment for International Peace, June 2011 at http://www.carnegieendowment.org/2011/06/15/afghanistan-impossible-transition/1ij (Accessed on December 27, 2011).
19. Walter K. Andersen, "US, India and Afghanistan: An Evolving Triangle," Foreign Policy Research Centre, August 2011, pp. 48-57.
20. P. M. Kamath, "India-Afghanistan Relations: The US and Pakistan as Conditioners,"

Foreign Policy Research Centre, August 2011, pp. 71-77.

21. Dan Caldwell, "US Policy Towards Afghanistan, Pakistan, and Iraq," Academic Conference Call, Council on Foreign Relations at http://www.cfr.org/afghanistan/us-policy-toward-afghanistan-pakistan-iraq-audio/p24732 (Accessed on January 22, 2012).
22. "Statement by the President on the Afghanistan-Pakistan Annual Review," Office of the Press Secretary, The White House, December 16, 2010 at http://qa.uspolicy.sidonia.be/headline/president-obama-afghanistan-pakistan-annual-review (Accessed on January 1, 2012).
23. "Foreign Policy," The White House, at http://www.whitehouse.gov/issues/foreign-policy (Accessed on January 24, 2012).
24. Kenneth Katzman, no. 1.
25. Venkat Lokanathan, "The US Factor in Indo-Afghan Relations," Foreign Policy Resource Centre, pp. 129-34, August 2011.
26. Arvind Kumar, "Future of Afghanistan: India's role," *Defense and Security Alert*, 2 (11), August 2011, pp. 49-51.
27. G. D. Bakshi, "Endgame in Afghanistan: India's Stakes and Options," *Defense and Security Alert,* 2 (11), August 2011, pp. 12-16.

10. Conflicting Imperatives of India and Pakistan in Afghanistan

Anwesha Ghosh

The importance of a cooperative regional effort towards peace and stability in Afghanistan has been recognised by policymakers and analysts alike. With the announcement of the United States (US) to gradually withdraw its troops and hand over the responsibility to Afghan forces by 2014, the role of neighbouring countries in helping to fill the expected political vacuum has again gained significance. From this perspective the question today is: Will there be a repetition of the behaviour witnessed after the Soviet withdrawal in 1989, where their influence on different warring ethnic groups contributed to further deterioration of the situation and to the civil war of 1992-1996? Or will they be able to exert positive influence over the Afghan state and contribute to regional stability? While an optimist will see possibilities of stabilisation in Afghanistan, a cautious policy approach relies on a more realistic analysis of the interest of states in the bilateral and trilateral relationships with Afghanistan.[1] This chapter tries to understand the dynamics of a triangular relationship between three South Asian countries: India, Pakistan and Afghanistan and assess the competitive role played by India and Pakistan in Afghanistan and its implications for the future of Afghanistan and the region at large. The chapter also attempts to understand how this tripartite relationship is likely to impact each other in the near future.

Indo-Pak Contest in Afghanistan

> *Afghanistan has been a prize that Pakistan and India have fought over directly and indirectly for decades.*
>
> —*Robert Kaplan*[2]

Both India and Pakistan, since their independence in 1947 have had ties with various Afghan Governments. Pakistan being an immediate neighbour and by virtue of sharing Afghanistan's longest border, could have been in an advantageous position vis-à-vis India, but despite this physical proximity, the two have not enjoyed the most cordial of relations, courtesy issues such as the Durrand Line and claims over Pashtunistan. India, on the other hand, had a relatively smooth beginning and during the long rule of Zahir Shah (1933-73) had better relations with Afghanistan with high-level visits, expanding trade, aid projects and facilities for training. India's cautious approach during the first fifty years restrained her from supporting Afghanistan on issues that were regarded critical. The Afghans demonstrated their disappointment by following an even-handed approach during and after Pakistan's aggression in 1965.[3]

India managed to maintain close ties with the communist regimes that came to power after Zahir Shah. Moreover, a long-standing rivalry over the Afghanistan-Pakistan border had escalated tensions between the two since the end of British rule in India. Afghanistan refused to abide by the treaties it signed with the British Government prior to Pakistan's independence. This included the demarcation of the Durrand Line. With the Soviet intervention in Afghanistan, Pakistan got the ideal opportunity to position itself as the regional bulwark against communism. From that time, Pakistan's involvement with Afghanistan was focused on training, equipping and planning of operations for the resistance fighters to tie down Soviet forces.[4] It was during this period that the US and others used this to their advantage in funding Mujahideen (Islamic holy warrior) groups, via Pakistan, based in the region which could easily cross back and forth between the two countries in the decade-long insurgency against the Soviet presence in Afghanistan. After failing to engage Pakistan with the prospects of a regional solution to the Soviet invasion and faced with substantial American military and economic assistance to Pakistan ($ 3.2 billion for six years), India avoided any public censure of the Soviet occupation.[5] It chose instead to work with successive Soviet puppet regimes in Afghanistan and underestimated the Islamist ideological orientation shared by a bulk of the Afghan Mujahideen groups that Pakistan was supporting on behalf of the US. India was also loath to cede its military superiority over Pakistan and relied on the Soviets to provide advanced weaponry at bargain-basement prices.[6] Throughout the Cold War, India provided lip service to the idea of "Pashtunistan" with the goal of keeping Pakistan's army occupied on its restive western border.[7] Throughout the Afghan War, India supported Ahmed Shah Massoud's Northern Alliance because of its hostility towards Pakistan-supported Mujahideen groups.

Although a founding member of the Non-Aligned Movement, India had moved into closer cooperation with the Soviet Union and signed the Indo-Soviet Treaty of Friendship and Cooperation in 1971 and since then had been receiving Soviet military aid. Pakistan for its part had fallen into the US sphere of influence, signing a security agreement in 1959 and in time becoming a conduit for billions of dollars in US aid to the Mujahideen. With the war in Afghanistan fuelled by the two superpowers, the border also became another front in the conflict between India and Pakistan, which, after flaring into full-scale wars in 1965 and 1971, was then being carried out in several parts of South Asia. As the Research & Analysis Wing (RAW) already had a close relationship with the *Komitet gosudarstvennoy bezopasnosti* (KGB), this extended to cooperation with Afghanistan's intelligence agency, Khadamat-e Aetela'at-e Dawlati (KhAD), the predecessor of National Directorate of Security (NDS).[8] The KGB and KhAD carried out assassinations and sabotage in Pakistan, and RAW found its cooperation with them useful; in particular for intelligence on Sikh groups training in military camps, according to the memoirs of Bahukutumbi Raman, a former RAW officer.[9]

After ten years of a fruitless counterinsurgency campaign, the Soviet Union withdrew from Afghanistan, and a brutal civil war engulfed the country. India's ability to maintain good relations with Afghanistan drew to a close with the Pakistani-aided and abetted Taliban victory in 1996.[10] The Taliban emerged out of the plans conceived by Inter-Services Intelligence (ISI), grew through chaos and anarchy of various brawling Mujahideen groups, recruited by the Jamiat-al-Ulama-i-Islam led by Maulana Fazlur Rahman from the Afghan refugee camps in North-West Frontier Province and Baluchistan.[11] The ISI took charge of providing logistic support and brokered an alliance of General Dostam, General Shahnawaz Tanai and former commander Jalaluddin Haqqani with the Taliban.[12] With this, Pakistan's politico-military establishment got what they believed to be a ductile regime in Afghanistan that would grant it strategic depth against India. Pakistan's advantage meant just the opposite for India, and it was forced to abandon its embassy and withdraw its diplomatic mission after the violent killing of former President Najibullah by the Taliban.

To counter the Taliban, Russia, Iran and India gave weapons, money and supplies to the United Front, commonly known as the Northern Alliance, which included in a loose confederation, Abdul Rashid Dostam and his Uzbek militia in the North-west, Ismail Khan in the West in Herat, Karim Khalili in the Hazara-dominated central highlands, along with the forces of Ahmed Shah Massoud, whose Shura-e-Nazar drew on a core of loyalists from the Tajik-inhabited Panjshir Valley, North of Kabul. Eventually, Dostum and Ismail Khan were forced to flee Afghanistan while Massoud's forces were pushed by the Taliban into a tiny northern corner of the country. India reportedly provided Massoud's forces with high-altitude warfare equipment, defence advisers and helicopter technicians. Indian medical personnel were also believed to have treated Northern Alliance members at a hospital in Farkhor on the Afghan-Tajik border.[13] Massoud was killed in a suicide attack two days before those at the World Trade Centre and a Taliban victory seemed near, but 9/11 and US military intervention abruptly altered the course of Afghanistan's history. As Massoud's deputies were swept into power on the back of a US-led bombing campaign, a stark improvement in the relationship with India became visible and India reciprocated with substantial support, committing billions of dollars in development projects, making it the largest bilateral donor in the region.

A Rejuvenated India-Afghanistan Relationship

India's engagement with Afghanistan readily became multidimensional after the defeat of the Taliban and the installation of an Interim Authority in 2001.[14] India actively participated in the Bonn Conference and was instrumental in the emergence of the post-Taliban governing and political authority in Afghanistan. Since then, India's main focus has been to support the Afghan government, and the political process in the country as mandated under the Bonn agreement of 2001.[15] A variety of factors contributed in improving relations between India and Afghanistan. Unlike Pakistan, ties are not hampered by the existence of contested borders. Secondly, India's support for the Northern Alliance against the Pakistan-backed Taliban in the 1990s strengthened its position in Kabul after 2001. Many members of the Alliance became members of the government or held influential portfolios. Thirdly, India has restored the balance in its engagement with a range of different ethnic groups and political affiliations in Afghanistan. The balance was tilted towards the Tajik-dominated Northern Alliance during the 1990s as a counter to the Pakistan-controlled hardline Pashtun factions, led by the Taliban. India has used its vocal support for Karzai, an ethnic Pashtun educated in India, to demonstrate its keenness to revive its close ties with Pashtuns.[16]

Significance of Indian Presence in Afghanistan

For the first time in Afghanistan's history, there was an interior minister, a foreign minister and a chief of intelligence—all from Panjshir Valley. These were men who had been, a month before, fighting desperately against a Pakistani-supported Taliban while taking military and financial aid from India.[17] These were remarkably positive times for Indo-Afghan relations and India responded by adopting a multi-pronged strategy in Afghanistan. Some observers have claimed that India's unusually proactive Afghanistan Policy since 2001 was driven by her growing regional and global ambitions.

India's commitment of $ 1.3 billion in development projects such as roads, dams, telecommunications, Salma Dam Project, Indira Gandhi Children's Hospital, a power line between Kabul and Uzbekistan and sponsorships for Afghan students to India, made her the fifth largest overall donor after the US, Britain, Japan and Germany. Even the new parliament building on Darulaman Road is being built by India for $ 83 million, though Afghans are beginning to wonder when it will ever be finished (the government says 2011).[18]

India has embraced cooperation in security matters as well, seeing it as a crucial battleground in fighting terrorism in the region. Public opinion is divided in India on whether India should get militarily involved in Afghanistan or not. Though India, primarily due to US objections stemming from Pakistan's concerns, has not sent its military to be part of the NATO-led International Security Assistance Force (ISAF), it has helped build the capacity of the Afghan security forces, providing pilot and counterinsurgency training and even monitoring the Afghan Army's marching band.[19] According to Indian officials, there are currently about four thousand Indian workers and security personnel working on different relief and reconstruction projects in Afghanistan. Since 2006, following increased incidents of attacks, India has sent the country's mountain-trained paramilitary force tasked to guard its workers; there are about five hundred police deployed in Afghanistan currently.[20] India's investment at the Iranian port at Chabahar will allow it to gain trading access to Afghanistan, bypassing Pakistan. Pakistan currently allows transit rights to Afghanistan for its exports to India, but does not allow goods to move from India to Afghanistan.

For India, Afghanistan is also a potential route for access to Central Asian energy. The signing of Strategic Partnership Agreement just after the assassination of former President Rabbani, is seen by some observers as consolidation of gains made by India's soft power approach, as well as expansion of India's plans to secure its national security interest.[21] India, an observer in the Shanghai Cooperation Organisation (SCO), has been pursuing better relations with Central Asian states for energy cooperation as well. "India is looking to ensure that other countries in the region favour or at least are neutral on its conflict with Pakistan," according to Alexander Thier.[22]

Although Afghanistan's economy has recovered significantly since the fall of the Taliban, with the real Gross Domestic Product (GDP) growth rate exceeding 7 per cent in 2008 (Central Intelligence Agency, 2009), it still remains largely dependent on foreign aid. The only way the central government in Kabul can enhance legitimacy is by bringing the economy on track. India has an interest in ensuring that Afghanistan emerges as a stable and economically integrated state in the region and therefore has played an important role by laying foundations for sustainable economic development in its neighbourhood.[23] The Preferential Trade Agreement signed by India and Afghanistan gives substantial duty concessions to Afghan products while entering India. India also piloted the move to make Afghanistan a member of the South Asian Association for Regional Cooperation (SAARC), with the hope that, with this, issues related to transit and free flow of goods across borders in the region can be addressed, thereby leading to greater economic development of Afghanistan and the region at large.

Pakistan-India in Afghan Battlefield

It might be fallacious to assume that this unusually proactive Afghanistan policy by India stems only from the desire of promoting security and stability in the country. India seeks to restrict Pakistan's influence over any emergent regime in Afghanistan and wants to ensure that no regime emerges in Afghanistan that is fundamentally hostile towards India. By helping rebuild a new Afghanistan, India strives for greater regional stability, but also hopes to counter Pakistan's influence in Kabul, say experts.[24] One of the major imperatives of Indian policy in Afghanistan is to prevent the rise of the brand of Islamist militancy that has been prevalent over the past six decades. India therefore aspires to develop a sufficient diplomatic and intelligence network within the country to be able to monitor Pakistan's activities within Afghanistan and if necessary work to curtail them.[25] Pakistan, on the other hand, has viewed Afghanistan as a good means of balancing India's preponderance in South Asia.[26] Good India-Afghanistan ties are seen by Pakistan as damaging to its national security interests as the two countries flank two sides of Pakistan's border. A friendly political dispensation in Kabul is viewed by Pakistan as essential to escape the strategic dilemma of being caught between a powerful adversary in India in the east and an irredentist Afghanistan with claims of Pashtun-dominated areas in the west.[27] Pakistan considers its role to be privileged in Afghan affairs because of its ethnic Pashtun linkages. Due to these conflicting imperatives, both the countries have tried to neutralise each other's influence in Afghanistan's affairs.[28] Both are stuck in a classic security dilemma in so far as their policy towards Afghanistan is concerned.[29] Any attempt by either of the countries to augment their own security leads the other to act in response, thereby resulting in deterioration in the overall regional security environment.

The security problem in Afghanistan today can be linked to the Pakistani military's predominant position which has, since the 1990s, viewed the Taliban as a means of controlling Afghanistan and undercutting India's influence there.[30] Having focused extensively on the Taliban, it is struggling to abandon it now. The cost of such a policy to Pakistani polity and society is evident with the growing hold of the Taliban within Pakistan. Pakistanis themselves are arguing, "the common belief in Pakistan that Islam's radicalism is a problem only in the Federally Administered Tribal Areas (FATA) and madrasas are the only institutions serving as jihad factories. This is a serious misconception." This mindset, it is suggested "may lead to Pakistan's demise as a nation state."[31] The increasing pattern of insurgent assaults against high profile government and civilian targets in Pakistan suggests that militancy has spun out of government's control. Kabul has repeatedly blamed Islamabad for resurgence of the Taliban over the past few years and has slammed Pakistan for its terror links.[32]

Forestalling Pakistan

What makes the issue of Indian and Pakistani actions in Afghanistan so thorny is that, to some observers, all three parties have overriding national interests in the situation.[33] While Pakistan along with Saudi Arabia and United Arab Emirates (UAE) was the main supporter of the Taliban, India, along with Russia and Iran, threw its weight behind the United Front fighters. As a consequence, Pakistan's influence in Afghanistan peaked with the coming to power of the Taliban in 1996. Pakistan has long believed that it can gain "strategic depth" vis-à-vis India by influencing the domestic politics in Afghanistan, something Islamabad felt it achieved during the 1980s and the 1990s. It is also keen to prevent its strategic encirclement as a result of close Delhi-Kabul ties.[34] Pakistan's frustrations at the loss of political influence after the ouster of the Taliban have been compounded by the welcoming attitude of the Karzai Government towards India. India opened consulates in Herat, Mazar-e-Sharif, Kandahar and Jalalabad, in addition to its Embassy in Kabul. Pakistan has accused India's embassy in Kabul of spreading anti-Pakistan propaganda and views the establishment of the consulate as a way for Delhi to improve intelligence gathering against it. Pakistan claims much of the funding and arms for the Baluch tribal leaders, grouped under the umbrella of the Baluchistan Liberation Army, is funnelled through the Indian consulates in Jalalabad and Kandahar.[35] Barnett Rubin sees Pakistan's concerns over India's involvement in Afghanistan as one of its "legitimate interests."[36] Richard Holbrook, President Obama's special envoy for Afghanistan and Pakistan, however had clarified in an interview that "there is no evidence at all that Indians are supporting miscreants."[37] Some have even equated Holbrook's statements to an explicit "bail out" of New Delhi by the United States.[38]

Countering India

"Afghanistan ... in many ways has replaced Kashmir as the main arena of the still-unsolved struggle between Pakistan and India."[39] Ahmed Rashid has argued that the road to Kabul is partly through Kashmir. Pakistan has worked hard to limit India's involvement in Afghanistan. Large-scale suicide car bomb attacks on the embassy in 2008 and 2009 were suspected to have been orchestrated by Lashkar-e-Taiba with the help of the Haqqani network and the ISI. Immediately after the 2008 bombing, Manmohan Singh announced another additional $ 450 million in aid to Afghanistan, a sign to Pakistan that India would not be deterred from its involvement there. At this, an Indian observer in Kabul said, "Every time India gets attacked, the government responds with another pledge of millions of dollars."[40] Pakistan made transit rights to Afghanistan conditional upon a resolution of the Kashmir issue. By doing so, Pakistan has sought to leverage Afghanistan's reliance on the Karachi port as its only gateway to the world. Pakistan has been conscious of limiting India's military involvement in Afghanistan. It did not even allow India to send a few hundred military transport vehicles to Kabul, which India had to ultimately route through Iran.[41] Despite Pakistan's objections, Afghanistan has sought Indian assistance in the defence sector, and defence equipment has been serviced by Indian technicians. At the London Conference held in early 2011, Pakistan could successfully marginalise India (who was more inclined to establish the fallacy of making a distinction between "Good and Bad Taliban") when the West was only interested to know when and how to exit from Afghanistan. It was established that a negotiated settlement was necessary with the Taliban leadership. Pakistan seems to have convinced the West that it can play the role of a mediator in negotiations with the Taliban. With the arrest of Mullah Baradar, the number two figure in the Quetta Shura, Taliban's Senior Leadership Council, Pakistan's message was clear—you go through us or not at all.

Will Pakistan Exit Afghanistan?

Turkey's condemnation of the destabilising role ISI plays in Kabul at the Istanbul Conference held in 2011 has helped in the development of a general consensus outside Islamabad that Pakistan must refrain from interfering in Afghan politics and exit from Afghanistan for the region to stabilise. As the Afghan President Hamid Karzai had pointed out time and again that Pakistan and Afghanistan are tied to each other with an umbilical cord, the question remains—would it do so? The fact is the Afghan tragedy of the past three decades has impacted Pakistan more than any other country in the region. President Musharraf had to make an uneasy choice after 9/11 under

US pressure; Islamabad swiftly disavowed the Taliban regime and supported the US military operations against them. However, now that the prospect of US withdrawal from Afghanistan looms large, Islamabad (and particularly the military and more specifically the ISI) appears to be following a policy of running with the hare and hunting with the hound—cooperating with the US programme of stabilising the Karzai Government and simultaneously opening a back channel with the Taliban.[42]

Apart from the perception that Pakistan army is wedded to the idea of Afghanistan providing strategic depth against an Indian invasion—an article of faith since the 1990s but one that makes Pakistani scholars now dismiss as sheer paranoia—what is generally ignored about the Af-Pak scenario is that Pakistan bore the brunt of refugee problems unleashed by Soviet presence in Afghanistan. Three million Afghan refugees have crossed borders transforming the demographic character of two frontier provinces of Pakistan—Khyber Pakhtunkhwa and Baluchistan, and also FATA. These were traditionally "Hindku" speaking regions but with an overwhelming majority of Pakhtuns settling in that region, Pashtu became the dominant language. In Baluchistan, the transformation can be measured by the fact that Baluch is no longer the predominant language spoken in the provincial capital, Quetta. It has been replaced by Pashtu. This in turn has resulted in the resurgence (with greater intensity than earlier in the 1970s) of a secessionist movement in Baluchistan, as also massive internal migration out of Khyber Pakhtunkhwa into Punjab and Sindh, which in turn has increased sectarian tensions among Sunnis in Punjab as well as between Shias and Sunnis in Afghanistan.[43]

The unrest in Khyber Pakhtunkhwa and Swat was met by a military response bringing the army to the tribal area. By 2009, in a stated attempt to bring peace to this region, the Government of Pakistan signed a peace accord with the Taliban and agreed upon the imposition of Sharia law in Swat and to the suspension of military offensives against them. A look at the current state of terrorism and Talibanisation in Pakistan also shows that the threat to militancy is higher in areas with marked social, economic and political disparities such as FATA, Baluchistan, interior Sindh and southern Punjab.

Moreover, Pakistan's approach in the post-bin Laden environment is now one of head-on opposition to the US. It appears to be more distrustful of the US than they are of Al Qaeda.[44] Pakistan would like to see the negotiated departure of the US in order to bring Afghanistan under its sphere of influence. According to recent reports, Pakistan army's support for the Taliban is not decreasing, on the contrary, and Pakistan's opposition to direct

US actions involving drones and Central Intelligence Agency (CIA) agents largely limits the possibility of fighting the insurgency in Pakistan itself. In particular, Pakistani army offensives have had no impact on the insurgents in border areas; if anything, the insurgents have grown stronger in recent months.[45] Pakistan's intentions and security perceptions are the crux of her problem. Pakistan has to understand that shutting down militant groups in its territory is in its core national security interests. Until Pakistan's strategic managers and citizenry alike embrace this belief, Pakistan will not strategically renounce militancy as a tool of foreign policy.

India Debates Its Options

The primary objective of India's policy has been to pre-empt the return of Pakistan's embedment in Afghanistan's strategic and political firmament.[46] Ironically, it is India's success in Afghanistan that has driven Pakistan's security establishment into panic mode with a perception gaining ground that India was taking over Afghanistan. According to an ABC poll conducted between December 30, 2008 and January 12, 2009, 74 per cent of Afghans hold favourable opinions towards India, while 8 per cent hold a favourable opinion towards Pakistan.[47] The Obama Administration's desire for rapid disengagement in Afghanistan coupled with their deteriorating relations with Pakistan, has given the Indian government enough reason to debate over its policy options in the strategic space. Its traditional stance of no direct engagement in security operations is becoming hard to sustain. Two major strands can be discerned in the present debate. One strand maintains that despite setbacks, New Delhi should continue to rely on Washington to secure its Afghanistan and Pakistan interest.[48] They identify a converging point between the Manmohan Singh and Barack Obama Administrations in viewing Pakistan as the source of Afghanistan's insecurity and believing that the world must act together to cure Islamabad's political malaise. The other side is becoming impatient with New Delhi's continued reliance on Washington, which has systematically ignored Indian interests and sensibilities.[49] They argue that while Washington may have no vital interest in determining who actually governs the country so long as Afghan territory is not used as a springboard for attacks on American soil, New Delhi most certainly does. The Taliban—good or bad—are hostile to India in many fundamental ways. The abandonment of the goal of establishing a functioning Afghan state and a moderate Pakistan is liable to put greater pressure on Indian security.[50] Another point of view is in favour of India's exit from Afghanistan in return for a firm anti-terror commitment from Pakistan. For them, a way forward would be "to address Pakistan's fear—of being boxed-in by India from two sides—by systematically exiting from Afghanistan, while extracting in turn a verifiable Pakistani commitment to abandon the use of its home-grown terror groups against India."[51]

Conclusion

Progress towards stabilisation and development in Afghanistan is being heavily influenced by India-Pakistan and the rivalry between them. For some members of the Indian strategic community, Afghanistan is a litmus test for their country's ascendance as a regional and global power.[52] India's capacity to deal with instability in its own backyard will, in the final analysis, determine its rise as a significant global power; therefore, success in Afghanistan becomes crucial. India has a number of interests in Afghanistan, notably containment of Islamist extremism, the use of Afghanistan as a gateway to the energy-rich Central Asian region, and affirmation of its regional predominance that it would like to maintain and uphold. Yet, the most important goal for New Delhi remains the prevention of Pakistan regaining its central role in Afghan affairs. Pakistan on the other hand, tries to ensure that India does not achieve this goal and hopes for a repetition of the 1990s scenario, in which India's security interest suffered to an unprecedented degree. But, unlike now, India was a weaker state, marginal in the strategic equation of the major global players, and therefore, could be easily snubbed. Today, India considers itself a rising global power with many more cards to play in Afghanistan than ever before, and it is highly unlikely that it would give up Kabul without a fight.[53] However unclear the future scenario might be, one thing is certain: the tragedy for ordinary Afghans, Indians and Pakistanis is likely to worsen as long as the India-Pakistan rivalry continues in Afghanistan.

Notes

1. Tom Gregg, *Is a Regional Pact to Stabilize Afghanistan Possible?* Centre on International Cooperation, New York University, 2010.
2. Jayasree Bajoria, "India-Afghanistan Relations," Council of Foreign Relations at http://www.cfr.org/india/india-afghanistan-relations/p17474#p3 (Accessed on December 31, 2011).
3. I. P. Khosla, "Indo-Afghan Relations: Looking into the Future," in Sreedhar (ed.), *Afghanistan in Transition* (New Delhi: ICWA, 2003).
4. Arpita Basu Roy, *Contemporary Afghanistan: Conflict and Peace-Building* (New Delhi: Har-Anand Publications, 2010), pp. 114-20.
5. Sumit Ganguly and Nicholas Howenstein, "India-Pakistan Rivalry in Afghanistan," *Journal of International Affairs,* 63(1), Fall/Winter 2009, p. 127.
6. S. Nihal Singh, "Why India Goes to Moscow for Arms," *Asian Survey,* 24 (7), July 1984, pp. 707-20.

7. Barnett R. Rubin and Abubakar Siddique, "Resolving the Pakistan-Afghanistan Stalemate," US Institute of Peace Special Report, no. 176, October 2007.
8. Mathew Aikin, "India in Afghanistan: Nation Building of Proxy War" *The Caravan,* 2(10), October 2010, p. 28.
9. Ibid. p. 31.
10. On Pakistan's ties to the Taliban, see Ahmed Rashid, *Taliban* (New Haven: Yale University Press, 2001).
11. K. Warikoo, *The Afghanistan Crisis: Issues and Perspectives* (New Delhi: Bhavana Books and Prints, 2002).
12. Arpita Basu Roy, *Contemporary Afghanistan: Conflict and Peace-Building* (New Delhi: Har-Anand Publications, 2010), pp. 114-20.
13. Sumit Ganguly and Nicholas Howenstein, no. 5.
14. P. P. Basu, "India and post-Taliban Afghanistan: Stakes, Opportunities and Challenges," *Third World Quarterly,* 63 (3), 2007.
15. Agreement on Provisional Arrangements in Afghanistan at http://www.afghangovernment.com/AfghanAgreementBonn.htm (Accessed on December 27, 2011).
16. Harsh V. Pant, "India in Afghanistan: a test case for a rising power," *Contemporary South Asia*, 18 (2), 2010, pp. 133-53.
17. Mathew Aikin, no. 8, p. 32.
18. Ibid., pp. 28-39.
19. Ibid., pp. 28-39.
20. Jayasree Bajoria, no. 2.
21. Shanthie Mariet D'Souza, "India-Afghan Strategic Partnership: Perceptions from the ground," *The Af-Pak Channel*, October 26, 2011 at http://afpak.foreignpolicy.com/posts/2011/10/26/indian_afghan_strategic_partnership_perceptions_from_the_ground (Accessed on January 1, 2012).
22. Jayasree Bajoria, no. 2.
23. Harsh V. Pant, no. 16.
24. Jayasree Bajoria, no. 2.
25. Sumit Ganguly and Nicholas Howenstein, no. 5.
26. M. G. Weinbaum, "Pakistan and Afghanistan: The Strategic Relationship," *Asian Survey* 31(6), 1991, pp. 489-99.
27. R. Hussain, "Pakistan's Relations with Afghanistan: Continuity and Change," *Strategic Studies*, 22(4), 2002, at http://www.issi.org.pk/old-site/ss_Detail.php?dataId=227 (Accessed on January 2, 2012).
28. Harsh V. Pant, no. 16.
29. J. Herz, *Political Realism and Political Idealism*, University of Chicago Press, Chicago, 1951.
30. R. Hussain, no. 27.
31. P. Hoodbhoy, "The Saudi-isation of Pakistan." *Newsline,* January 2009.
32. "Karzai Slams Pak's Terror Links," *The Times of India,* September 8, 2011.
33. "The Great Game Revisited: India and Pakistan are playing out their rivalries in Afghanistan," *Asia Today*, September 30, 2009.
34. Harsh V. Pant, no. 16.
35. Ibid.
36. No. 33.

37. Chidananand Rajghatta, "US endorses Indian role in Afghanistan," *The Times of India,* April 27, 2009.
38. Chidananand Rajghatta, "US Bails out India from Baluchistan Wrangle," *The Times of India,* July 31, 2009.
39. Barnett R. Rubin and Ahmad Rashid, "From Great Game to Grand Bargain: Ending Chaos in Afghanistan," *Foreign Affairs*, 87 (6), 2008, pp. 30-34.
40. Mathew Aikin, no. 17, p. 38.
41. C. Raja Mohan, "India's New Road to Afghanistan," *The Hindu,* September 6, 2003.
42. Kingshuk Chatterjee, "Would Pakistan Exit Afghanistan?" Institute of Foreign Policy Studies, December 2011 at http://www.caluniv.ac.in/ifps/Pak-Afghan-kingshuk.pdf (Accessed on January 2, 2012).
43. Ibid.
44. Christine Fair, "Time for Sober Realism: Renegotiating Pakistan Relations with US," *Washington Quarterly*, 32 (2), 2009, pp. 149-72.
45. Durronsoro Gilles, "Afghanistan: The Impossible Transition," The Carnegie Paper, *South Asia,* June 2011.
46. Harsh V. Pant, "The Afghanistan Conflict: India's Challenging Role," *The Middle East Quarterly*, Spring 2011, pp. 31-39.
47. Anthony Cordesman, "Afghan Public Opinion and the Afghan War: Shifts by Region and Province," Breakout of the data in the ABC News Poll, CSIS Report, April, 10, 2009.
48. *The Indian Express,* July 27, 2010.
49. *The Tribune* (Chandigarh), August 19, 2010.
50. *Hindustan Times,* March 2010; *Business Standard*, September 15, 2010.
51. Maroof Raza, "The Quagmire Next Door," *The Times of India,* October 25, 2011.
52. Harsh V. Pant, no. 46.
53. Ibid.

11. Saudi Arabia's Long-Term Policy towards Afghanistan: The Consequences

Mirwais Balkhi

Introduction

A brief study of Saudi Arabia's policy towards Afghanistan shows that it has a long history of engagement in Afghanistan. This can be seen in three historical stages, starting from the traditional policy which revolved around security and Pan-Islamism to the policy during the Cold War; working alongside the United States (US) and Pakistan to aid the Mujahideen in defeating the Soviet Union during and after the Cold War by opposing Iran, and cooperating with Pakistan as a strategic partner and preserving international prestige by claiming to be the regional hegemonic power in West Asia after the Gulf War.

Although the Kingdom's policy towards Afghanistan is time-bound and based on the prevailing international, regional and national situation in both the countries—which Riyadh had to respond to and take initiatives—certain long-term policies are also formulated in Riyadh towards Afghanistan that may not change drastically depending on the global conditions. In other words, Saudi Arabia has had certain potential in Afghanistan that could engage it positively without having to deal with Washington or Islamabad, its two strategic allies. Most of the regimes in Afghanistan sought their legitimacy among the people with the support of Saudi Arabia. The communist regime in Afghanistan did try not to face Riyadh in war against the US allies. Also the Kabul regime ignored many Saudi attacks on the Afghan Communist regime.

Riyadh shapes its long and short-term policy towards the individual states based on such a policy. Its policy towards Afghanistan was overshadowed by the four-point policy of Saudi Arabia since at least the 1980s. An analysis of this in Afghanistan in the past three decades is enumerated in the succeeding paragraphs.

Principles and Objectives of Saudi Foreign Policy

It is said that the principles and purposes of a state are reflected in its foreign policy. The foreign policy is the key element in the process by which a state translates its broadly conceived goals and interests towards concrete courses of action to attain these objectives and preserve interests. The principles and objectives of the foreign policy of Saudi Arabia are not outlined by any individual leader. It is derived from the determinants of the policy that Riyadh had to formulate from the beginning. This is contrary to many countries of the world where a charismatic political leader emerged and shaped the foreign policy of the country. This is invisible in Afghanistan where the kings or leaders have changed the trend of foreign policy based on their individual choice. Nehru also in India shaped the foreign policy of the country soon after India's independence in 1947. His charisma affected the trends of Indian foreign policy which are visible till now.

Keeping Balance of Power

For survival and preserving the kingdom, the regime in Saudi Arabia adopted the policy of keeping balance of power as a strong instrument of foreign policy to compete with equal regional powers like Iran, Israel, Egypt and Iraq. The Gulf War in 1991 was the turning point in the history of Saudi Arabia and its foreign policy formulation, combined with a shift in the global strategic balance following the end of the Cold War. This was the time when Riyadh gave a strong shape to the principles and method of its foreign policy in relation to its new position in the region.[1]

The method of keeping the balance of power in Saudi foreign policy had begun in the 1970s vis-à-vis Israel and Egypt, under which the Saudis organised the Organisation of the Islamic Conference (OIC) to counter Egyptian nationalism, while Pan-Arabism and Pan-Islamism were targeted against Israel.[2] During the Gulf War, the Saudis supported the US against Saddam Hussein due to which the course of the War changed and resulted in victory for the US. This had given a special position for Saudi Arabia as a close ally of Washington. In the formulation of the "New World Order" by George W. Bush, Riyadh was given the importance and freedom to shape its policy for the benefit of the Kingdom. The leadership in Riyadh convinced the Ulema that it is only the Kingdom of Saudi Arabia which can represent Islam and support other Islamic societies. Riyadh also spread the propaganda that the enemies of the Kingdom are Jew, Shia, and Communists. Such propaganda was aimed at Israel, Iran and other Arab States ruled by leftists or Communists.[3]

One of the pillars for reaching and maintaining an equal balance with Iran, Israel and Iraq for Saudi Arabia had been the presence of the American troops in the Kingdom besides its rich reserves of oil, geographical centrality and hub of Islamic credence, being home to two holy places of Islam.[4] But stationing US troops in Saudi land was not easy. The radical elements were active in the Kingdom's political decision making and viewed Washington with pessimism. The Al Saud family convinced a group of Ulema that Saddam Hussein is the real danger for Islam, more than the presence of US troops. The formal state clergy who were influential in the Islamic world had supported the presence of US troops in Saudi Arabia. Sheikh Abdul Aziz Bin Baaz the Grand Mufti of Saudi Arabia issued a fatwa regarding this controversy to help Riyadh come to terms with criticism in the Islamic world.[5] Riyadh even used the fatwa of Bin Baaz for Pan-Islamic goals to unite Arabs and Muslims in supporting anti-Iraqi forces in West Asia. As a result, thousands of volunteer fighters from many Islamic countries entered Saudi Arabia to dispel the danger of communism. The Afghan Interim Government in Peshawar also sent three hundred soldiers.

For keeping the balance of power intact, Afghanistan has been always a geopolitical pocket[6] in the long-standing policy of Saudi Arabia for two main reasons: first, to oppose Iran and second, to convince the Arab world that Saudi Arabia's sphere of influence stretches up to Afghanistan. Afghanistan, which is located on the eastern borders of Iran while at the same time being far from the Arab region, has been convenient for Riyadh to carry on an indirect war with Tehran. Riyadh always had tried to put pressure on Tehran from Kabul mainly to overshadow Tehran's anti-Saudi policy in Bahrain, Yemen and Lebanon. As a second step, a friendly and loyal government in Kabul towards Riyadh strengthens its position in the Arab World. It shows the expanded influence of Saudi policy.

With the isolation of Egypt and Iraq in the 1980s and 1990s, it was only Tehran which could confront Saudi Arabia in the quest to represent the Islamic world. Both were expanding their spheres of influence over West and Central Asia as well as North Africa. Both were in a position to represent their own model of Islamic fundamentalism—Saudi Arabia as the leader of Sunni Islam with its Wahhabi model and Iran with Vilayat-e-Faqih in Shia Islam. Riyadh had always avoided a direct confrontation with Tehran. But, indirectly, the Kingdom has followed an anti-Iranian policy and it always has supported Sunni Afghan radicals. Saudi Arabia also sponsored the Wahhabi Mujahideen in Afghanistan and Central Asia.

The period immediately after the Gulf War of 1991 led the Saudis to broaden their outlook on the Afghan issue. Riyadh's political role in Afghanistan took more practical overtones and representatives were trying to gain direct contact through Pakistan and Washington. All this was happening during the presidentship of Dr. Najibullah who was confined to the city of Kabul. Different Mujahideen factions supported by different external powers were capturing parts of the country, where bloodshed and civil war could be seen before their final victory.[7] Afghanistan was a Hobbesian state of nature. In the absence of support from the international community, especially the US, after the withdrawal of Soviet troops from the country, a clash of interests for influence by many regional powers started. Saudi Arabia was concerned about its own position in the future of Afghanistan, because after the demise of communism, its rival, Iran, was also trying to extend influence using its historical and cultural ties.

Afghanistan was passing through a crucial time in her history when Soviet troops withdrew from the country after the Geneva Accord, and the communist regime of Kabul was saddled among various Afghan insurgents with their foreign allies.[8] A big change in the country was predictable to all interested powers especially when, during 1991, for the first time the Mujahideen captured many cities and provinces and progressed towards Kabul. This was mainly due to the weakness of Dr. Najibullah's regime and the strength of Jihadi groups.[9] At this time, external powers formulated policy how to expand their interests while opposing their rivals. Regional powers like Saudi Arabia, Iran, Pakistan and Turkey were dictating policy to the friendly Jihadi groups to shape future interests and prove their strength in the region. For achieving goals, they encouraged Afghanistan's young leaders to use any means to contest the opposition groups which Najibullah anticipated about the future when he said, "The near future of Afghanistan shows that streams of blood will flow in Kabul."[10]

For Saudi Arabia, Afghanistan became a factor to keep the balance of power intact by cutting Iran's influence in the country. All Shiite parties were influenced and supported by Iran and the seven Peshawar-based Sunni parties were also supported by Saudi Arabia after entering Kabul. It should be noted that Jamiat-e Islami Afghanistan—a Tajik (Persian) party under the leadership of Burhanuddin Rabbani was by ethnicity and language close to Iran. Gulbuddin Hekmatyar and Rasool Sayyaf—two other main parties—were opposed to Saudi Arabia, because of the presence of US troops in Saudi Arabia and the rest were weak parties who were not capable of furthering Riyadh's goals in Afghanistan.

Iran's active interest in Afghanistan during the 1980s became a source of tension for Riyadh especially when it became more active after the end of the Iran-Iraq War in 1989.[11] Iran had applied pressure on encouraging Shia Hazara leaders to form the Hezb-e-Wahdat, or the Party of Unity, to which it was now providing assistance. At the same time, Tehran encouraged the Wahdat to seek rapprochement with Kabul and signalled to Moscow and the United Nations (UN) its support for a political settlement.[12] Riyadh understood that Tehran could play any role to weaken its position in Afghanistan. With the disintegration of the Soviet Union and the gradual weakness of the communist regime in Kabul, the nature of war also changed. Jihad in Afghanistan was a finished task for Tehran. Further, anti-communist action meant the gradual growth of the Saudi position in the post-communist regime in Afghanistan. That is the reason why Tehran was looking to negotiate between the Mujahideen and the regime in Kabul. Tehran encouraged Shia parties among the Mujahideen to negotiate with Kabul and the join the central government.[13]

The Saudis established policy towards particular groups in Afghanistan against Tehran, which enjoyed the support of Shia and Hazara parties towards Pan-Shiaism.[14] It was mainly due to two reasons: firstly, the conservatism of the House of Saud was criticised by the radical Islamists, and secondly, the Wahhabi model of Riyadh's fundamentalism was viewed with scepticism by Hanafi leaders who were inspired by Deobandi madrasas. Shia Hazara parties, Tajik/Persian and Uzbek parties all aligned with Tehran when the victory of the Mujahideen was expected, while the radical groups like Hekmatyar and Sayyaf returned to the Saudi fold, as the main supporters of the Mujahideen were losing power and influence in Afghanistan against Iran. This led to Riyadh changing sides and supporting the regime in Kabul which was under Tajik/Persian rule, after 1992. Though Rabbani aligned with Riyadh and was avowedly anti-Iran in fighting with the Wahdat parties, this could not be a price for what Saudi Arabia paid during the Afghan Jihad. The Mazari-Hekmatyar and Dostum alliance under the name of Cooperative Council (CC) turned against Kabul supported by Iran.[15]

Afghanistan herself was now a threat to Saudi Arabia because after the victory of the Afghan Mujahideen backed by the Afghan Arabs, the security and survival of the Kingdom were in danger. Arab extremists, who were free from overthrowing a Soviet-backed regime in Kabul, looked to the Arab world once again with a strong impetus. After Egypt's Camp David Accords with Israel (1978-79), a universal front was closed for various Islamic movements which were busy in liberating Palestine. After the liberation of Palestine these movements had plans to overthrow monarchical and communist regimes in the Arab World. The withdrawal of these groups homewards resulted in chaotic conditions in Saudi Arabia where Islamists were free and returned to the country and once again their target was to overthrow of the Al Saud family. But a miracle happened when the Soviet Union invaded Afghanistan. To the mutual benefit of the Saudi Arabian government and the Islamists, these extremists left Saudi Arabia and other Arab states to participate in the Afghan Jihad while pursuing their own goals from there to use Afghanistan as an expanded front for achieving their dreams in the Arab World. Riyadh knew that these Arab Islamists known as "Afghan Arabs," were in Afghanistan besides the Afghan Mujahideen and could find favourable conditions for monitoring further operations, and would need to be quickly annihilated. But these extremists could not be controlled as they were spread across in the erstwhile Soviet territory supporting liberation movements, and only a few of them returned home.

The obvious point in the study of Saudi Arabia's policy towards Afghanistan is that Riyadh played an inconsistent role both during the Mujahideen government as well as the Taliban regime. Domestic factors had a strong impact on foreign policy formulation in Saudi Arabia. Studies show that this kind of scenario complicates decision making, and there is always a contradiction while a policy is formulated. This resulted in the ambiguous politics within Saudi Arabia. This complication caused difficulties for Saudi Arabia to formulate clear policy guidelines in Afghanistan.[16]

The influence of Iran in the country following the demise of the communists in Kabul worried Riyadh, and the Kingdom lost its opportunity to play a systematic role during Mujahideen rule whereas the Kingdom was looking for factors to facilitate her interests in Afghanistan. She used the OIC and some of the Gulf Cooperation Council (GCC) states like the United Arab Emirates (UAE) to help, as the UAE recognised the Taliban regime along with Saudi Arabia. Saudi Ulema did not issue fatwa to ban drug cultivation and drug trafficking in Afghanistan because it was an easy source of funds for them.

Supporting the Interests of the Strategic Alliances

The second long-standing policy of Saudi Arabia in Afghanistan derived from its strategic policy with its two main alliances, the US and Pakistan. Since the Soviet invasion of Afghanistan in 1979, the convergence of interests between Soudi Arabia, Pakistan and the US has been explicit. All three powers shaped a triangle in seeking individual and common interests in Afghanistan. It would be correct to say that US strategy and weapons, Saudi finance and Pakistan's manpower worked simultaneously to oppose the Soviet Union in the country.[17]

Since its establishment in 1932, Saudi Arabia has always been in search of a strategic alliance in the region or internationally. This is mainly because of the two explicit goals that Riyadh is pursuing. The first goal is the result of the regional rivals who are seen as a threat to the security and survival of the Kingdom. This has always forced Riyadh to be aligned with an international power to exert its presence against rivals. In the 1980s, Saudi Arabia was already surrounded by Soviet allies such as Iraq, South Yemen, Syria, Libya and Ethiopia. Iran and Egypt were also regional opponents and this external pressure put Riyadh in a critical situation. Riyadh had to start somewhere to oppose all three rivals, and the Arab Socialists, Iran and the extremists within. Islamabad's invitation to join the anti-Soviet resistance was a rational choice and a chance for Saudi Arabia to face all the mentioned challenges. Saudi support to Afghan Mujahideen had three aims: first, to involve all fundamentalists who were a threat to the internal security in Saudi Arabia; second, to deal with regional issues. When in the 1980s the country was surrounded by Soviet allies such as Iraq, South Yemen, Syria, Libya and Ethiopia, as well as Iran and Egypt who were also regional opponents—Afghanistan was an opportunity to defeat communism and prove the strength of Saudi Arabia in West Asia; and third, to have an international presence where Saudi Arabia has been a close ally of the US as a strategic partner. In its quest for regional stability and national interests, Riyadh is seeking supremacy in its own region by consolidating its roots outside the neighbourhood.[18] No doubt in both cases, either Saudi Arabia was seeking a guarantee or looking for an ally to oppose a regional opponent; it had to adhere to certain promises. This compelled the state to look towards bilateral ties. The alliance had been characterised by reciprocal dealings and while Riyadh expected some support, it also had to support its allies. The allies of the Kingdom recognised the potential and hence became part of the alliance.

The US and Pakistan are two main strategic alliance partners of Saudi Arabia both regionally and internationally. Following the end of the Second World War and in a shift of power from Great Britain to the US, the dependence of Britain also shifted. In post-Second World War bloc politics which was termed the Cold War, the world mainly came to be divided into the Soviet Union and the Western blocs. Saudi Arabia stood strongly with the West. This close relationship took on a more explicit character when the Arab world came to be divided into three main power centres, namely, Egypt, Iraq and Saudi Arabia, in which Iraq and Egypt joined the Soviet bloc, and the Iranian revolution in 1979 also resulted in a diplomatic failure for the US.

Saudi Arabia had to support the US's strategic interests in the region which were under Saudi Arabia's sphere of influence. Riyadh would have used all its resources to help Washington in the region if it was in need of a power which would give it security from regional powers. This cooperation would be done in two ways: either Riyadh had to act directly with the US or support an ally of the US. To oppose the Soviet invasion in Afghanistan in 1979, the US formed an extraordinary anti-communist alliance with militant

Islamic forces in South Asia. John Cooley describes the development of US foreign policy and the Central Intelligence Agency's (CIA) covert activity in the 1980s, which facilitated the training and arming of almost a quarter of a million Islamic mercenaries drawn from around the world. Cooley marshals a wealth of evidence to demonstrate the devastating consequences of this alliance between the US government and radical Islam—from the assassination of President Anwar Sadat, the destabilisation of Algeria and Chechnya and the emergence of the Taliban, to the bombings of the World Trade Centre and the US embassies in Africa.[19]

Riyadh was interested in a strategic alliance with Pakistan for two reasons: firstly, to use its potentiality from the US strategic friendship; and secondly, to accept Pakistan as a second Sunni pillar in the Islamic world to oppose Shia Iran and the influence of communism in Afghanistan. For this, Islamabad had a more active role to play than Riyadh. The leadership in Islamabad convinced Riyadh that Pakistan can fulfil many of Riyadh's plans in its international relations. Saudi Arabia's two strategic alliances have had deep strategic interests in Afghanistan but their separate strategies did not work effectively which resulted in the common approach for their individual and group interests.

References to the convergence of interests between Saudi Arabia, the US and Pakistan have been explicit while we review the literature on Afghanistan and the region. It is believed that the strategic alliances of Saudi Arabia with the US and Pakistan also had a direct influence in Afghanistan. The closeness of the relationship among the three countries was reflected while Saudi Arabia dealt with Russia, China, India, Central Asia and Iran, as was the case during the Cold War; the CIA, Inter-Services Intelligence (ISI) along with Saudi Arabia's intelligence, created the Mujahideen as a front against the Soviet Union.[20]

From the beginning, the strategy of the US towards Afghanistan in the 1950s was overshadowed by the consequences of the Cold War. Competition was on in Afghanistan between the US and the Soviet Union. After the visit of President Eisenhower to Kabul in 1959 and the US$ 500 million support to King Zahir Shah, Moscow felt threatened on its southern borders. Afghanistan was a factor in the US's long-term strategic interests in its regional policy. With the rise in influence of the Moscow-backed faction in Kabul, the overthrow of Muhammad Daud Khan, and the rise of the communists to power, Washington drew up the Afghanistan doctrine in which the US supported the anti-Kabul groups. Washington's policy towards Afghanistan changed after the disintegration of the Soviet Union which resulted in the independence of many new republics rich in natural resources and the substitution of Islamists for communists who began to attack American interests around the world. For this threefold policy—creation of a regional pocket for long-term strategic interests, access to the Central Asian Republics (CARs), and the suppression of Islamists—Afghanistan was seen as playing a major role. Washington could not afford to ignore the importance of the country in fulfilling its strategic goals.

Washington achieved a major success in 1979 while mediating between Anwar Sadat and Menachem Begin, and closed a major front against a strategic alliance inimical to it. But, in the same year, things went wrong for Washington in other parts of West Asia—in Saudi Arabia, Iran and Afghanistan. Closing the front in Israel resulted in active operations of Islamists within the Arab world. In 1979 the seizure of Mecca by the Islamists led by Juhaimyan was soon followed by the Islamic revolution in Iran and the invasion of Afghanistan by Soviet troops. The year was ominous for Saudi Arabia and the US.

Notwithstanding these friendly ties, relations between Saudi Arabia and the US were unstable. Saudi Arabia has always maintained close relations with the West and particularly the US because of its assistance for Al Saud's safety. King Fahd was considered to be more pro-West than other royal family members. But the deterioration of King Fahd's health at the end of 1995 and the temporary transfer of power to the conservative Crown Prince Abdullah, known for his different approach towards the US, complicated matters.[21]

On the other hand, Pakistan has had its own assessment regarding its interests in Afghanistan. The partition of India and Pakistan did not suit Afghanistan when a large part of southern Afghanistan was seized by the new state of Pakistan called North-West Frontier Province (NWFP), now Khyber Pakhtunkhwa, something with which the regime in Kabul never could come to terms. This resulted in long-term hostility between the two countries. Islamabad felt further threatened when in 1971 East Pakistan proclaimed independence as Bangladesh, and India came closer to Afghanistan on two sides of Pakistan. Jihad in Afghanistan in the 1980s forced Islamabad to draw a long-term strategy in Afghanistan which was based solely on self-interest.

It is argued that Pakistan plays an important role for Saudi Arabia's interests in the region. Sometimes Pakistan assumes greater importance than Afghanistan. Rais B. Rasool discusses Pakistan as a factor in Saudi Arabian interests in Afghanistan. He writes, "Saudi Arabia's political and religious influence have been linked in Afghanistan since the 1950s, when Wahhabi elements began to establish religious schools in Pakistan in which a number of Afghan Mullahs were trained. In more recent times, Saudi Arabia's objectives in Afghanistan were first to drive out the Soviet Communists and then to counter Iran's influence."[22]

Briefly, Pakistan is looking at certain policy options in Afghanistan which are: enhancing its sphere of influence, competing with regional powers like Iran, assessing its role in government formation in Kabul, exploring Afghanistan as a market seeking access to Central Asia, and recruiting Afghans for anti-India operations in Kashmir and Xinxiang. In other words, Pakistan is Saudi Arabia's strongest Sunni ally to oppose Shiaism and to spread Wahhabism. This is the reason why Saudi Arabia has a genuine interest in bringing peace in Afghanistan because it will help stabilise Pakistan. Sometimes, their strategic ties are close and clandestine to the extent that even the US has no influence. In 1985, Saudi Arabia, Ikhwan and Jamah't Islami Pakistan formulated a policy to support radical Islamic groups within Afghanistan and oppose Iran's influence, besides avoiding the influence of Western culture among the Mujahideen and migrants. Pakistan can help Saudi Arabia in its intelligence activities in Afghanistan much in the same way as Turki-al-Faisal, the former head of Saudi Arabia's intelligence in Afghanistan was monitoring operations from Pakistan with the support of the ISI.[23]

Of course, the triangular strategy works on matters other than political issues as well, but it also revolves around oil interests, as was clear in the meeting for Union Oil Company of California (Unocal) plans in Afghanistan. It included Saudi Arabia-based Delta Oil, Pakistan's Crescent Group and Russia's Gazprom. It is being viewed that close friendship with the US is not supported by Saudi Arabia's people, as a majority of the conservative nationalist intelligentsia in Saudi Arabia are resentful with the US's politics in West Asia and its dual role and two-faced policy.[24]

Spreading the Wahhabi Model of Fundamentalism

The third long-standing policy of Saudi Arabia towards Afghanistan is the spread of the Wahhabi model of Islamic Salafism. The terms Wahhabi or Salafi are seen as interchangeable and frequently misunderstood. However, as Madawi al-Rasheed explains in a fascinating exploration of Saudi Arabia in the twenty-first century, even the Saudis do not agree on the meaning of these terms. Under the influence of mass education, printing, new communications technology, and global media, they are coming to their own conclusions and debating religion and politics in traditional and new venues, often violating the official taboos and the conservative values of Saudi society. Drawing on classical religious sources, contemporary readings and interviews, al-Rasheed presents ethnography of consent and contest, exploring the fluidity of the boundaries between the religious and political. Bridging the gap between text and context, the author also examines how states and citizens manipulate religious discourse for purely political ends, and how this manipulation generates unpredictable reactions whose control escapes those who initiated them.

Since the eighteenth century there has been a discourse among different schools of theology within Islam. Wahhabism is one of the latest versions which came out of the Hanbali School of theology called Ahl Hadith or the people of Hadith (Speeches of Prophet Muhammad). David Commins gives a very thematic picture of Wahhabism in his book, and writes in its preface:

> What is the Wahhabi mission? To answer that question is to risk taking a position on a controversy that has divided Muslims for more than two centuries. A neutral observer could define the Wahhabi mission as the religious reform movement associated with the teachings of Muhammad ibn Abd al-Wahhab (1703-1792). He and his followers believe that they have a religious obligation to spread the call (in Arabic, da'wa) for a restoration of pure monotheistic worship. Thus, the mission's devotees contend that "Wahhabism" is a misnomer for their efforts to revive correct Islamic belief and practice. Instead of the Wahhabi label, they prefer either salafi, one who follows the ways of the first Muslim ancestors (salaf), or Mujahid, one who professes God's unity. On the other hand, a Muslim critic would say that Wahhabism is a deviant sectarian movement started by an ambitious, misguided religious leader from a remote part of Arabia that has spawned heretical movements since early Islam. Muslims sharply disagree on this question of definition because the pivotal idea in ibn Abd al-Wahhab's teaching determines whether one is a Muslim or an infidel. In his opinion, Muslims who disagreed with his definition of monotheism were not heretics, that is to say, misguided.[25]

The spread of Wahhabism to the rest of the Islamic world has been one of the pillars in Saudi foreign policy. The Saudi government comprises an easy alliance between its royal family and its conservative religious clergy. The Saudi clergy followed an unusual, puritanical doctrine of Islam often referred to as Wahhabism.

Riyadh was following its own policy in the 1980s during the jihad in Afghanistan. The Kingdom defined Arab jihadists as strategic assets or in other words, they were defined primarily as catalysts by Western observers. Saudi Arabia, under Cold War influence, told Washington that Muslim revivalists who participated in the jihad in Afghanistan are part of the Cold War contest between the Soviet Union and the US. Riyadh allowed preachers like Abdullah Azzam, Osama bin Laden and Omar Bakri Muhammad to attract Arabs into Afghanistan. This was a chance that Riyadh took in the process of Wahhabinisation of the country which failed in the nineteenth century. Commins writes:

> What observers of the war minimised, or missed completely, was its function as a crucible for the synthesis of disparate Islamic revivalist organisations into a loose coalition of like-minded jihadist groups that viewed the war as a struggle between Islam and unbelief. In brief, the war in Afghanistan amplified the jihadist tendency from a fringe phenomenon to a major force in the Muslim world.[26]

The Wahhabinisation process of Saudi Arabia is mainly an opportunistic policy. Riyadh would avail any kind of privilege to influence other Islamic sects to avert the threat. For that purpose, Wahhabinisation is a constructive process. Steve Coll writes, that "the ministry of Hajj and Awqaf of Saudi Arabia had strong relation[s] with Taliban via charity institutions and Wahhabi preaching groups."[27]

In Afghanistan, the Saudi policy of Wahhabinisation fructified with the support of radical jihadis during the1980s. The semi-independent clergy in Saudi Arabia began to support the Afghan Arabs in order to convey the message of Salafism to the Mujahideen and to the people of Afghanistan in general. For this purpose, the Jamiat-ul-Ulema of Pakistan which was a close ally of the Afghan Mujahideen was also supportive of the process. Maulana Mawdudi's writings, while being more anti-establishment than what Saudi Arabia's self-protecting monarchy might tolerate at home, nonetheless promoted much of their Islamic moral and social transformation sought by the Saudi clergy.[28]

In Afghanistan, from the eighteenth century onwards, Wahhabism was taken as a sect that deviated from Islamic principles and therefore their followers were not considered true Muslims. The prevalence of an anti-Wahhabi sentiment in Afghanistan or in a broader sense in South or Central Asia was mainly due to their principles and objectives preached by colonial powers which diverted Muslims with a view to destroying Islam. Five slogans of Muhammad ibn Abd al-Wahhab respectively—the Unity of Allah, khatamat of Prophet Muhammad, Quran as the law, Jihad in the path of Allah as the end and martyrdom as a wish—all were construed as anti-colonial which challenged their interests. In the first half of the twentieth century individual preachers were stoned to death by the verdict of Hanafi Ulema in charge of preaching Wahhabism in eastern Afghanistan. Wahhabism was introduced by non-Islamic groups in the same way as Baha'ism and the Qadyani sect.

The Assembly of Mujahideen ended within two weeks with the formation of an Afghan Interim Government (AIG) under the presidency of a moderate leader, Sibgatullah Mojaddadi. In the ensuing weeks, this government was recognised by Saudi Arabia on March 10, 1989 as the first to turn against Riyadh. The leaders in Kabul introduced Saudi Arabia as a Wahhabi face which interferes in Afghanistan for its own interests to spread Wahhabism in the country and the media in Kabul termed Arab Mujahideen as Saudi Arabian terrorists, Arab advisers to Wahhabis and Saudi spies who tried to create factions among the Mujahideen to oppose Saudi Arabia. On May 26, *Bakhtar* newspaper in Kabul carried a headline stating "9 Wahhabi Mercenaries from Saudi Arabia killed in Nangarhar." Again, in the same month, *News* talked of a Saudi citizen killed in eastern Afghanistan. In August, rumours were afloat about Wahhabi mercenaries being present among the Mujahideen.[29] The Afghan government even enlisted the help of influential local people and the Ulema for anti-Wahhabi propaganda and asked them to issue a fatwa of Jihad against them. Many tribal groups and Ulema issued a fatwa of Jihad against the Wahhabis in Afghanistan and asked Afghans not to allow them to be spread in the country.[30] Yonis Khalis, the Peshawar-based Jihadi leader in an interview with the *Voice of America* in October 1990, said that Wahhabis are creating problems in Afghanistan. Sayyaf also condemned Saudi Arabia for financial support to Moscow and vowed that Riyadh is supporting the enemies of Islam. Riyadh was trying to protect small parties from extermination by extremists. In September 1991, Abdu Shams Turki, King Fahd's special envoy, visited Afghan resistance leaders and discussed Mujahideen expansion towards Kabul, but the real message of Turki was negotiation between Gulbuddin Hekmatyar and Malawi Jamil-ur-Rahman, a Salafi leader in eastern Afghanistan who was under serious attack from Islamists.[31]

The religious clergy understood that an Afghan jihad was a rare chance for closer cooperation between Wahhabis and Muslim revivalists. Riyadh knew that some reactions would be expected from Afghan traditionalists and conservative leaders but Arabs and Pakistanis did not have such expectations from Wahhabism. Perhaps the Saudi Wahhabi Ulema were optimistic about the change of Afghan conservatism towards the Wahhabi mission. But the tension which was created by the Afghans and the fatwa of Abdullah Azzam as the leader of the revivalists, led these Ulema to find support elsewhere among the Afghans themselves. Only moderate leaders like Shibghatullah Mojaddadi and Gailani were supporters of Riyadh as the Mujahideen interim government under Mojaddadi's presidency sent 300 army personnel to Saudi Arabia in support of the coalition forces to fight against Iraq where extremists condemned it and supported Iraq. For the extremists, the US invasion of Iraq was an attack on an Islamic land and Saudi Arabia's hostile anti-Iraq stance as support to the US.[32]

In November 1991 a high-powered Mujahideen delegation comprising Burhanuddin Rabbani, Muhammad Nabi Muhammadi, Ayatollah Muhsini, Amin Wiqad and Sayyid Ahmed Gailani visited King Fahd before leaving for Moscow. The delegation visited King Fahd on their return from Moscow too, but extremists like Hekmatyar and Khalis condemned these visits and support. Jamil al-Rahman was the pseudonym of an Afghan Mujahideen leader named Maulavi Hussein who had parted ways with Gulbuddin Hekmatyar's Hezb-e-Islami on ideological grounds in 1985. Around 1986 he set up an independent organisation in Kunar with the encouragement and financial support of conservative Saudi and Kuwaiti businessmen. This organisation drew many Saudis because it was rigidly Salafi and thus enjoyed the support of the official Saudi Ulema. Saudi sheikhs considered Jamil al-Rahman's group more doctrinally pure than the Muslim Brotherhood-dominated Services Bureau or the revolutionary Egyptian and Jordanian factions in Peshawar. Jamil al-Rahman had studied with Ahl-e-Hadith in Pakistan, and his "Society for Da'wa" had a stronger focus on social and ritual issues than other factions. They engaged in violent enforcement of the Wahhabi ban on grave worship and other local practices considered religious innovations (*bid'a*). Al-Rahman's group had extensive contacts in Saudi Arabia and published a magazine in Peshawar called *Al-Mujahid*, which was even more widely available in the Kingdom than Azzam's *Al-Jihad* magazine. The flow of Saudis slowed down after the assassination of Jamil al-Rahman in 1991 and all but ceased after the fall of Kabul in 1992.[33]

When the Taliban rose to power and imposed a harsh regime of Islamic law and morality, it was common to view it as a manifestation of Wahhabism. While it is true that Saudi Arabia's government and Wahhabi establishment lent support to the Taliban, the Afghan puritans emerged not from Wahhabism but from the Indian Deobandi movement. But Salafis and Deobandis since the 1980s in Pakistan figured as a fairly minor part of its religious scene until the regime of General Zia-ul-Haq (1977-1988), who used an Islamic policy to buttress his military dictatorship. Part of his policy to "Islamise" Pakistan was a campaign to expand religious education with funds for thousands of new madrasas.

Keeping International Prestige

The fourth principle in the foreign policy of Saudi Arabia towards Afghanistan is the matter of prestige in which Saudi Arabia has been recognised as an influential regional actor in Afghanistan. This was more visible during the 1980s when Saudi Arabia was supporting the Mujahideen against the communist regime in Afghanistan. Saudi Arabia has not become important and influential since the invasion by Soviet troops in Afghanistan but the Kingdom has been playing its major role in the country since the seventh century when the people of Afghanistan converted to Islam and Mecca and Medina turned holy cities. Since then, Afghans have looked upon Saudi Arabia as the land of miracles and the cradle of Islam. Throughout history the Ulema of Saudi Arabia have had a direct influence over the Muslims in Afghanistan.

During Jihad, while Riyadh was supporting the Mujahideen, the regime in Kabul still did not want to confront Saudi Arabia, considering its role among the people. Taraki and Amin followed a policy of appeasement to gain Riyadh's support against the Mujahideen. Babrak Karmal's policies were termed anti-Saudi, but they were replaced by a call to friendship by Dr. Mohammad Najibullah who replaced Babrak Karmal as president. For the preservation of its prestige, Riyadh was even involved in many negative policies in the region which in the end turned against it. The rulers sought to appease the religious purists and Imams by supporting and financing Islamic causes and movements abroad, such as the Mujahideen of the Afghan resistance; the Arab volunteers who fought on the Muslim side in Bosnia and in Kosovo; the Wahhabi-inspired fundamentalist movements in Central Asia and the Taliban in Afghanistan. Saudi foreign policy has been facetiously described as "realpolitik." The most articulate exponent of Wahhabism was the Saudi rebel, Osama bin Laden, who broke with the Saudi regime on the issue of the presence of non-Muslim armed forces on Saudi soil during the Gulf War.[34]

Saudi Arabia was politically active in Afghanistan but economically and culturally the Kingdom has been always absent in the region. A survey of historical literature shows that at every stage when the war reached its end and Afghanistan experienced a partial peace, when regional and international powers streamed in to participate in post-war reconstruction, Saudi Arabia kept a low profile; whereas during each war, it played an active support role. One cannot ignore the fact that millions of dollars were given to Afghanistan by the Kingdom in all three stages of the war, during the Mujahideen period, during the rise of the Taliban and after 9/11 and the establishment of the present government, but such support was influenced by ideological, religious and political support. If Afghans are asked about Saudi Arabia's role in the reconstruction of Afghanistan at any stage, they will respond negatively with anger or a bitter smile and will say "they only know how to eat, wear and sleep."

Culturally, Afghanistan has strong ties with Saudi Arabia in the sphere of Islamic culture, being a Sunni country. In Afghanistan, a small minority of Arabs also reside, who have migrated to Afghanistan in two distinct phases. The first migration took place during the Arab expedition to Afghanistan with the intention of spreading Islam, during which the migrants stayed on and in due course of time got assimilated within the Afghan society. Today they are known as Arabs by name. Secondly, the October Revolution in Russia and the rise of communist regimes in the Central Asian states also resulted in a large wave of Muslim migration to Afghanistan in which a large portion of these migrants were Central Asian Arab people who were living in northern Afghanistan, and some of their tribes like Bani, Tamim, preserved their language and culture.

Riyadh has always used all its potential to preserve its name as an active player in Afghanistan. For this, it used all its political, religious and economic clout at its disposal. For example, in 1992, with the victory of the Mujahideen and the gradual fading of the Saudi role in Afghanistan, the Kingdom for the first time thought of the small Arab minority who had migrated to Afghanistan during the 1920s from Central Asia because of communist pressure on the religious groups of the region. Many leaders of Arab community were invited to Saudi Arabia by the King. The Arabs were provoked to form a single political party, the Unity of Arabs of Afghanistan Party. There is little doubt that this idea was given by Riyadh to awaken its pressure groups inside Afghanistan and to exploit the resources for the Kingdom's benefit. But this policy did not work because a majority of the Arabs of Afghanistan had absorbed the local culture and way of life. Besides, they had participated with different Mujahideen groups and were not ready to give up their alliances. The efforts of a small number of Arabs were in vain and the attempt failed.[35]

Saudi Arabia did not retreat from this failure in Afghanistan because of the negative responses by the Arab community. Riyadh formulated another policy making strategic assets work for the interests of the Kingdom. This time Riyadh asked the Sayyids of Afghanistan to form a political party. Riyadh promised them financial support. The Sayyids are the community who belong to the family of Prophet Muhammad. In the family tree they reach up to Fatima and Ali, who are the daughter and son-in-law of the Prophet. In Saudi Arabia's theological belief, the Sayyids do not occupy a special place in the religious system of the Kingdom. Sayyids are like any Muslims in Saudi Arabia and they do not have special privileges. Sheriff Hussein of Mecca was the last influential leader from the Sayyid community of Saudi Arabia who was expelled by the Al Saud family with the help of the Wahhabi forces.[36]

But now in Afghanistan they were being provoked to work as a special and privileged community with the support of Saudi Arabia. Some famous personalities from Kunar province in eastern Afghanistan announced the formation of the Sayyids Party of Afghanistan, which was not supported wholeheartedly by other Sayyids in other parts of the country as it was by the Arabs. Riyadh also asked many famous Muslim Brotherhood leaders to negotiate with the Afghan Mujahideen for a closer alliance with Saudi Arabia. Turki al-Faisal on many occasions had taken with him some Ikhwan Ulema to Afghanistan. It was because of this policy that Professor Sayyaf, a radical Islamist leader, came close to the Rabbani regime in Kabul.

Many argue inside Afghanistan that Saudi support for the Taliban movement even overshadowed this policy of Riyadh. In 1994, Turki al-Faisal in an interview with the *Pakistan Times* said that the Islamic parties in Afghanistan forgot the support of Saudi Arabia during Jihad and now we do not have any role in the reconstruction. This complaint by al-Faisal shows his anticipation about the plausible end of this weak role of Saudi Arabia in the recent past. When Saudi Arabia was losing her prestige and role in a zero-sum game policy with Iran, in Afghanistan, a new political movement was being molded within tribal Islam by the US and Pakistan—the two major players in the Afghan Jihad who also lost their role in the Mujahideen regime in Kabul. Both the US and Pakistan were looking for new ways to avoid a vacuum in the continuation of their interests in Afghanistan and through Afghanistan in Central Asia, India, China and Russia. The Taliban was an Islamic group which had a fascist interpretation of Islam inspired from their tribal reading of Islam which appealed to Saudi Arabia's Wahhabi interpretation of Islam with a common tribal characteristic. The Taliban showed their loyalty to Saudi Arabia's interests in the country and gained the trust of the Kingdom. In 1998, when they captured Mazar-e-Sharif, they killed nine Iranian diplomats.

Conclusion

Thus for Saudi Arabia, Afghanistan became a factor in the balance of power by cutting Iran's influence in the country. But all Shiite parties were influenced and supported by Iran and the Taliban-based Sunni party was also propped up by Saudi Arabia after 2006. It should be noted that the

Jamiat-e Islami Afghanistan—a Tajik (Persian) party under the leadership of Burhanuddin Rabbani was by ethnicity and language close to Iran. Gulbedin Hekmatyar and Rasool Sayyaf—two other main parties were opposed to Saudi Arabia, because of the presence of US troops in the country and the rest were weak parties which were not active to help further Riyadh's goals in Afghanistan. But the obvious point in the study of Saudi Arabia's policy towards Afghanistan is that Riyadh played an inconsistent role both during the Mujahideen government as well as the Taliban regime. Internal factors had a strong impact on foreign policy in Saudi Arabia. Studies show that this kind of situation complicates decision making and a contradiction always emerges while a policy is formulated, and this resulted in ambiguous politics within Saudi Arabia. This complication created difficulties for Saudi Arabia in drawing up clear policy guidelines on Afghanistan.

Afghanistan also had always been aware of the economic and religious importance of Saudi Arabia. In its economic and legitimacy concerns throughout recent history, almost all regimes which came to power in Afghanistan tried to have friendly relations with Riyadh. Even communist regimes used the policy of appeasement on many occasions to befriend Saudi Arabia. The rapid political changes and fragmentations in Afghanistan confused Saudi Arabia when it dealt diplomatically with Afghanistan. The main opposition parties in Afghanistan and factions within them were the source of confusion for Riyadh in its friendly relations with the country. In the 1990s, there were four divided power centres in Afghanistan: the Democratic Republic of Afghanistan, the moderate Afghan Islamic oppositions heading Afghanistan's interim government in Pakistan, the Afghan Islamic extremists in Pakistan and the Afghan anti-communist Shia leaders based in Iran. Some Shia leaders like Ayatollah Sheikh Mohammad Asif Mohsini, the leader of the Islamic movement of Afghanistan, was also unfriendly with Tehran. He was a strong critic of the Vilayat-e-Faqih and a strong critic of Imam Khomeini. Riyadh had to deal with him to prevent Iran's influence in Afghanistan but Gulbedin Hekmatyar, the Sunni extremist, was unhappy with this policy. Riyadh had to play a role to bring all its pro-Saudi political parties upfront to oppose both Iran's influence and anti-Riyadh groups, besides being friendly with Pakistan. From 1932 to 1990, the Kingdom tried to play a defendant's role for the survival and security of its territory. All its major policies—Pan-Islamism, Pan-Arabism, economic policy, anti-Israel slogans, and supporting the Islamic cause overshadowed self-protection. Riyadh used Afghanistan for this purpose against Russia. It also exterminated its radical elements inside Afghanistan.

Many studies have analysed that Saudi Arabia's foreign policy is based on petro-diplomacy when it deals with Arabs, as it is a case of Islam and Arab identity inside the Arab world; but as far as Afghanistan is concerned, Riyadh has two aims in Afghanistan, namely, security of oil-oriented interests by using Afghanistan as a buffer state for depriving Soviet Union access to the Persian Gulf, and propagating Islam for limiting the spread of Shia Islam in South Asia and Central Asia.

Looking at the above considerations, the Saudi role in post-communist reconstruction in Afghanistan depends on two factors: first, continuation of the reconstruction with international cooperation leading the process where major powers are actively involved; second, assumption of its appropriate role in the region and inside Afghanistan as an individual player. However, it can be said that Saudi Arabia's Afghan policy is in poor shape. It is believed that the Saudis have followed a policy of double standards in Afghanistan. After the fall of communism and the presence of Mujahideen troops in the country, there have been direct and indirect interventions in Afghanistan since 1992. Overall, the future policy of Saudi Arabia towards Afghanistan can be investigated in three areas, i.e., Islam, economics and security. In the area of religion, the Islamic cultural loop governs the cultural relations between both the countries as it is a dominating culture in Afghanistan too. The multidimensional problems in Afghanistan and mass camping of Afghan leaders in Saudi Arabia, the traditional dependency for work in that country by Afghans because of the economic imbalance in their country, are the major reasons why the Afghans are being absorbed in Saudi Arabia. This is also a factor in Saudi Arabia focusing its attention on Afghanistan.

Historically, one can claim that Saudi Arabia has had an influential role in Afghanistan since the birth of Islam when in the first century of the Islamic calendar the people of Afghanistan converted to Islam. For two hundred years the Arabs ruled Afghanistan and since then Saudi Arabia has been the centre where every year thousands of Afghan Muslims visit Mecca for Hajj. Saudi Ulema have had a deep influence over Afghans over centuries. In modern times, relations improved after the emergence of the Kingdom of Saudi Arabia in 1932. Initially, the Afghan King, Nadir Shah, recognised the declaration of the Saudi state and a high-level official was sent to Jeddah for the fulfilment of the formalities. This warm relation became warmer when King Faisal visited Kabul in 1953. In 1973, in a bloodless coup, Muhammad Daud Khan overthrew the monarchy and declared Afghanistan a Republic. Subsequently, Daud Khan came closer to Riyadh. He supported the Saudi policy against Israel in the West Asian crisis and visited Saudi Arabia thrice. The condition of bilateral relations remained stable till 1978 when a group of communist soldiers in the Afghan army revolted against the regime of Muhammad Daud Khan which resulted to his murder in the presidential place.

Thus the study of Afghan-Saudi ties shows that both countries have had to face many challenges in the history of their foreign relations. The ties have been unstable and based on the internal situations of both states as well as international situations. The friendly relations deteriorated after the communist revolution in 1978 and then the invasion by the Soviet Army a year after.

Notes

1. Ahmad Hamid, "لماوع و للع :نابلاط [Taliban: Reasons and Factors]" *Political and Economic Quarterly*, 2002, pp. 131-35.
2. Ahmed Rashid, "Taliban: Exporting Extremism," *Foreign Affairs*, 76(6), 1999, pp. 22-35.
3. David B. Edwards "Summoning Muslims: Print, Politics, and Religious Ideology in Afghanistan," *Journal of Asian Studies*, 52 (3), 1993.
4. Gulbedin Hekmatyar, ؟دراد لح هار نانستاغفا نارحب ایآ [*Does Afghanistan Crisis have a Solution?*] (In Persian), Qisa Khwani, Peshawar, 2002.
5. Ahmed Rashid, "Back with a Vengeance: Proxy War in Afghanistan," *The World Today,* 52(3), 1996, pp. 60-63.
6. William Maley, "Dynamics of Regime Transition in Afghanistan," *Central Asian Survey*, 16(2), 1997, pp. 167-84.
7. Group of Migrants in Delhi,هطبار رد هللا بیجن روتكد دیهش یاه هینایب زا یشخب هعومجم هب یشم یحلاصم یلم [*A Collection of Martyred Dr. Najibullah's Speeches about National Conciliation*] (In Persian) (New Delhi: Zarnosht Publications, 1999), p. 79.
8. Chintamani Mahapatra, "Afghan Turmoil: Problems and Prospects," *ICC Quarterly*, 24(1), 1997, pp. 131-43.
9. Mohammad Hassan Kakar, *Afghanistan: The Soviet Invasion and Responses 1979-1982* (California: University of California Press, 1995).
10. "Speech to the Teachers," Chiraq-e-Shaheed, a documentary movie made on Dr. Najibullah's life in 2005.
11. Prince El-Hassan bin Talal, "Afghanistan: Parallels and Anti-Parallels," *Perceptions,* 7(1), 2002, pp. 5-27.
12. Amin Saikal, "The Afghanistan Conflict, International Terrorism and US Responses," *Perceptions,* 7(1), 2002, pp. 84-71.
13 یسایس ماظن هدنیآ و ناتسناغفا [*Afghanistan and the Future of Political System*] (In Persian), Zulal Kousar, Qom, 2002, p. 54.
14. Miraqa Haqjoo, یجراخ تالخادم و ناتسناغفا [*Afghanistan and External Interferences*] (In Persian) (Tehran: Majlisi Publishers, 2000), p. 213.
15. Ahmed Rashid, "Afghanistan: Heart of Darkness," *Far Eastern Economic Review*, 1999, pp. 10-13.
16. Prince El-Hassan bin Talal, no. 11.
17. Citha D. Maas, "Afghanistan Conflict: External Involvement," *Central Asian Survey,* 18(1), 1999, pp. 65-78.
18. Ralph H. Magnus, "Afghanistan in 1996: Year of Taliban," *Central Asian Survey*, 37(2), 1997, pp. 111-17.

19. John K. Cooley, *Unholy Wars: Afghanistan, America and International Terrorism* (London: Pluto Press, 1999), p. 89.
20. David B. Edwards, "Summoning Muslims: Print, Politics, and Religious Ideology in Afghanistan," *Journal of Asian Studies*, 52 (3), 1993.
21. Ahmed Rashid, "Back with a Vengeance: Proxy War in Afghanistan," *The World Today,* 52(3), 1996, pp. 60-63.
22. Wahid Mozhda, *Afghanistan wa Panj Sal Sulta Taliban* [*Afghanistan Five Years under Taliban*] (Tehran: Nai Publishers, 2002), p. 24.
23. Khouja Bashir Ahmad Ansari, *Afghanistan dar Atash Naft* [*Afghanistan in the Fire of Oil*] (Kabul: Maiwand Publishing House, 2002), p. 22.
24. Abir Mordechai, *Saudi Arabia: Government, Society and the Gulf Crisis* (London: Routledge, 1996), p. 123.
25. David Commins, *The Wahhabi Mission and Saudi Arabia* (I. B. Tauris & Co. Ltd., 2006), p. 85.
26. Ibid., p. 91.
27. Steve Coll, *Ghost Wars: The Secret History of the CIA, Afghanistan, and Bin Laden: From the Soviet Invasion to September 2001* (London: Westview Press, 2001), p. 213.
28. Ibid., p. 154.
29. *Bakhtar News,* July 8, 1989.
30. Ibid. November 2, 1989.
31. Ibid.
32. Ibid.
33. Carol J. Riphenburg, "Ethnicity and Civil Society in Contemporary Afghanistan," Middle East Institute, *Middle East Journal*, 59 (1), Winter, 2005, pp. 31-51 at http://www.jstor.org/stable/4330095 (Accessed on August 11, 2010).
34. Olivier Roy, "Rivalries and Power Plays in Afghanistan: The Taliban, the Shari'a and the Pipeline," *Middle East Report*, 202, Cairo: Power, Poverty and Urban Survival Winter, 1996, pp. 37-40 at http://www.jstor.org/stable/3013041 (Accessed on August 11, 2010).
35. Zalmay Khalilzad, "Afghanistan in 1994: Civil War and Disintegration," *Asian Survey,* 35 (2), A Survey of Asia in 1994: Part II (February 1995), pp. 147-52 at http://www.jstor.org/stable/2645023 (Accessed on August 11, 2010).
36. Jamil Ur Rahman Kamgar, کرونولوژی حوادث تاریخی افغانستان: از جمهوریت تا اداره موقت *[Chronology of the Historical Events in Afghanistan: From Republic to Interim Government] (in Persian) (Kabul: Maiwand Publishing House, 2004), p. 267.*

12. Afghanistan's Political Future and the Shanghai Cooperation Organisation

P. Krishna Mohan Reddy

The relationship between the Shanghai Cooperation Organisation (SCO) and Afghanistan is relatively a new area of research. This chapter will discuss the interplay between the SCO, Afghanistan and China, vis-à-vis the Bonn Conferences held between 2001 and 2011.

Shanghai Cooperation Organisation

The SCO was founded in 2001 in Shanghai by the leaders of China, Kazakhstan, Kyrgyzstan, Russia, Tajikistan, and Uzbekistan. Except for Uzbekistan, the other countries had been members of the Shanghai Five, founded in 1996. After the inclusion of Uzbekistan in 2001, the members renamed the organisation. In 2001 at the annual summit in Shanghai, the five member nations first admitted Uzbekistan in the Shanghai Five mechanism. Then all the six heads of state signed the Declaration of Shanghai Cooperation Organisation, on June 15, 2001. In July 2001, Russia and the People's Republic of China (PRC), the organisation's two leading nations, signed the Treaty of Good-Neighbourliness and Friendly Cooperation. In June 2002, the heads of the SCO member-states met at St. Petersburg, Russia. There they signed the SCO Charter, which expounded on the organisation's purposes, principles, structures and form of operation, and established it officially from the point of view of international law. By 2007, the SCO had initiated over twenty large-scale projects related to transportation, energy and telecommunications and held regular meetings of security, military, defence, foreign affairs, economic, cultural, banking and other officials from its member-states. The SCO has now established relations with the United Nations (UN), where it is an observer in the General Assembly, the European Union (EU), Association of Southeast Asian Nations (ASEAN), the Commonwealth of Independent States (CIS) and the Organisation of the Islamic Conference (OIC). The Secretariat of the SCO which is the primary executive body of the organisation is located in Beijing. The SCO is primarily centred on its member nations' Central Asian security-related concerns. In October 2007, the SCO signed an agreement with the Collective Security Treaty Organisation (CSTO), in the Tajik capital Dushanbe, to broaden cooperation on issues such as security, crime, and drug trafficking.

Over the past few years, the organisation's activities have expanded to include increased military cooperation, intelligence sharing, and counterterrorism. There have been a number of SCO joint military exercises. The first of these was held in 2003, with the first phase taking place in Kazakhstan and the second in China. Since then China and Russia have teamed up for large-scale war games in 2005 (Peace Mission 2005) and yet again in 2007 and 2009, under the auspices of the SCO. Following the successful completion of the war games, Russian officials began speaking of India joining such exercises in the future and the SCO taking on a military role. The Peace Mission 2010, conducted between September 9 and 25 at Kazakhstan's Matybulak training area, saw over 5,000 personnel from China, Russia, Kazakhstan, Kyrgyzstan and Tajikistan conduct joint planning and operational manoeuvres. The SCO has served as a platform for larger military announcements by members. During the 2007 war games in Russia, with leaders of SCO member-states in attendance, including Chinese President Hu Jintao, Russia's Prime Minister Vladimir Putin used the occasion to take advantage of a "captive" audience and announced that Russian strategic bombers would resume regular long-range patrols for the first time since the Cold War.

In the 2008 summit address, Putin said that "We will witness and take part in the transformation of the global and regional security and development architectures adapted to new realities of the twenty-first century, when stability and prosperity are becoming inseparable notions." Although the declaration on the establishment of the SCO contained a statement that it "is not an alliance directed against other states and regions and it adheres to the principle of openness," it is believed that one of the original purposes of the SCO was to serve as a counterbalance to the North Atlantic Treaty Organisation (NATO) and the United States (US) and in particular to avoid conflicts that would allow the US to intervene in areas bordering both Russia and China. The US applied for observer status in the SCO, but the request was denied in 2005.

At the Astana summit in July 2005, with the wars in Afghanistan and Iraq foreshadowing an indefinite presence of US forces in Uzbekistan and Kyrgyzstan, the SCO urged the US to set a timetable for withdrawing its troops from SCO member-states. Shortly afterwards, Uzbekistan asked the US to leave the K-2 air base. In November 2005, Russian Foreign Minister Sergey Lavrov reiterated that the "Shanghai Cooperation Organisation is working to establish a rational and just world order" and that "The Shanghai

Cooperation Organisation provides us with a unique opportunity to take part in the process of forming a fundamentally new model of geopolitical integration." A Chinese daily expressed the matter as: "The Declaration points out that the SCO member-countries have the ability and responsibility to safeguard the security of the Central Asian region, and calls on Western countries to leave Central Asia. That is the most noticeable signal given by the Summit to the world."[1]

China's Interests in SCO and Afghanistan

Since the Bonn 2001 Conference which was almost simultaneous with the launching of the SCO, China has been following a very careful and unique policy till 2011 with regard to Afghanistan. Many scholars feel that China places its economic interests above everything else in Afghanistan; however, factors like geopolitics, border security, regional balance of power, and Islamic terrorism also influence its policies. The shift in Chinese policy towards Afghanistan seems to have gained momentum around 2006 though China showed little interest in the reconstruction of Afghanistan following the overthrow of the Taliban.[4] Bilateral assistance and aid have thus far been extremely limited, even if bilateral trade has steadily increased. Chinese companies, ZTE and Huawei, partnered with the Afghan Ministry of Communications to implement digital telephone switches, providing roughly 200,000 subscriber lines. The political ties between China and Afghanistan also have been relatively cordial since 2001, and President Karzai has publicly reiterated his ambition to emulate "America's democracy and China's economic success." China and Afghanistan have signed a number of agreements for the establishment of bilateral business councils and other similar institutions devoted to the development of bilateral ties.

As can be observed elsewhere in the developing world, Chinese state-owned companies launched bids almost doubling those of their foreign rivals. The copper mine in Aynak was estimated to go for US$2 billion but the Chinese far outbid the competing Strikeforce (which is part of Russia's Basic Element Group), Kazakhmys Consortium, Russia's Hunter Dickinson, and the US company, Phelps Dodge.[5] The tender forms part of Afghanistan's national privatisation programme, which has resulted in international tenders for most of the major state-owned companies during 2007-2008, while legislation is continually being adjusted to allow foreign investments.

There are frustrations over the US providing security in Afghanistan and China doing its business smoothly without committing any troops to ISAF. An NBC News Production in October 2009 by Adrienne Mong says, with regard to the indirect role of the US in protecting the Chinese business establishments in Afghanistan, that: "The problem is that while America is sacrificing its blood and treasure, the Chinese will reap the benefits. The whole direction of America's military and diplomatic effort is toward an exit strategy, whereas the Chinese hope to stay and profit ... China will find a way to benefit no matter what the United States does in Afghanistan. But it probably benefits more if we stay and add troops to the fight."[6] In an article in *Foreign Affairs* in April 2010, Christian Le Mière analysed that when Afghan President Hamid Karzai visited China in March 2010, Karzai met with Chinese President Hu Jintao, Premier Wen Jiabao and the Politburo Standing Committee member, Wu Bangguo, during his three days stay in Beijing. Karzai signed agreements with Chinese leaders on economic cooperation, technical training and preferential tariffs for Afghan exports. It was after Karzai's fourth trip to China as Afghanistan's president and Washington's show of impatience with the Karzai regime on issues like electoral reform that Kabul had begun to look for new supporters and patrons. As the regional hegemon, China was the obvious choice. A successful courtship with Beijing, Kabul reasoned, could yield benefits in terms of trade, economic assistance, and even military training.[7] The interest appears to be mutual. With US President Barack Obama having decided to withdraw troops from Afghanistan, China is increasingly aware that it will soon have a pivotal role in Afghanistan's security and that of the whole region.

China's interests in Afghanistan are twofold: security and trade. Afghanistan remains a source of instability to China's west, particularly as it abuts the restless Xinjiang Uighur Autonomous Region (XUAR). Concerns about Islamist militancy on its western border have only heightened since the Uighur riots of July 2009 and are likely to increase with the US withdrawal. The Turkistan Islamic Party (TIP) which Beijing often blames for attacks within China is based in Afghanistan and the borderlands of Pakistan. In September 2003, Hasan Mahsum, the then TIP's leader, was killed in South Waziristan by Pakistani security forces supported by Chinese intelligence officers. In February, a US drone strike killed Abdul Haq al-Turkistani, the TIP's most recent leader, in North Waziristan. Beijing can pursue its agenda of promoting trade and combating insurgent groups, while Kabul will gain a reliable, long-term partner that makes few demands with regard to corruption and democratic governance.[8] As the US begins its military withdrawal and such drone strikes become less frequent, China worries that the TIP will gain greater freedom of movement. Even if the group remains unable to launch cross-border operations into Xinjiang, the TIP's mere existence in Afghanistan and Pakistan will continue to be a serious concern for China.

China has an active interest in ensuring that the Afghan military is able to effectively guard the border separating the two countries. This goal was evidently the purpose of the meeting in March 2010 between Afghan Defence Minister Abdul Rahim Wardak and Chinese Minister of National Defence Liang Guanglie. China's Defence Ministry pledged to continue its low-key support to Afghan forces in the form of military supply and personnel training. Trade and development assistance are the most significant and integral part of Afghan-Chinese relationship. Such trade agreements also help China in developing its western regions. Despite the ethnic violence, Beijing has redoubled its efforts to boost the economies of its two western provinces, the XUAR and the Tibet Autonomous Region, which also witnessed ethnic riots in 2008. In March 2010, Hu said that development of the western region is a priority of China's Twelfth Five-Year Plan, which will run from 2011 to 2015. These concerns appear to be driving China's development of local infrastructure in the Wakhan Corridor—the thin strip of land that leads to the only direct border crossing between Afghanistan and China. Beijing is funding the construction of the new road, supply depot, and mobile communications centre that will allow greater movement and trade across the border.[9] At a conference on Afghanistan in Istanbul in January 2010, China's foreign minister, Yang Jiechi, said that China has provided ¥900 million ($132 million) in reconstruction assistance to Afghanistan since 2002. This development assistance pales in comparison to the contributions of other countries, most notably the US, which provided $ 5.87 billion between 2002 and 2007 and budgeted $ 3.77 billion for 2008 and 2009. The United Kingdom's (UK) Department for International Development spent £147.5 million ($220 million) in 2008-2009 in Afghanistan. Even the International Committee of the Red Cross spends approximately $70 million per year in Afghanistan.

The growing interest of China in Afghanistan cannot be separated from its long-standing concern over spheres of influence. Beijing is uncomfortable with more than 100,000 US troops stationed just across its border. India's expanding presence in Afghanistan is also a concern. India is among the top donors to Afghanistan, ranking fifth behind the US, UK, Japan and Canada. Overall, New Delhi has pledged $1.2 billion in reconstruction assistance, including funds for building a new parliament building in Kabul. Ultimately, Beijing would like to see, in the words of Christian Le Mière, the influence of foreign powers in Afghanistan decrease so that "it can continue its *policy of non-interventionist intervention,* building trade relationships and avoiding political interventions."[10] China has followed this policy with regimes in countries like Iran, Sudan and Venezuela.

Richard Weitz, writing in the *Huffington Post* in August 2011, traces the pure economic interests of China, and how it is using the US in Afghanistan. According to him, China's limited support for the US-led counter-insurgency campaigns in Afghanistan and Iraq, despite the growing Chinese economic stake in these countries, has provoked some irritation among US observers over China's "free riding" on the back of dead European, American and Afghan or Iraqi soldiers.[11] The Chinese government has continued to reject suggestions that it contribute combat forces to the NATO-led ISAF seeking to pacify Afghanistan. China has also dismissed inquiries about whether NATO could send supplies, even non-lethal ones such as food and clothing, through Chinese territory to Afghanistan to support the coalition forces there. China's security policies in Afghanistan resemble Beijing's policies in Iraq, which have focused on investing in the Iraqi energy sector while shunning any major security role. In both Afghanistan and Iraq, Chinese policymakers are ambiguous about the US's military role. They certainly do not want Islamist extremists to triumph there, since they could then use these territories to attempt to spread extremism throughout China. America taking the lead in fighting Islamist insurgents in Afghanistan and Iraq relieves China of having to fight them directly. China prefers the US and its allies to bear the burden of countering radical Islamist movements outside China, especially as alarm grows at how Islamist extremists are depicting their policies in Xinjiang as anti-Muslim. Chinese leaders do not challenge the legitimacy of the US military operations in Afghanistan or Iraq. Beijing indeed wants the US to continue to fight Islamist terrorism and promote Afghanistan's and Iraq's economic and political reconstruction. They do not support maintaining a long-term Western military presence in these countries. Given these conflicting pressures, the Chinese government has publicly supported the Afghan and Iraqi governments. However, it sought to distance itself from the US-led counter-insurgency campaigns in both countries by refraining from endorsing any lengthy Western military presence in these regions.

China has encouraged its companies to invest in developing these countries' natural resources. Recent Chinese investment activity has concentrated on gaining access to raw materials and developing the infrastructure required to transport these goods to China. After Afghanistan opened its energy, mineral and raw material sectors to foreign investment in 2007, China rapidly became Afghanistan's largest foreign investor with the Metallurgical Corporation of China (MCC) proving to be the surprise package, acquiring a controlling stake in the Ayanak copper field. The November 2007 bid of more than $3 billion made that transaction the single largest foreign direct investment in Afghanistan. The state-owned MCC could offer a package of benefits that its private sector competitors could not match, and in July 2009, MCC and Jiangxi Copper Co. started development work at the mine. Subsequent revelations of vast untapped mineral resources in Afghanistan have undoubtedly peaked Chinese interest in developing rail connections and related commercial infrastructure in Afghanistan. According to recent reports, US geologists have rediscovered around $1 trillion worth of iron, copper, cobalt, and lithium reserves scattered around Afghanistan.[12]

Energy security considerations also influence Chinese policy toward Afghanistan. In addition, China has been expanding its access to energy assets in the surrounding countries of Central Asia. The security of these resources, and the land-based transportation routes linking them to China, depends in part on the situation in Afghanistan. In December 2009, China opened a major energy pipeline that transports natural gas from Turkmenistan through Uzbekistan and Kazakhstan through areas sufficiently close to Afghanistan. The pipeline could be attacked by guerrillas operating from Afghan territory. Afghanistan is thought to have unexplored or underdeveloped reserves of oil, natural gas, iron, gold, copper and other raw materials that China imports in abundance.

By acquiring these goods from Afghanistan, China could further diversify its source of imports away from more distant world regions, whose products are transported to China along lengthy ocean shipping routes vulnerable to pirates, foreign navies, and other interruptions. Importing materials from Afghanistan also allows Beijing to pursue a more geographically balanced process of internal economic development. China's western provinces need readily available natural resources for development. Trade with Afghanistan would accelerate the economic growth of the sensitive Xinjiang region, which borders Afghanistan as well as Pakistan and the Central Asian Republics. Foreign trade and investment are perhaps seen by the Afghan officials as their best means for reducing their dependence on international assistance, which currently covers 90 per cent of the Afghan government's budgetary expenditure. While the US and NATO forces protect other foreign investments and infrastructure from insurgent attacks, China's prominent and growing economic presence remains unaccompanied by a commitment from Beijing to send Chinese soldiers to Afghanistan to assist in the country's defence.[13]

At the moment, China's preferred outcome is a negotiated peace settlement amongst the Afghan government, the Afghan Taliban and the other Afghan combatants, supported by Afghanistan's neighbouring countries and the great powers. These international partners would agree to preserve Afghanistan's neutrality and collectively contribute to the country's political development and economic reconstruction. This scenario would establish a more favourable environment for Chinese investment in Afghanistan, reduce some sources of regional terrorism and narcotics trafficking and facilitate the use of Afghanistan's territory as part of the Afghan-Pakistan-Central Asian "Silk Road" connecting China's trade and investment with the rest of Eurasia, Europe and beyond.[14]

In another significant move to gain access to oil and natural gas, Afghanistan's government signed a deal on December 28, 2011 with China's state-owned National Petroleum Corporation (CNPC), allowing it to become the first foreign company to exploit the country's oil and natural gas reserves. The contract, which covers the north-eastern provinces of Sari Pul and Faryab, is the first of several such blocks to be put on the market in the coming months, said Afghan Minister of Mines, Wahidullah Shahrani, during the signing ceremony. Afghanistan has been seeking to find ways to exploit some of its mineral wealth to offset the loss of revenues when foreign aid and spending drops after the international combat troops leave by the end of 2014. The government has been keen to develop an oil-extraction and refining capability for the landlocked nation, which is entirely reliant on fuel imports from neighbouring Iran and the Central Asian Republics. The ministry listed the initial value of the project with CNPC as \$ 700 million. But the total could be ten times greater if more reserves are found and developed and if international oil prices remain at today's levels. The fuel pact allows the Chinese firm to research oil and natural gas blocks in Sari Pul and Faryab. CNPC will also build a refinery (Afghanistan's first) within the next three years, after the real size of the reserves is established with greater accuracy, according to Lu Gong Xun, the President of CNPC's international branch.[15]

Russia's interests in the SCO differ from those of China as Russia's main concern is countering the US influence and power in Europe. Russia is mainly concerned with the presence of NATO. Russia seeks a balance in the spheres of military and defence in which the US dominates. As far as Afghanistan is concerned, unlike China, Russia's economic participation is minimal. By 2010, the trade between Russia and Afghanistan was only US\$ 500 million. However, when the Afghan President Hamid Karzai visited Moscow in 2011, both the Russian and Afghan businessmen met and discussed the future business and trade prospects between these two countries. But, nothing concrete seems to have happened.[3]

Is China using SCO for Its Interests in Afghanistan

According to Elizabeth Wishnick, the SCO as a stabilising force in Afghanistan is likely to be weak after the withdrawal of US troops, and China cannot gain from the SCO in Afghanistan.[16] China's interest in Afghanistan revolves around natural resources and Xinjiang Province. Fitting Afghanistan into the region's economic and resource-oriented network can further develop Xinjiang's economy, thereby stemming the growth of extremist groups. China's central government is aiming to import more energy via overland routes, rather than sea lines of communication like the Malacca Strait that are vulnerable to the US Navy in the event of conflict. The CNPC, as stated before, recently signed an agreement with the Afghan government to explore oil in Afghanistan, marking the first of its kind. China has also begun a $3 billion project to mine copper in Logar Province, Afghanistan.

The SCO as the most obvious stabilising force during the post-withdrawal scenario in Afghanistan, when contemplated, seems to be too weak. The SCO failed to reach a basic consensus to help Kyrgyzstan, a member country, to resolve its problems back in 2010. It further has no military and represents a very weak linkage between member countries.[17] However, taking into account the collective statements made by the SCO members at the 2002 conference and the subsequent clear statements against the American and the international presence and their emphatic statements that any international forces should work under the UN norms, it is clear that the SCO members have a strong sense of unity amongst themselves. Similarly, the fact that the SCO itself is a collective security organisation, and the signals it sends through its joint military exercises along with the statements made by its members, both collectively and individually, indicate that the SCO indeed wants to play a dominant role in the new world order. As far as Afghanistan is concerned, all the members of the SCO have keenly followed the developments in Afghanistan from the Bonn 2001 to 2011 conferences. They have given freedom to China to take advantage in Afghanistan through the SCO. Therefore, Elizabeth Wishnick's remarks seem untenable. Jagannath P. Panda feels that China has been successfully using the SCO for furthering its own economic interests.[18] According to him, three factors coincide in this emerging relationship: withdrawal of US troops from Afghanistan; the SCO's tenth anniversary; and the debate about expanding the SCO's mandate and membership. Although China shares only a 46-mile long border with Afghanistan, Chinese investment in that country is increasing consistently to exploit Afghanistan's energy and mineral resources. Yet, going beyond the conventional strategy of engaging

Afghanistan bilaterally, Beijing is considering an alternative SCO-based approach that could ease regional concerns while still serving Chinese interests. While Afghanistan has been keen to join the SCO as an observer, China has been keen to receive Afghanistan. This is not surprising given Afghanistan's geopolitical situation at a time when the SCO is on the verge of expansion. Notably, most of Afghanistan's neighbours are either SCO members or observers. Beijing—at least, according to Sun Weidong, the Deputy Director-General of the Ministry of Foreign Affairs (MFA) Asian Department—envisions that the SCO should play a bigger and productive role in Afghanistan's reconstruction process.[19] In Beijing's formulation, Afghanistan is a vitally strategic location that connects South Asia and Central Asia and that both China and the SCO must take seriously. Establishing closer linkages with the region through the SCO-Afghanistan Contact Group is one such method. China understands this group is an interesting SCO initiative, which could be used to discuss various security issues beyond the Sino-Afghan bilateral framework. Seeing this initiative as an opportunity to strengthen institutional linkages within the region, Zhang Deguang, the first SCO Secretary-General, hoped the SCO would work with this group to address the Afghanistan issue.[20]

Beijing's current focus is to integrate the region economically with China's west by prevailing over Central Asian reservations to remove trade barriers. To resolve these, China may opt for multilateral engagement with Afghanistan through the SCO rather than only relying on bilateral contacts. Interactions with Chinese experts give the impression that if the SCO's mandate and membership expands, Beijing would like to use the SCO to influence Afghanistan. Chinese foreign policymakers are well aware of the strategic opportunities and challenges Afghanistan offers after the US troop withdrawal. To seize those opportunities, "multiple considerations" are being considered in China currently. One of those considerations is how to employ Afghanistan as a common factor for a broader Central Asia and South Asia policy. The reference point for the Chinese here again remains the US. Chinese experts are concerned about the US's proposal of tying Central Asia and South Asia together through trade and energy corridors.[21] While China would prefer to develop a similar strategy like that of the US, the most appropriate option for the Chinese at the moment seems to be the establishment of a strong connection between Central Asia and South Asia by granting SCO membership to Afghanistan. Hence, SCO expansion is a matter of utmost importance in China today.

Afghanistan and SCO

Afghanistan, while not being an observer, is currently a part of the SCO-Afghanistan Contact Group. The Contact Group was established in 2005, and serves as a mechanism for SCO member-states to jointly contribute to the reconstruction and stability of Afghanistan. In June 2011 Russia decided to support Afghanistan for observer status. In October 2011, Russian Ambassador in Kabul explained that Moscow supports Afghanistan's bid for becoming a member-state. In the Beijing conference on January 7, 2002, the SCO issued a joint statement which indicates that it was concerned about the events in Afghanistan since the Bonn 2001 Conference.[2] The important statements made were as follows:

- The SCO member-states fully support the measures provided by UN Security Council Resolutions 1373, 1377, 1383 and 1386 and engage in full-scale cooperation with the Counter-Terrorism Committee of the Security Council, established by Resolution 1373.
- We want Afghanistan to become a peaceful and neutral state respecting and observing human rights and basic freedoms, maintaining friendly relations with all neighbour countries and complying with its international obligations.
- The SCO member-states support the Bonn Agreement of December 5, 2001, and the efforts by the Afghan people to establish a widely representative authority with the participation of the various ethnic groups. We will render vigorous support to the Interim Administration of Afghanistan.
- At the same time we believe that only the first step has been made on the difficult road of a post-crisis dispensation in Afghanistan. We call upon the international community to cooperate within the UN with a view to preventing a new destabilisation of the situation in Afghanistan that could jeopardise the process of political settlement.
- The determination of a future political dispensation in Afghanistan, and the choice of a structure and character of the bodies of power is an inalienable right of the Afghan people itself. All members of the international community should respect the sovereignty, territorial integrity and state unity of Afghanistan and avoid any interference in its internal affairs, thus creating favourable external conditions for the normal development of Afghan society. Any attempts to impose on Afghanistan some or other forms of government and the drawing of the country into the sphere of somebody's influence may lead to a new crisis in and around Afghanistan.

- The operations of the International Security Assistance Force (ISAF) should be carried out in accordance with the UN Security Council mandate and with the consent of the lawful authorities of Afghanistan.
- The SCO member-states are unanimous in the view that the leading role in the international struggle against terrorism belongs to the UN and its Security Council. All anti-terrorist operations should be in line with the purposes and principles of the UN Charter and other universally recognised rules of international law, their scope may not be extended arbitrarily, and they must not be accompanied by interference in the internal affairs of sovereign states.
- The SCO is ready for a constructive dialogue and cooperation with the Interim Administration of Afghanistan and future Afghan power structures and calls upon the lawful Afghan leaders to closely cooperate with the SCO.

From the above discussion, we may broadly understand that SCO is mainly inspired and driven by China and Russia. It aims to balance and even counter the American influence not only in terms of NATO in the Eurasian region but also in Afghanistan. As the SCO is dominated by China and Russia, their respective interests seem to be somewhat different. Russia's main concern has been to contain the American and NATO influence in Afghanistan since 2001. It is also concerned with the likely outcome after the NATO-dominated ISAF withdraws after 2014.

Afghanistan is concerned about the likely situation after 2014 and is aware of its dependence on China for investment not only in the energy sector but also in infrastructure. Through the SCO, Afghanistan can have the assistance of China and Russia without any negativity from the US or countries like India. Moreover, it can tackle the Jihadi elements operating from the Af-Pak region with Chinese support. Therefore, Afghanistan needs SCO both for Chinese investment and for strategically balancing Pakistan.

In early November 2011, an Afghan delegation led by the Vice-President of the Islamic Republic of Afghanistan, Karim Khalili, visited St. Petersburg and participated in the summit of the SCO as a guest. In St. Petersburg, Karim Khalili held separate talks with Russian Prime Minister, Vladimir Putin, Kazakh Prime Minister, Karim Masimov, and the heads of delegations from Uzbekistan, Kyrgyzstan and several other countries. During the summit, Vladimir Putin urged the SCO member-countries to render assistance to Afghanistan which is in trouble. He also expressed Russia's readiness to assist Kabul to strengthen its borders and promote agriculture. Notably, the Vice-President formally called on the SCO member-countries to grant Afghanistan the observer status of this prestigious organisation. Russia supported Afghanistan's bid to join the SCO. It was emphasised that earlier, Afghanistan's admission to the SCO was discussed with the Chinese officials.

In August, a memorandum on cooperation in the fuel and energy sector was signed. In November, under agreements concluded between the oil and gas departments of Afghanistan's Ministry of Commerce and Industry and Russia's state-run Gazprom-Neft Company, a contract was signed to supply 10,000 tons of oil products to Afghanistan. The supply of Russian oil products ahead of the winter is very important for Afghanistan. This not only reduces Afghanistan's energy dependence on other countries but also gives the Afghan government an opportunity to establish price control on the country's fuel and lubricants market by market-control methods. Moreover, most importantly, the SCO summit in St. Petersburg declared the creation of an SCO bank which would finance concrete infrastructural projects in Afghanistan.[22]

Afghanistan is keen to forge a relationship with the SCO although right now Afghanistan's foreign affairs do not have any official engagement with the SCO as an organisation. This is obvious because it has not yet obtained observer status. The official website of the Ministry of Foreign Affairs of Afghanistan, in its policy areas, lists the EU, NATO, the US and the Islamic World, but SCO is a notable omission.[23] However, the statements by Hamid Karzai at the 10th Summit of the Heads of State of the SCO at Astana, Kazakhstan in June 14-15, 2011, reveals Afghanistan's anxieties and interests:

> In Afghanistan, we have been pursuing peace and reconciliation with those Taliban who are ready to sever their association with terrorist groups and accept the Afghan Constitution. We look for the support of the SCO Members and Observers in the pursuit of this endeavour.
>
> At present, Afghanistan is going through a transition; this process will see Afghan security forces taking responsibility, in an incremental manner, from the US and NATO forces. We are determined to take full responsibility of our security by 2014. This will allow the military forces of our international partners to withdraw from Afghanistan.
>
> Afghanistan's long-term stability and economic development will, however, require the support and cooperation of the international community well beyond 2014. In this context, we are negotiating long-term negotiations and comprehensive partnerships with our regional and international partners, including the United States of America.

At the same time, it is the wish of the Afghan people that the presence of the United States and other NATO/ISAF forces in our country be regulated. We are a sovereign country and it is natural that the laws enforced in Afghanistan be those of Afghanistan. We are working to ensure that the presence of all NATO/ISAF forces adhere to our national laws and the requirements of a sovereign nation.

In our bilateral and multilateral discussions with the United States and NATO, we are mindful of the regional dimensions, as well as the concerns of our neighbours. We will not enter into a partnership if we have reason to believe that it might jeopardise the security of our neighbours or that of our region.

We see our future deeply rooted in this region. Our region has enormous potential to grow. Some among us, such as China, India and Russia, are experiencing extraordinary growth rates in their economies and standards of living. These nations can and should serve as the engines of growth for the rest of the region. We highly appreciate Chinese investment in our copper mines. We invite all our friends and partners to follow China's example in investing in our economy.

Over the past decade, we have focused on expanding our bilateral relations with each of the SCO member-states.

Our friendly relations are solidly rooted in the cultural, historical and economic ties that have flourished among us over centuries. We believe that these bonds can be nurtured and further strengthened under the SCO framework. We have valued our presence at the SCO as a guest country for the past years. Today, we seek to become an observer in this important forum. We hope that the Council of Heads of State of SCO would respond positively to our request. I thank the Russian Federation for encouraging us to take this step. I also deeply appreciate the support already expressed by other SCO members in this regard.

The future holds tremendous opportunities for prosperity and well-being for all of us. Solidarity and partnership must be the foundations of our shared future. Afghanistan stands ready to cooperate with the SCO to unlock our collective potentials and achieve a better, safer, and more prosperous region.[24]

The above statements make it obvious that Afghanistan is assuring the SCO that the Afghans would not like to rely solely on the US and the international community, but on the SCO for the political, economic, and strategic benefits in the future. Afghanistan also made it clear that it is a part of Asia and wishes to be a strong component of the SCO.

Conclusion

In a post-Bonn conference environment, the SCO is likely to play a key role in the political, economic, security and strategic future of Afghanistan. The main players in the SCO, namely China and Russia, are uncomfortable with the post-NATO withdrawal scenario in Afghanistan. If NATO and the Americans withdraw, then both Russia and China can play a meaningful role in Afghanistan. The Chinese policy of not committing troops to the ISAF, not publicly opposing the US presence, and in fact, using the US presence for its own security in trade and business establishments is unique. Though China's main agenda seems to be economic in Afghanistan, it does want to play a dominant role there through the SCO. Afghanistan on its part only welcomes the SCO in the post-NATO scenario, not only for the economic benefits but also to tackle its own problems of border security, Jihadi attacks from the Af-Pak region as well as to compensate for the absence of the US and the international community. Therefore, it offers a win-win situation for Afghanistan, China and the SCO.

Notes

1. For a brief history, nature and purpose of SCO see Enrico Fels, *Assessing Eurasia's Powerhouse: An Inquiry into the Nature of the Shanghai Cooperation Organisation* (Bochum: Winkler Verlag, 2009); Sznajder Ariel Pablo, *China's Shanghai Cooperation Organisation Strategy* (University of California Press, 2006); Sean L. Yom, "Power Politics in Central Asia: The Future of the Shanghai Cooperation Organisation," *Harvard Asia Quarterly,* 6 (4), 200, pp. 48-54.
2. Joint Statement of the SCO in 2002 at http://english.chinamil.com.cn/special/5army/txt/5.htm.
3. Dmitry Saveliev, "Hamid Karzai's visit to Moscow: Time for economic diplomacy," January 25, 2011 at http://en.afghanistan.ru/doc/213.html.
4. Nicklas Norling, "The Emerging China-Afghanistan Relationship," *The Central Asia-Caucasus Analyst,* May 14, 2008 at http://old.cacianalyst.org/?q=node/4858.
5. Ibid.
6. Adrienne Mong, "Resource-hungry China heads to Afghanistan," *NBC News* at http://worldblog.msnbc.com/news/2009/10/14/.
7. Christian Le Mière, "Kabul's New Patron? The Growing Afghan-Chinese Relationship," *Foreign Affairs*, April 13, 2010 at http://www.foreignaffairs.com/articles/66194/christian-le-miere/kabuls-new-patron.
8. Ibid.
9. Ibid.
10. Christian Le Mière, no. 7.
11. Richard Weitz, "Is China freeloading off the US Military's Work in Afghanistan and Iraq?" *Huffington Post*, August 15, 2011 at http://www.huffingtonpost.com/2011/08/15/.
12. Ibid.
13. Ibid.
14. Ibid.

15. Patrick Quinn, "Afghanistan, China sign first contract to develop northwestern oil blocks," *Associated Press*, December 28, 2011.
16. Lecture by Elizabeth Wishnick, "China's Afghanistan Policy and Implications for US-China-Afghanistan Relations," Weatherhead East Asian Institute at Columbia University, October 30, 2011 at http://globalcenters.columbia.edu/eastasia/2011.
17. Ibid.
18. Jagannath P. Panda, "China or the SCO: Who will supervise Afghanistan?" *China Brief*, The Jamestown Foundation, 11 (15), August 17, 2011 at http://global-security-news.com/2011/08/17/.
19. *Khaleej Times*, June 8, 2010, cited in Jagannath P. Panda, no. 18.
20. *China Daily*, February 4, 2010, cited in Jagannath P. Panda, no.18.
21. *Beijing Review*, July 21, 2011, cited in Jagannath P. Panda, no. 18.
22. Mohammad Khaism, "Afghanistan and SCO are coming closer," November 18, 2011 at http://en.afghanistan.ru/doc/284.html.
23. For foreign policy of Afghanistan in general and with the regional organisations, see the official website of Afghanistan at http://mfa.gov.af/en/page/3873#rc.
24. See http://www.gmic.gov.af/english/index.php/features/241.

13. India in Afghanistan: The Saga of India's Role in Afghanistan's Political Future

Yow Peter Raiphea

Introduction

The fall of the Taliban and the Bonn Agreement paved the way for Afghan groups to form an interim government under the leadership of Hamid Karzai in 2001 in Afghanistan. On December 22, 2001, India's Minister for External Affairs, Jaswant Singh visited Afghanistan and participated in Karzai's inauguration and reopened the Indian Embassy that was closed on the eve of the Taliban's seizure of Kabul in 1996. Since then, India has been able to steadily re-establish its presence in Afghanistan while engaging there under the United States (US) and the North Atlantic Treaty Organisation (NATO) security umbrella. India has always been enthusiastic and worked for the establishment of a stable and durable government in Afghanistan which would not only serve the best interests of the region, but the interests of all ethnic communities living inside Afghanistan. India's concerns and efforts have been appreciated by Afghanistan and some neighbouring countries. This chapter attempts to examine the role of India in Afghanistan's reconstruction and developmental activities. It will also look into the question as to why India should think of any possible political future for Afghanistan (to build a peaceful, prosperous and stable democratic country for Afghanistan), which direction India should take and the means India should use in order to direct Afghanistan out of its present spell of uncertainty.

Since the terrorist attacks of September 11, 2001, which we now refer to by the widely accepted designation "9/11," the policies of the US and its allies have been dominated by the threat of terrorism. The attack destroyed the World Trade Centre (WTC) in New York and a wing of the Pentagon in Washington, killing thousands of Americans and citizens of about 60 other countries.[1] The attacks mobilised support for the US by a very broad coalition of states, out of a realisation that terrorism threatens the interstate system itself. President George W. Bush, Jr. declared a "war on terrorism" that was expected to last years and span continents, employing both conventional and unconventional means. The US administration suspected that Al Qaeda operating from Afghan soil was behind the WTC attack. In late 2001, US-led coalition forces and their Afghan allies ousted the Taliban regime in Afghanistan which had harboured and supported the Al Qaeda network (led by Osama bin Laden) responsible for the attacks on the US.[2]

The subsequent fall of the Taliban paved the way for mending bilateral relations between India and Afghanistan which was at a low ebb in the 1990s during the Taliban era following the ouster of the Rabbani government in September 1996. With the help of the international community, the United Nations (UN) called a conference at Bonn, Germany. The Conference led to the formation of an interim government under the leadership of Hamid Karzai.[3] On December 22, 2001, India's Minister for External Affairs, Jaswant Singh visited Afghanistan and participated in Karzai's inauguration and reopened the Indian Embassy that had been closed on the eve of the Taliban's seizure of Kabul in 1996. Since then, India has been able to steadily re-establish its presence in Afghanistan while engaging there under the US and NATO security umbrella.[4]

Ambivalent complexities emerged in the aftermath of 9/11 in the domestic affairs of Afghanistan. "With the intervention of the international community, Afghanistan has only just emerged from the dark years of a reactionary, medieval and fundamentalist regime essentially created by Pakistan."[5] While the new government has international legitimacy, the task of reconstruction and rebuilding the institutions is formidable. Afghanistan today is at the crossroads with diversified changes in all its politico-socio-structural conditions which calls for multitude of interactions within and across her geographical boundaries. Afghanistan has remained the focal point of Indian regional policy because of its geostrategic location, neighbouring Iran, Pakistan and the Central Asian Republics. A rapid progress for democratisation has begun in Afghanistan since the Bonn Agreement was signed in December 2001 by representatives of various Afghan factions, excluding the Taliban. At the conclusion of the UN-sponsored Bonn Conference on Afghanistan, political and institutional reconstruction in Afghanistan faced daunting hurdles. Scholars and policymakers opined that institutions must be developed at the national, regional and local levels, and a means for interface among these institutions—and between them and an array of international actors—must be created. India joined the international efforts of post-war reconstruction process and economic development and engaged in Afghanistan in diverse areas.

India's Engagements in Afghanistan: Role and Challenges

India and Afghanistan are geographical neighbours and remained so till 1947 when Pakistan was formed. They have established a strong relationship based on their historical and civilisational relations which, in the post-9/11 period, have been strengthened by India's role in the reconstruction of Afghanistan. The principal objective of India's development partnership, covering the entire Afghanistan and all sectors of development, is to build indigenous Afghan capacity and institutions. India has played an active role in the development of Afghanistan based on the understanding that social and economic development is the key to Afghanistan becoming a source of regional stability.[6] India's pledged assistance to Afghanistan's reconstruction and nation-building in diverse sectors stands at US$ 2 billion and is the sixth largest bilateral donation to Afghanistan[7] (India is the largest regional provider of aid for Afghanistan). All the projects are undertaken in partnership with the Afghan government, in complete alignment with the Afghanistan National Development Strategy. India's engagements in Afghanistan cover four broad areas—infrastructure projects, humanitarian assistance, small and community-based development projects, and education and capacity development. The 218 km road project from Zaranj to Delaram in south-western Afghanistan to facilitate movement of goods and services to the Iranian border and onward to the Chahbahar Port was inaugurated by the Afghan President and the Indian External Affairs Minister in January 2009. India constructed a 202 km 220 KV DC transmission line from Pul-e-Khumri to Kabul and a substation at Chimtala bringing Uzbek electricity and lighting up the city of Kabul throughout the year. This project was completed in collaboration with the Afghan government, Asian Development Bank (ADB) and the World Bank, with inputs from the United States Agency for International Development (USAID) and international energy firms, and was an outstanding example of regional and international cooperation in Afghanistan. The other two major infrastructure projects, the construction of the Afghan Parliament in Kabul and the construction of Salma Dam power project in Herat province are in progress.[8]

For humanitarian assistance, India supplies 100 gm of fortified, high-protein biscuits to nearly two million schoolchildren in 33 of the 34 provinces of Afghanistan every day under a School Feeding Programme administered through the World Food Programme. During the visit of President Karzai to India in January 2009, India announced a gift of 250,000 metric tonnes of wheat to assist Afghanistan in overcoming its food shortage. The Indian medical missions are providing free medical consultations and medicines to over 30,000 Afghans every month.[9]

In August 2005, during Prime Minister Dr. Manmohan Singh's visit to Afghanistan, an innovative scheme focusing on small and community-based development projects, with a short gestation period and having a direct impact on community life, was unveiled. So far, 101 such projects with emphasis on local ownership and management in the field of agriculture, rural development, education, health, vocational training, and solar energy have been initiated.[10]

In education and institution development, India is providing 675 (increased to 1,000 in 2011) annual long-term university scholarships sponsored by the Indian Council for Cultural Relations (ICCR) for undergraduate and postgraduate studies for Afghan students, especially encouraging women students to avail of the additional slots in India. Similarly, another 675 annual short-term India Technical and Educational Cooperation (ITEC) training scholarships for Afghan public servants are provided in Indian technical and professional institutions. More than 20 Indian civil servants served as coaches and mentors under the Capacity for Afghan Public Administration Programme supported by the United Nations Development Programme (UNDP) and the Governments of Afghanistan and India. The Confederation of Indian Industry (CII) built an India-Afghanistan vocational training centre for training Afghan youth in carpentry, plumbing, welding, masonry and tailoring. Another innovative programme was executed by the well-known Indian non-government organisation (NGO) called SEWA (Self-Employed Women's Association), which built a Women's Vocational Training Centre in *Bagh-e-Zanana* in Kabul for training Afghan women (war widows and orphans) in garment making, creation of plant nurseries, and food processing and marketing.[11]

Capacity building programmes are also under way in the fields of diplomacy, media and information, civil aviation, agricultural research and education, health care and medicine, tourism, education, standardisation, rural development, public administration, electoral management and administration and local governance. Besides these, India is involved in reconstruction of the Indira Gandhi Institute of Child Health and Habibia School in Kabul. India has assisted in expansion of the Afghan National TV network by providing an uplink from Kabul and downlinks in all 34 provincial capitals for promoting greater connectivity. It has also gifted around 1,000 vehicles including buses, utility vehicles and ambulances to Afghanistan.

Agriculture being the key to the development of Afghanistan, India announced at the London Conference in January 2010, 100 fellowships for Masters and PhD programmes for existing faculty members and another 200 for fresh graduates each year for the next five years to assist in faculty and student development in the agricultural sector. To build indigenous Afghan capacity and institutions, India also announced its strong support to the proposed Afghan National Institution Building Project of the UNDP.[12]

Indian Prime Minister Dr. Manmohan Singh visited Afghanistan in May 2011, re-emphasising commitment to regional stability and Afghan development. In significant developments, emphasising the Treaty of Friendship between the Government of India and the Royal Government of Afghanistan of January 4, 1950, the resolve to draft a Strategic Partnership document was declared. As of now, a Strategic Economic Partnership has been established which would operate through the mechanism of a Partnership Council led by the two foreign ministers, and comprise Joint Working Groups in various fields, including education and human resource capacity building, people-to-people exchanges, regional economic cooperation and cooperation in the area of security and law enforcement.

Moreover, additional assistance to Afghanistan in term of a fresh package of US$ 500 million was announced by the Prime Minister during his visit to Afghanistan, taking India's existing commitments to the reconstruction and development of Afghanistan from a financial outlay of close to US$ 1.5 billion to $ 2 billion. This underlines India's undiluted commitment to the efforts of the government and people of Afghanistan to build a peaceful, prosperous and stable country. Indian engagements in Afghanistan have been guided by the principle of providing a safe, stable and secure Afghanistan, free from the threat of international terrorism or a base for global terrorists. The following are the aid commitments made during the visit:

- A fresh commitment of US$ 100 million for the third phase of India's programme of Small Development Projects, over and above the previous pledge of US$ 20 million;
- Donation of 1,000 buses for the Kabul and other municipalities with provision for maintenance support, training and infrastructure;
- A medical package consisting of the treatment of Afghan patients in select disciplines and hospitals in India over the next three years to be implemented through the Afghan Ministry of Public Health; the rehabilitation and professional upgradation of the National Malaria and Leishmaniasis Centre of Afghanistan; and the upgradation of the Indira Gandhi Institute of Child Health, including the neo-natal and maternal care unit;
- Upgradation of the agricultural department at the Kabul University to an agricultural university and providing scholarships for the study of agricultural sciences.
- Donation of 500 tractors for Afghan farmers; Provision of seeds and other assistance for the agricultural sector;

- The early finalisation of a US$ 50 million Buyers Credit Line to promote exports and attract Indian business to Afghanistan;
- A grant of US$ 10 million for the preservation and revival of Afghanistan's archaeological and cultural heritage and cultural exchanges;
- A grant of US$ 4 million to the Government of Afghanistan for the restoration of the historic Stor Palace in Kabul.
- Assistance in setting up an Afghan Institute of Mining.
- An enhancement of ICCR scholarships for students from 675 to 1,000 with a special focus on encouraging women students to avail of the additional slots;
- Assistance in setting up of a computer laboratory at Habibia School.[13]

While there are over 4,000 Indians working in Afghanistan on various projects, the main threat is to the Embassy in Kabul and the Consulates in Jalalabad which are under constant pressure and despite the increase in security measures are highly vulnerable. The threats to Indians in Afghanistan are therefore likely to increase. As the Afghanistan National Intelligence Agency spokesperson Lutfullah Mashal indicated with reference to the failed attempt on the Indian Consul-General of Jalalabad province, "Well, these two guys have very clearly confessed that they were hired by the Inter-Services Intelligence (ISI), they were paid by ISI and they were promised that if they killed the Indian Consul-General, they will be paid 1.20 lacs, which is a big amount of money in Afghanistan." The vulnerability of Indian assets is therefore likely to remain high.

India has genuine interests in a stable Afghanistan. It has chosen to be an important partner in reconstruction efforts having committed US$ 2 billion in economic assistance and reconstruction. But its political influence has been minimal. Since 2002, the Taliban have been vociferously demanding the departure of Indians involved in developmental activity, and these demands have been followed up with threats and action. The nature of attacks on Indian targets has varied from abduction and beheading to suicide attacks. In the wake of the attack on the Indian Embassy, the Afghan interior ministry has unambiguously stated that the attack was carried out "in coordination and consultation with an active intelligence service in the region,"[14] an obvious reference to the role of the Pakistani ISI. It appears that India's involvement in reconstruction of conflict-ridden Afghanistan has not been to the liking of the Taliban-Al Qaeda combine and their sponsors. Moreover, Pakistan continually points to the presence of Indian Consulates in the proximity of the Afghan-Pakistan border as a source of destabilisation in its territory.[15] But it is not in India's interest to see Afghanistan becoming a breeding ground for terrorism, particularly under Pakistan's dominance because of its geographical proximity and the possibility of exporting terrorism to India.

Against all odds, India has been keenly interested in the reconstruction and developmental activities in Afghanistan. Pakistan views India's growing influence in Afghanistan as a threat to its own interest in the region.[16] For Pakistan, the Taliban offers the best chance for countering India's regional influence. Pakistan's support for the Taliban has led to increased instability in Afghanistan, from the growth of terrorism to increased opium cultivation.[17]

Indian presence in Afghanistan through development and reconstruction activities is likely to continue for some time. India will have to expand leverages and defuse regional apprehensions while Pakistan plays the China card, and Iran, Russia, Central Asian Republics also pitch in with their own take. A reality check based on facts would also reveal that there is a considerable improvement in the security situation in the country including the North, where the spread of the insurgency is contained. Recent attacks by the Taliban in large numbers in Kandahar and Nuristan have been very effectively neutralised by the Afghan National Army and Afghan National Police, though there is a long way to go. At the end of the day, till the Afghans can stand up on their own, the familiar great game in different forms will continue. Therefore, India needs to carve out its own strategic space for linkage or access to Central Asia that the Pakistanis and Chinese have been denying to India. The fact that India does not have contiguous borders with Afghanistan puts India into a dependency mode.[18] India has several options that it can and must exercise given her material capacity and status of the most powerful country in the region and emerging great power on the world stage which can be beneficial for both Afghanistan and the region in the long run. Thus, Indian innovative and proactive engagements should continue as India's foreign policy dynamics towards Afghanistan and the region. India's big challenge is to see how it can help Afghanistan to rebuild with limited resources. Though the basic infrastructure to support the rebuilding initiatives of the Government of Afghanistan is built through donor assistance, the main challenge that will still remain would be its transparent and corruption-free maintenance, upkeep and management for its long-term sustainability and viability.

Afghan Socio-Political Universe

In order to understand the socio-political universe[19] of Afghanistan at present, we need to go back to the societal set-ups and its power relations of the past. Amin Saikal in his book, *Modern Afghanistan: A History of Struggle and Survival*, argues and brings out clearly how Afghanistan's politics and society in modern history have been shaped by interaction between variables of *royal polygamy*, *major power rivalry* and *ideological extremism*, with which few other countries have had to cope. He concludes that the confluence of these variables, in conjunction with certain peculiar geostrategic aspects of Afghanistan as a traditional, ethno-tribal and a mountainous land, a large part of which is too dry and rocky for cultivation, and which is a landlocked Muslim country, has played a determining role in the evolution of the Afghan state and politics and in influencing the material life and psyche of its citizens as well as the country's relevance to the outside world.[20]

B. D. Hopkins[21] in his book, *The Making of Modern Afghanistan*, concludes that the three idioms defining the Afghan political universe, to which they turned, were tribe, Islam and royalism. These were the normative orders on which political authority rested, representing what David Edwards has termed the "moral fault lines" of the Afghan political community. Amin Saikal also argued that the three variables have undoubtedly been the subject of much scholarly research and writing. But this has been conducted with a focus on them individually, rather than in an integrative manner. This emphasises the primacy of intersection between royal polygamist power struggles and major power rivalries and interventions as contributing centrally to the kind of conditions which have kept the Afghan state weak and vulnerable to ideological extremism. A significant outcome of Afghanistan's historical journey has taken a very turbulent and violent path punctuated by only one long period of relative peace and stability, that is 1930-1978.[22]

P. C. Yadav's *Soviet Intervention in Afghanistan*[23] clearly dealt with the role of tribal chiefs, feudal lords and the clergy which form the political universe of the Afghans. Administratively, Afghanistan was organised into provinces each under a governor. The appointment of the provincial governors by the Afghan Government notwithstanding, the authority of the State was practically non-existent outside of the main cities and towns. The real population had been unaware of any authority except that of tribal chiefs, feudal lords and the clergy who did not care much for the government in Kabul. As they had a nominal existence, the provincial governors had no authority or say in the running of the administration. The local tribal chieftains were the *de facto* autonomous rulers in their respective areas. The legislative institution of pre-revolutionary Afghanistan was the Loya Jirga (the Great Assembly), comprising nominated members whose only qualifications were relationship with the court or traditional influence.

After the First World War, both King Amanullah and the Bolshevik regime were striving for international recognition. The Union of Soviet

Socialist Republics (USSR) was the first country to recognise Afghanistan as a sovereign nation and its action was reciprocated by Afghanistan. While Afghanistan was aspiring for nationhood, it was yet to mature into effective statehood. King Amanullah wanted to modernise the socially and economically primitive Afghanistan. He introduced social reforms, a new code of laws and educational reforms on secular lines. Education and equality for women was anathema to the backward society of Afghanistan dominated by such vested interests as tribal chiefs, feudal lords and the mullahs.

Amanullah's well-intentioned schemes could not be sustained by the weak economy of Afghanistan. Even the expenditure of royal court burdened the country's meagre finances. This added to a long list of grievances. The primitive social milieu of Afghanistan was not conducive to these reforms. The leaders interpreted these reforms to be a violation of Islam. These leaders organised a rebellion against Amanullah Khan. Amanullah was compelled to meet various tribal chieftains and was forced to yield to conservative demands in the Loya Jirga. He was compelled to forgo social reforms and interference in the affairs of individual tribes. In order to satisfy the rebels some of the new laws were withdrawn. This was a blow to the Amir's prestige.[24] Amanullah established diplomatic relations with other nations. In spite of his forced retreat in the matter of social reforms, he continued to strive for the modernisation of Afghanistan. But he failed to develop an independent and cohesive army for imposing national unity. The army was faction-ridden by rivalry and it could not develop primary allegiance to him. This was essential because change breeds tremendous resistance in the modernisation of a primitive set-up. The lack of a substantial degree of unity and absence of central authority over Afghanistan, coupled with increasing opposition of religious leaders and tribal chieftains to the social reforms of Amanullah, added to the general unrest which ultimately led to an open rebellion by the vested interest holders. This time the king could not contain the rebellion. The religious elements decried that the reforms were anti-Islamic. Thus, the resistance movement was given religious colour and sanction.[25]

Ahmed Shah Abdali, who is generally considered the founder of modern Afghanistan, made a promising start. In a quarter of a century of Ahmed Shah's patrimonial, centralised and charismatic rule, not only had Afghanistan crystallised as a political and territorial entity, but it had also developed a number of political and institutional practices which laid the foundations for the growth of a central authority with some distributive and administrative attributes. What substantially thwarted the progress of this state beyond what had crystallised under Ahmed Shah was not the fact that the micro-societies successfully revolted against the Centre and one another resulting in an internal breakdown, but rather that Afghanistan witnessed a fragmentation of power, largely due to dynamic interaction between royal polygamist power struggles and outside power[26] rivalries over Afghanistan. Indeed, the Afghan polygamist fragmentation of power would not have attracted much outside attention had it not been accompanied by certain geostrategic imperatives.

Though we may not completely agree with the above socio-political universe of Afghanistan to be as effective as bygone years and the recent past, the truth is that the established social order and norms that have shaped their political behaviour has resulted in the present stalemate and uncertainty in Afghanistan and will continue to shape the political future of Afghanistan in the years to come. Thus, Amin Ṣaikal's interaction between variables of *royal polygamy*, *major power rivalry* and *ideological extremism*, D. Hopkins' three idioms defining the Afghan political universe, tribe, Islam and royalism, and P. C. Kapur's idea of tribal chiefs, feudal lords and the clergy forming the political universe—need to be taken into account when we look for a policy option for a better, stable, prosperous, democratic Afghanistan. To substantiate their importance it may be noted that the British failure of 1842 was a consequence of a series of policy miscalculations themselves caused by a poor institutional understanding of the Afghan political unity.[27] Due to Afghanistan's role as a transit corridor linking the economies of West, Central, East and South Asia, outside forces are at times responsible for internal discord in Afghanistan. I. P. Khosla writes that Afghanistan's immediate neighbours, and the more distant powers that could play a role in this matter, have no particular self-interest in ensuring Afghan unity. The latter especially have presided over the break-up of other nations. Their interests in Afghanistan lie in another direction, that of a global geostrategic entity, and may neither be adversely affected nor would benefit from such a break-up. Given the equation of Afghanistan's global geostrategy, it is necessary that Afghanistan be enabled to play its due role in the South Asian region. He further observes that the spirit of nationalism and the political desire for unity among all the tribes and ethnic groups have been dominant through its history of the last two and a half centuries.[28]

Afghanistan's Political Future and India's Options

Following September 11, 2001 and the beginning of the global war on terror with full American political and military and international support, the Taliban was ousted in Afghanistan. The US and its allies, especially Britain, pledged not to leave Afghanistan in the lurch again as had happened after the Soviet intervention in Afghanistan.[29] History is a great teacher for the world. They promised to do everything possible to help the Afghans to reconstruct their county, and achieve peace and stability, with a lasting "democratic" order, as soon as possible, so that the country would never again become a source of international terrorism. The Karzai government initially came into existence as an interim administration for six months, starting from December 22, 2001. It originated from the Bonn Agreement of 2001, signed between the United Islamic Front for the Salvation of Afghanistan, led by the forces associated with the late Ahmad Shah Massoud, the Zahir Shah group, and two smaller Pashtun groups. Under the Bonn Agreement, in whose formulation the UN and the US, as well as Germany, played a critical role, Karzai was appointed as a compromise choice to head the Interim Administration, one of whose central tasks being to convene an Emergency Loya Jirga to appoint an 18-month-long Transitional Administration to pave the way for holding a general election for the creation of a popularly-mandated regular government. In the meantime, whereas the US established bases in Afghanistan to stamp out the remnants of the Taliban and Al Qaeda and help America's anti-terror operations beyond Afghanistan—again as provisioned in the Bonn Agreement—an International Security Assistance Force (ISAF) was deployed in Kabul to protect the Karzai government and maintain security in the capital. The Emergency Loya Jirga was convened in Kabul from June 11 to 19, 2002. It claimed to be probably the most democratic Loya Jirga ever held in Afghanistan. Over 1,600 delegates, the majority of whom represented various ethnic groups within Afghanistan, participated in the Loya Jirga. Some were appointed by various warlords and power brokers; others came from abroad representing Afghans living around the world. After lively and at times heated debate, an overwhelming majority, 1,295 of the delegates, voted for Karzai as the head of state. Concurrently, the UN—and for that matter the international community—commenced large-scale aid operations to sustain the Karzai government, to rebuild Afghanistan. But Afghanistan's problems are by no means over. On the contrary, the challenges facing the Afghans in building a viable polity, with an assertive, full state sovereignty, are enormous. It may be safe to surmise that Afghanistan is now in the grip of a situation where power still remains seriously fragmented and the American pre-eminence has once again proved that rarely in modern Afghan history has a government come to power and remained in power without a foreign force backing it. The Karzai government has little writ outside Kabul and its authority is limited by various power centres, ranging from local charismatic and religious leaders to armed commanders and warlords in different parts of the country.

Given the fact that US involvement in Afghanistan has been more motivated by America's war on terror than what might be best for the Afghan people in the long run, one cannot but be sceptical of the US's commitment to rebuilding the war-torn country, and empowering the Afghans to run and protect their country independent of any foreign military involvement. There is every chance that Washington will let its Afghan policy be guided more by fluctuations in its war against international terrorism and America's global interests.

The present scenario in Afghanistan is that the Taliban, the fundamentalist regime driven out in 2001, have come back in force. The biggest problem faced by Afghanistan today is the deteriorating security situation concurrently with the rise of regional warlords, increased drug trade and opium cultivation. Both the civilian and military deaths are rising. According to a recent UN report, it is reported that in the first eight months of 2011, the average monthly number of violent incidents in Afghanistan was more than 2,100, a 39 per cent increase from the same period a year earlier. This upsurge in violence, the withdrawal of international security forces; potential negotiations and reconciliation process to seek a peace agreement with the Taliban and the relationship between Afghanistan and other countries after 2014, will determine the fate of this geostrategically significant country.[30]

Amidst these political realities, India has been assisting Afghanistan in diverse areas realising that Afghanistan floundered and fell into a morass because the roots of its economic life had been sapped by Pakistan's policy of restricting its deep-rooted economic, cultural and people-to-people contacts with India to ensure that it can remain Pakistan's economic and strategic backyard.[31] India has a strong interest in ensuring that Afghanistan remains sovereign, stable and united and free from outside influence. India would not want Afghanistan to come under Pakistan's exclusive sphere of influence.[32] India is concerned about the revival of the Taliban which their sponsors have always used for cross-border terrorism and deny India's interests in Afghanistan. India's policy supports the unity, independence, integrity and sovereignty of Afghanistan. It wants a strong and stable Afghanistan which would naturally, given its geostrategic location and socio-economic composition, be on friendly relations with the US and contribute to peace and security in the region.[33] In his article, "Afghanistan on the Brink: Alternative Futures," and taking into account various ground realities in Afghanistan and the role of various national and international actors, Arun Sahgal writes that, "Afghanistan's future remains largely dependent on US strategies, developments in Pakistan and the manner in which reconciliation between moderates and radicals is structured." He asserts that the Pakistani military establishment is convinced that Western forces lack commitment as well as resolve for a sustained fight and is waiting to reclaim its strategic depth in Afghanistan after their eventual withdrawal. It is therefore going to be catastrophic if the US and NATO rely on Pakistan to fight the Taliban and settle Afghanistan's political uncertainty when Pakistan itself is reeling under multiple terror attacks as a backlash from its failed policies of supporting jihadi terror groups. When the Western coalition withdraw from Afghanistan the Taliban is more likely to act autonomously, throwing more challenges to Pakistan, the region itself and the international community.[34]

Given Afghanistan's geostrategic importance due to the fact that it is surrounded in the north by Tajikistan, Uzbekistan and Turkmenistan, in the west by Iran, in the south and east by Pakistan together with a short common border in the east with China, it is time for India to consider other policy options for a stable and durable peace in Afghanistan besides the soft option of development assistance. Therefore, establishing contacts with important domestic players in Afghanistan is imperative. Understanding its unique socio-political universe as discussed above and thus forming a regional consensus with key stakeholders like Iran and Russia, talking to China, as well as opening back channels with Pakistan, can determine a peaceful and durable political future for Afghanistan.

Conclusion

Despite the difficult internal situation in Afghanistan, bilaterally, India and Afghanistan achieved significant progress. Indian presence in Afghanistan is now evident and intensive. India has provided generous assistance amounting to US$ 2 billion worth of commitment for Afghanistan's reconstruction and nation-building in diverse sectors. Through various developmental and reconstruction activities India has been playing an innovative and proactive role in bringing durable stability in Afghanistan. In spite of political uncertainty in Afghanistan, adverse security situation for personnel, constrained by geography and the Pakistan factor, India has been carrying out its engagements successfully in Afghanistan. India's objective of current development and reconstruction efforts in Afghanistan is to help build a stable, democratic and prosperous country that contributes to regional and global security. Given Afghanistan's geostrategic importance and the fact that it is the gateway to the energy-rich Central Asian Republics, India's security is deeply affected by what happens in Afghanistan. India should also involve itself in Afghanistan's security in a meaningful way. It must ensure that terrorism and fundamentalist forces which are a common threat for both the countries are defeated. Institutional and capacity building should continue to be India's engagement priorities, as these will in the long-term bring positive development and bilateral goodwill. It is a common view within and outside Afghanistan that the country's future peace and stability rests very much on how rapidly its economic and social life is rebuilt as a precondition to prompting the Afghans to change their culture of the gun to that of peace.

In order to look for a viable political future of Afghanistan from the present political uncertainty, it is important that besides constitutional understanding and institutional state building, national character, topographical, and the socio-political universe of the past needs to be considered. All the factors which form the socio-political universe of Afghanistan need to be examined and given proper autonomy to function without hampering national unity. Moreover, a strong Centre in Kabul should be backed by an independent and cohesive army for imposing and maintaining national unity. We can agree with Amin Saikal that the challenge ahead is to establish an appropriate legal-rational framework and culturally relevant processes and institutions to ensure the development of a governmental system and polity whose operations would be underpinned by principles of public participation, transparency, accountability, administrative-bureaucratic efficiency, social equity, observation of basic human rights, and promotion of merit rather than family connection and ethnic affiliation as the basis for governmental appointments.[35] Therefore, it is required as of now to stress the establishment of the necessary processes and institutions, and above all, building a professional national army and security force. To expand its authority and create national unity, the Karzai government urgently needs to subordinate such individuals to the authority of the central government. Yet, this cannot be done as long as Pakistan's uncontrolled and repeated declaration of support for the new order in Afghanistan continues and is proven ineffective. Moreover, it is necessary that the Afghanistan-Pakistan border remains controlled and settled through necessary bilateral arrangements with international assistance.

Notes

1. Aijaz Ahmad, *Iraq, Afghanistan and the Imperialsm of our Time* (New Delhi: Left Word Books, 2005), p. x.
2. Joshua S. Goldstein, *International Relations* (New Delhi: Dorling Kindersley, 2006), pp. 72-73.
3. Sven Gunnar Simonsen, "Ethnicising Afghanistan: Inclusion and Exclusion in Post-Bonn Institution Building," *Third World Quarterly*, 25 (4), 2004, p. 712.
4. C. Christine Fair, "Under the Shrinking US Security Umbrella: India's End Game in

Afghanistan," *The Washington Quarterly,* Spring 2011, p. 180.
5. Annual Report 2002-2003, Ministry of Defence, Government of India, New Delhi, p. 3.
6. Government of India, "India's Assistance Programme in Afghanistan," Ministry of External Affairs, New Delhi, 2008 at http://www.diplomatie.gouv.fr/en/IMG/pdf/India-s_Assistance_Programme_in_Afghanistan_-_May_2008.pdf. (Accessed on May 13, 2011.)
7. "Outcome document on Indian Prime Minister's visit to Afghanistan," May 13, 2011 at http://strategicchaat.blogspot.com/2011/05/outcome-document-on-visit-of-indian.html. (Accessed on May 17, 2011.)
8. Government of India, Annual Report: 2008-2009, Ministry of External Affairs, New Delhi, p. 1.
9. Ibid., p. 2.
10. No. 6.
11. No. 8, p. 2.
12. Government of India, Annual Report: 2010-2011, Ministry of External Affairs, New Delhi.
13. No. 7.
14. Shanthie Mariet D'Souza, "Should India continue its present course in Afghanistan?" Institute for Defence Studies and Analyses, July 9, 2008 at http://www.idsa.in/idsastrategiccomments/ShouldIndiaContinueItsPresentCourseinAfghanistan_SMDSouza_090708.
15. Ibid.
16. Mondira Dutta, "India-Afghanistan Relations: Opportunities and Challenges," *World Focus*, 29 (11), November-December, 2008, pp. 412-18.
17. Vishal Chandra, "The Afghan Maze and India's Options," Institute for Defence Studies and Analyses, September 4, 2009 at http://www.idsa.in/event/TheAfghanMazeandIndiasOptions_vchandra_04092009.
18. Archana Thakur, "India's Role in the Afghan Reconstruction," *Third Concept,* May 2011, p. 15.
19. Socio-political universe in the context refers to the societal set-ups of hierarchical structure of a society and their power relations in yielding to a certain social and political outcome. Afghanistan has a unique socio-political universe in the form of tribes, feudal lords, great power rivalries and Islam that have been determining the changes throughout. It is therefore a prerequisite to the proper understanding of Afghanistan's present political situation.
20. Amin Saikal, *Modern Afghanistan: A History of Struggle and Survival* (London: I. B.Tauris, 2004), p. 131.
21. B. D. Hopkins, *The Making of Modern Afghanistan* (New York: Palgrave Macmillan, 2008), p. 163.
22. Amin Saikal, no. 22, p. 132.
23. P. C. Yadav, *Soviet Intervention in Afghanistan*, Dissertation, Master of Philosophy, North-Eastern Hill University, Shillong, August 13, 1984, pp. 54-67.
24. Ibid., pp. 5-9.
25. Ibid., pp. 11-15.
26. Amin Saikal, no. 22, pp. 232-34.
27. P. C. Yadav, no. 25.
28. I. P. Khosla, "India and Afghanistan," in Mohta, Madhup and Atish Sinha (eds.), *Indian Foreign Policy: Challenges and Opportunities* (New Delhi: Foreign Service Institute,

2007), p. 529.

29. Amin Saikal, no. 22, pp. 233-337.
30. "Germany Bonn hosts major conference on Afghanistan," December 5, 2011 at http://www.newsahead.com/preview/2011/12/05/germany-5-dec-2011-bonn-hosts-major-conference-on-afghanistan/index.php.
31. Rajiv Sikri, *Challenge and Strategy: Rethinking India's Foreign Policy* (New Delhi: Sage Publications, 2009), p. 55.
32. Ibid., p. 52.
33. I. P. Khosla, no. 30, p. 550.
34. Arun Sahgal, "Afghanistan on the Brink: Alternative Futures," *Jindal Journal of International Affairs,* 1 (1), October 2011, pp. 337-38.
35. Amin Saikal, no. 22, pp. 237-38.

RESEARCH NOTE

1. Parliamentary System for Afghanistan: Advantages and Disadvantages

Mohammad Ashraf Rasooli

After Montesquieu's theory of separation of powers, legal experts argued in two different ways about it, which later resulted in the establishment of two types of political systems: parliamentary and presidential. Some experts believed that Montesquieu's view (i.e., providing security and civil rights in a society) will not be feasible unless sovereignty is equally divided among the three branches of the political system—the executive, the legislature and the judiciary. In this case, the powers of each will be completely separated from one another, and none of them would be able to intervene in the affairs of the other. These schools of thought sought equality of powers and complete autonomy to prevail in society. However, the other group argued that absolute separation of powers will not be feasible because sovereignty is essentially indivisible; secondly, each of the three institutions of state implements policies in the name of the people and for the well-being of a society. Therefore, absolute separation of powers should be replaced by partial separation or cooperation and coordination, which is emphasised by the parliamentary system.

In the system of partial separation of powers, the government's power is gradually transferred through election to different institutions of a state. Morris Doworja in his book on political sociology has defined the partial separation of powers as "distinction of powers, cooperation in tasks, and body interdependency." In fact, partial separation of powers is different from both the absolute separation of powers and centralisation of power. In this system, the authorities and responsibilities of every institution of the state are defined and separated; similar responsibilities are assigned to individual institutions. On the other hand, these responsibilities and authorities at specific junctures, make them dependent on one another. They have instruments that are effective in reinforcing each other, resulting in cooperation.

Parliamentary System

Parliamentary system is a system where the executive or the government (Prime Minister and Cabinet) is responsible to the parliament. The ministers must get voted into the parliament. The parliament monitors the performance of the government; therefore, in this system the notion of "government of the people, for the people, by the people" and "national sovereignty" is practised. The parliamentary system is based on cooperation and coordination of the three branches of the government. The three branches of the political system share the responsibility of the nation's sovereignty. Irrespective of certain distinctions in their authority and responsibilities, they cooperate and maintain a system of checks and balances. This system is more likely to provide sovereign power to the people.

The parliamentary system worldwide has certain broad features:

1. Existence of executive power with two pillars: in which both the President/King and the Prime Minister head the state; and the Prime Minister heads the Cabinet meetings. In this system, usually the President/King has a symbolic role and mainly has no responsibility against the government's performances. The real executive power is vested in the Prime Minister, who runs the government with the assistance of the ministers.
2. The legislature, in addition to amending and approving laws, has the authority to approve the budget. It mainly elects the Prime Minister and the executive as well (the Prime Minister is chosen by the majority party after election to the legislature).
3. Legislatures can monitor the government's performances, and if the need arises, it can call the government and the executive for clarification and ask specific questions and if they are unable to answer satisfactorily, the legislative body can give them a vote of no-confidence and dismiss the government and/or any of its members.
4. The government has the authority to draft laws and amendments and send them to parliament for approval or, in some special cases, draft regulations, attend relevant legislative meetings and its various committees and provide information to the legislature.
5. The President/King has the authority to dissolve the legislature and call for fresh elections.

In a parliamentary system an equality of powers is thus created, which in a way makes the government and the executive responsible before the parliament—both from the voting point of view and by controlling and evaluating their performances and proposing a no-confidence vote against them. On the other hand, the parliament cannot act independently in all areas because the President/King also has the authority to dissolve it and order fresh elections; hence the parliament cannot act totalitarian.

Parliamentary System in Afghanistan

Evaluating the history of governments in Afghanistan and the Constitutions in the past, the Constitution of Afghanistan in 1923 and 1931 provided for a Prime Minister. In the parliamentary system that existed before the promulgation of the Constitution in 1964, the King's relatives were often serving as the Prime Minister. During the "Decade of Democracy" and in the Constitution of 1964, though the King had no responsibility, apart from being the holder of the highest political office in the country, he appointed the Prime Minister who was responsible for the formation of the government and seeking parliamentary approval for it through a vote of confidence by the House of People (Wolesi Jirga).

During Mohammad Daoud's republican regime, the Constitution of 1976 did not provide for the office of the Prime Minister; the President was the Head of State as well as the leader of the government. The political system was similar to the presidential system. During the era of the leftist Khalq and Parcham regimes, they re-established the system, having a Prime Minister on two occasions. The office of the Prime Minister also existed in the Constitution of 1987-1990 and the authority of the government was determined by law.

Advantages and Disadvantages of the Parliamentary System in Afghanistan

The parliamentary system, like the presidential system as an accepted system worldwide, has its own advantages and disadvantages. If the parliamentary system meets the conditions, requirements and functionality of a society, obviously the society will benefit from its advantages. It depends on the socio-political conditions of a society. It is a fact that absolute separation of powers is impossible. Even in the presidential systems it is not possible to have absolute separation among the state's three branches. Since the three branches constitute three pillars of a state's polity, irrespective of their separate roles and authorities, they are interdependent and work in cooperation with each other while performing their specific duties.

But for societies that have always suffered from dictatorships and totalitarianism in which those in power were aggressive—adoption of a parliamentary system is the best way to avoid centralised power in the hands of one individual. Even some leaders who gained power through legal and democratic means, have tried to dominate the system by concentrating powers in their own hands and rejecting those of others. The best way to tackle the problems of a dictatorship and limit the powers of such leaders is to implement the parliamentary system.

The parliamentary system has its own disadvantages too. The governments may not have enough stability under the parliamentary system, especially in countries that have multiple political parties. In such societies, the government is usually formed through consensus, and in case one of the parties is dissatisfied, it would leave the government and consequently the government may lose support in parliament. On the other hand, the President/King can, in certain cases, dissolve parliament and order fresh elections. Furthermore, possible emergence of tensions between the President and the Prime Minister can be considered another major disadvantage of the parliamentary system in present Afghanistan. However, it is worth mentioning that society is the milieu in which the political system operates. The political regime is a social institution. Without analysing the initial causes of problems in a society, determining and selecting a political system for a society cannot resolve problems. Therefore, the system that we select must respond to the needs of the society.

The System of Government in Afghanistan

According to Article 4 of the Constitution, sovereignty depends on the nation and the nation practises sovereignty through their elected representatives. It states that, "national sovereignty in Afghanistan shall belong to the nation, manifested directly and through its elected representatives." The nation of Afghanistan is composed of all individuals who possess the citizenship of Afghanistan. As per Article 81, Section 1 of the Constitution, "The National Assembly of the Islamic Republic of Afghanistan, as the highest legislative organ, shall manifest the will of its people as well as represent the entire nation." In Afghanistan and other similar democratic nations where sovereignty is people-driven, people directly elect the President and by electing the members of the parliament, indirectly implement and practise sovereignty. Therefore, sovereignty is mainly practised through election of representatives to the parliament through general elections. The parliament is responsible for creating legal frameworks, monitoring and enforcing of laws promulgated by the government. Parliament has the authority to call the Prime Minister and/or other ministers, who are appointed by the President, for enquiries and clarifications. It also has the authority to issue a vote of no-confidence against them, approve the budget and make decisions relating to the financial affairs of the government. Conversely, the President/

King has the authority to dissolve the parliament. However, according to the 2004 Constitution of Afghanistan there is no Prime Minister and the system that the Constitution talks about is that of a presidential one. But by merely gauging the authority of the President and the parliament, and particularly the authority of the House of People (Wolesi Jirga), one cannot identify whether the new political regime of Afghanistan is based on a presidential, parliamentary, or a combination of the two systems.

One of the main characteristics of the parliamentary system, as stated earlier, is that ministers are elected by the parliament. Based on Section 11 of Article 64 of the Constitution, the President selects ministers, and then they are introduced to the parliament for obtaining the vote of confidence. Section 3 of Article 91 of the Constitution states that approval and disapproval of these candidates is the particular authority of the Wolesi Jirga. This is more like the parliamentary system. Similarly, according to Section 12 of Article 64 and Section 3 of Article 91 of the Constitution, the head and members of the judicial institutions should get the parliament's approval.

Another characteristic of the parliamentary system is that ministers accept their political responsibility before the parliament. As stated by Article 92 of the Constitution, "The House of People, on the proposal of twenty per cent of all its members, shall make inquiries from each Minister. If the explanations given are not satisfactory, the House of People shall consider the issue of a no-confidence vote. The no-confidence vote on a Minister shall be explicit, direct, as well as based on convincing reasons. The vote shall be approved by the majority of all members of the House of People."

Monitoring of the government's performance is another characteristic of the parliamentary system. As per Article 89 of the Constitution, "The House of People shall have the authority to establish a special commission, on the proposal of one-third of its members, to review as well as investigate the actions of the government. The composition and method of operation of the afore-mentioned commission shall be determined by the Regulations on Internal Duties." At the same time, Article 93 states that, "Any commission of both houses of the parliament can question any Minister about special issues. The individual questioned shall provide an oral or written response."

As per Article 77, "The Ministers shall perform their duties as heads of administrative units within the framework of this Constitution as well as other laws prescribed. The Ministers shall be responsible to the President and House of Representatives for their specified duties" in the same way as is usual in the parliamentary system. Article 64, Section 2 describes that the President will "determine the fundamental lines of the policy of the country with the approval of the National Assembly." Article 69 of the Constitution describes that, "the President shall be responsible to the nation as well as the House of People." According to the provisions of this article if the President commits certain crimes such as human rights violations, treason, and criminality, the lower house with one-third majority can sue him/her. Explanations of such crimes against humanity, national treason as well as a crime against the President shall be demanded by one-third of all members of the House of People and if this demand is approved by two-thirds of the House of People, the House of People shall convene the Loya Jirga within one month. If the Loya Jirga, by two-thirds majority, approves the accusation, the President shall be released from duty and the issue shall be referred to a special court, which shall be comprised of the President of the House of Elders, three members of the House of People, and three members of the Supreme Court appointed by the Loya Jirga. The case shall be presented by the individual appointed by the Loya Jirga. In such a situation the provisions of Article 67 of this Constitution shall be applied.

Keeping in mind the above-mentioned authorisations, though the country's regime is similar and has affinity towards the presidential system, the national assembly and particularly the Wolesi Jirga that consists of the people's representatives has certain powers that are similar to the parliamentary system. What is missing in this system is the Prime Minister. Apart from being the head of the state, the President also leads the executive. This apart, avoiding centralisation of powers, authorisation of different institutions for supporting rule of law, and ensuring separation of powers, are some of the standards that help the practice of democracy in a society. As mentioned earlier, absolute separation of power is not possible anywhere in the world; even the presidential systems that are operating under the theory of autonomy do not have absolute autonomous powers. It is necessary to have a balance among the executive, legislative, and judicial branches of the government since it creates continuous tension among them. On the contrary, cooperation and control of these powers by one another creates equality and ensures implementation of their specific tasks within the limits of their authority.

It is required that specific tasks are given to each one of the three branches in accordance with their roles as a first step to ensure good governance. For instance, laws are made and amended by legislative power, the judiciary implements them, and the executive enforces the laws. Secondly, the three branches should be able to evaluate the actions of one another and have a horizontal relationship among them, so that they can create state-level equality and balance of power. The legislative power that makes and amends laws must not intervene in the affairs of the judiciary that implements the laws. And, inversely, the judiciary that is authorised to implement the laws should not use the authority of the legislature and make/amend the laws. It is very important that each one of these institutions performs its duties according to the roles assigned to it and stays in close contact with other branches to ensure effective governance of a state. The main idea of separation of powers should be respected and maintained to support the rule of law. This principle must precisely be included as an Article in the Constitution, and its implementation should be assured.

RESEARCH NOTE

2. Neutrality as an Institution of International Law: The Case of Afghanistan

A. N. Medvedev

Afghanistan's neutrality has been closely watched by various international fora of late, with many experts maintaining that Afghanistan's reinstatement of neutrality is *sine qua non* for ending the 30-year-long Afghan crisis. In 2011, the Centre for Political Technologies, an independent non-profit organisation, in cooperation with its partners from Afghanistan, Kazakhstan, Tajikistan and Russia held three international events: one in Almaty in June, another in Dushanbe in July and yet another in Dubai in November. A positive feature of the aforesaid events dedicated to Afghanistan was that its participants included current Afghan politicians, academics, representatives of various Afghan ethnic groups and representatives of Afghan diasporas and experts from 15 countries, including India. The series of events was dedicated to discussing a wide spectrum of issues pertaining to the Afghan crisis. The need for Afghanistan to restore its status of permanent neutrality was rather high on the agenda. Ahmad Wali Massoud, Founder and Head of the Ahmad Shah Massoud Foundation; Aziz Arianfar, Director of the Centre for Afghanistan Studies and Research (Germany); Prof. Vladimir N. Plastun, Oriental Studies Department of Novosibirsk State University; Suleiman Layek, an academician and member of the Afghan Academy of Sciences; Waheddulla Sabawoon, Presidential Tribal Affairs Advisor-Minister and others shared their views on the subject.

Experience has shown that the discussion on Afghanistan's prospects of restoring its status of permanent neutrality have been gaining momentum. The discussion centres on how topical and realistic is Afghanistan's neutrality within the context of the particular foreign policy situation. On the whole, international experts were unanimous on the need for Afghanistan to restore its permanent neutrality. But they seriously disagreed on the feasibility of the process, when it could start and end, mechanisms to restore permanent neutrality and what the notion "Afghanistan's permanent neutrality" signified. Foreign military presence in a neutral state was a critical issue in the discussion. Prof. V. N. Plastun said in his speech in Almaty that "the term 'neutrality' calls for substantiation from the point of view of today's international law. For when we utter the word 'neutrality' in its common meaning, it means the lack of foreign troops in neutral states. Hence, if neutrality is declared tomorrow, it would be questioned due to the presence of foreign troops here. However, the idea is very good."

A brief historical digression is called for, to clarify the situation and answer a number of questions. Neutrality is the oldest institution of international law. Neutrality in international affairs existed as a common approach and a principle. In earlier times, the rights and obligations of neutral countries were not, or rather could not be, defined based on a treaty or a law. Most often, neutrality was defined as the obligation of a non-warring party to not follow the steps of the state waging an "unjust" war and abstain from supporting the aggressor in any way. Neutrality in war is the first and most widespread form of neutrality. The early international agreements on neutrality are the Hague Convention of 1907 respecting the Rights and Duties of Neutral Powers and Persons in Case of War on Land; and the Hague Convention of 1907 concerning the Rights and Duties of Neutral Powers in Naval War. Proceeding from the conventions, neutrality in war is understood to be the legal status of a state under which it does not participate in a war and provide immediate assistance to the belligerents. Almost all states throughout the world are signatories to the Conventions.

It should be emphasised, however, that the nineteenth century had given the world a new form of neutrality much before the aforesaid Conventions were signed, namely, permanent neutrality bolstered by international treaties. For instance, the participants in the Congress of Vienna in 1815 recognised the eternal neutrality of Switzerland and assured the latter "of the integrity and inviolability of its possessions within the new borders" which proved to be a major advancement in the development of the institution of neutrality. The world's first internationally recognised permanent neutrality resulted from the emergence of certain foreign relations systems, such as the Vienna system, resting on an alliance of great powers. The neutrality of Belgium as a part of the same system of relations is a case in point here. Having gained independence in 1830, Belgium was declared "an independent and eternally neutral state" by the European powers; while the Netherlands—from which its southern provinces had split to make up a new state—recognised Belgium's independence and neutrality only in 1839. Later on, the status was reaffirmed by a series of treaties among Britain,

France and Prussia. One stipulated that Britain and Prussia would use military force to defend Belgium's neutrality if France violated it. The other bound Britain and France to defend Belgium's neutrality in a similar manner in case Prussia violated it. Actually, the system governing international relations between neutral and warring states had begun to emerge by the late nineteenth and early twentieth centuries. However, the process has not been completed and is likely to continue in the form of a further evolution of the international relations system. In this connection, Afghanistan's restoration as a permanently neutral state will turn a new page in the process that has both regional and international significance.

The twentieth century, which has been marked by two world wars and the subsequent confrontation of the superpowers, drastically gave a new meaning to the concept of neutrality. The First World War exemplified the declaration of war as the only response to violation of rights of an internationally recognised neutral state. When Germany set foot on Belgian soil in August 1914, this was used by Britain as a *casus belli* to declare war on the aggressor. Following the Second World War, a number of states, both in Europe and outside it, declared neutrality in the backdrop of the Cold War. The three traditionally neutral countries, namely, Sweden, Switzerland and Ireland (the latter's neutrality was declared in the 1930s after it had become independent) were joined by Austria, Finland and Malta. Cyprus became neutral, too, albeit for other reasons. Its neutrality resulted from its split into the Greek and Turkish states and the emergence of the self-proclaimed Turkish Republic of Northern Cyprus. Amongst the above examples of neutral states, Austria, which got the status in 1955, deserves special mention, study and understanding. The four victorious states of the Second World War—the Soviet Union, the United States, Great Britain and France (as is known, Austria, as part of the Third Reich took part in the war as an ally of Germany and was divided into occupational zones like Germany)—undertook certain measures to respect and comply with the permanent neutrality of Austria.

It needs to be understood that Austria assumed the status of permanent neutrality voluntarily. This obliged it to comply stringently with the requirements of neutrality that it had assumed as a result of its conviction to strengthen its independence and sovereignty, rather than pressure by other powers or due to vested interests. Secondly, Austria's neutrality is enshrined in an international treaty which the country cannot abandon unilaterally. Thirdly, Austria's permanent neutrality has been recognised by the international community. The states which have recognised it thus have undertaken to respect the territorial integrity and sovereignty of the nation. Fourthly, Austria's neutrality is of armed variety. Austria can have armed forces to defend its neutrality and territorial integrity. The aforesaid historical facts show unambiguously that each of the neutral states mentioned above got their neutral status under peculiar conditions that were unique. A brisk understanding of this is important for any further discussion on the prospects of Afghanistan's restoration of its neutral status.

In short, the historical experience of the European neutral countries proves that there are no common rules and ways to acquire or restore neutrality, for each neutral country gained the status in particular circumstances, with the guarantees of neutrality being equally special (some states, for example, Ireland, lack the neutral state status whatsoever). Neutral states appeared, as a rule, due to the then international situation and parity among the world powers. Neutral Sweden, Switzerland and Belgium were part and parcel of the international relations system based on the agreements at Vienna (Belgium had been until 1914) that emerged in Europe in the wake of Napoleon's defeat, while neutral Austria and Finland are an organic part of the system derived from the Yalta Conference after the Second World War. The gist of the policy of neutrality is determined by every state depending on how it understands it. In practice, permanent neutrality was often interpreted by the states in a broader manner, often lacking uniformity in the understanding rights and obligations of permanently neutral states. In this respect, the most telling example is that of Switzerland which had abstained from joining the United Nations (UN) for a long time, believing the neutral state status did not allow it to join. However, 55 per cent of the Swiss voted for joining the UN in March 2002, while 75 per cent of them had voted against joining 16 years before. Lately, there has been growing sentiment in the Swiss government and society for a more flexible interpretation of the principle of neutrality, with Switzerland cooperating with North Atlantic Treaty Organisation (NATO) under the Partnership for Peace programme in the present times.

The key difference between permanent neutrality and neutrality in war is in the latter being limited in time and being a single instance to a state. In other words, although a state can be neutral in one war, it can alter its stance in case of another military conflict without violating international law, while permanent neutrality precludes a state's participation in any ongoing or future war, except a defensive one, coinciding with individual self-defence. The aforesaid pertains to the experience of European countries. However, with Turkmenistan as an example, it has been proven yet again that the experience of every state which gained permanent neutrality status is no yardstick for other neutral states. Turkmenistan has exemplified a new form of neutrality.

On December 12, 1995, the UN General Assembly passed Resolution 50/80A Permanent Neutrality of Turkmenistan, stating, amongst other things, the following:

> The General Assembly,
>
> Having considered the question of the permanent neutrality of Turkmenistan,
>
> Reaffirming the sovereign right of every State to determine independently its foreign policy in accordance with the norms and principles of international law and the Charter of the United Nations,
>
> Welcoming the legislative confirmation by Turkmenistan of its status of permanent neutrality,
>
> Welcoming also the desire of Turkmenistan to play an active and positive role in developing peaceful, friendly and mutually beneficial relations with the countries of the region and other States of the world,
>
> Expressing the hope that the status of permanent neutrality of Turkmenistan will contribute to the strengthening of peace and security in the region,
>
> Taking note of the support by the Movement of Non-Aligned Countries and by the Economic Cooperation Organisation of the status of permanent neutrality of Turkmenistan,
>
> Recognising that the adoption by Turkmenistan of the status of permanent neutrality does not affect the fulfilment of its obligations under the Charter and will contribute to the achievement of the purposes of the United Nations,
>
> 1. Recognises and supports the status of permanent neutrality declared by Turkmenistan;
> 2. Calls upon States Members of the United Nations to respect and support this status of Turkmenistan and also to respect its independence, sovereignty and territorial integrity.

Turkmenistan's neutrality was a new foreign relations phenomenon whose form of neutrality was of unprecedented kind. It was unusual because an international act was passed first and Turkmenistan's domestic law was modified subsequently. Neutrality has enabled Turkmenistan to pursue an independent foreign policy and establish constructive relations with all countries and other parties. This example proves yet again that Afghanistan is not obliged to use anybody's experience for restoring its permanent neutrality, but is entitled to look into the experience of today's neutral states and use only what fits and benefits it. As far as Afghanistan is concerned, the key features of permanent neutrality should be as follows:

1. The principle of voluntary adoption of neutral status. This would commit Afghanistan to stringent adherence to all requirements of neutrality. The principle would become a legal cornerstone for creating the conditions for signing agreements with neighbouring countries pertaining to non-interference in domestic affairs with Pakistan in the first place and agreements on inadmissibility of aggression against each other and on renunciation of territorial claims to each other;
2. The nature of neutrality, enshrined in an international agreement, which would legally prevent Afghanistan from renouncing its permanent neutral status unilaterally;
3. The recognition of Afghanistan's permanent neutral status by the international community, which would oblige other states to respect its territorial integrity and sovereignty;
4. The armed nature of Afghanistan's neutrality, entitling the nation to maintain armed forces to support its neutrality and defend its territorial integrity and sovereignty.

A special conference under the auspices of the UN could become a mechanism of Afghanistan's restoration to its permanently neutral status. An invaluable support in initiating such a conference could be provided by the Non-Aligned Movement (NAM), Economic Cooperation Organisation (ECO) and other regional and international organisations, including the Shanghai Cooperation Organisation (SCO) in a manner similar to Turkmenistan attaining permanent neutrality.

As for the possible timeline for launching the mechanism, the international expert community is at odds on this issue. Some international experts believe that Afghanistan should get permanent neutral status prior to the pull-out of the US forces from the country. In their opinion, this can lead Washington to voluntarily limit its influence in order to honour Afghan neutrality and motivate similar attitude on the part of other nations. It should be realised, however, that the permanent neutral status is not only an international legal status, but also a conscious state philosophy and Afghan society's realisation of the place and role of its country within the system of international relations.

As applied to Afghanistan, the country's restoration of its neutrality has both domestic and foreign preconditions. As to the domestic preconditions concerned, the popularity of the concept of neutrality will be facilitated by the very mindset of the Afghans, which includes the lack of aggression and desire for outside expansion, coupled with aversion to the presence of foreign troops in their country. In addition, there is Afghanistan's own experience of the 1950s and 1960s, when the actual substance of neutrality was almost ideal in all its manifestations, including the system of mutual relations between such rivals as the US and the Soviet Union. To a certain degree, a similar experience has been gained by Finland, where neutrality stemmed from the Finnish-Soviet Treaty on Cooperation and Mutual Assistance of 1948. The country's neutrality policy has been realised de facto and has enabled Finland to cooperate with both opposing camps by means of symmetric treaties and, as can be seen now, become a flourishing country. However, it should be noted that the current domestic preconditions for Afghanistan's permanent neutrality are not sufficient. For the restoration of permanent neutrality to succeed, the idea has to become part of a broader set of concepts and projects to be implemented as part of the resumption of the national reconciliation policy—those that are capable of winning support of the Afghan intellectual elite of various ethnic hues and diasporas supporting the concept of a nationwide project tentatively called Multinational Neutral Afghanistan Striving Towards Stable State and Society.

International factors include the neighbouring states' interest in the restoration of Afghanistan's neutrality. It is important for Russia to have Afghanistan re-emerge as a permanently neutral state. Russia had appreciated Afghanistan's neutrality during the Cold War until the late 1970s, when the Soviet Union resorted to a military intervention there following the emergence of the threat of toppling the communist regime and the US filling the void. Today, there are no Afghanistan-related antagonisms among Russia and other world players. Russia tries not to get involved in the Afghan political processes. It signed an agreement for non-combat supplies, rail and air transit with the US, Germany, France and Spain. Washington deems its cooperation with Russia "critical," for the "northern route" is the only safe one. Today, the Afghan issue is an element of complicated relations between Russia and the US. However, the geopolitical arena of Russia-US rivalry is not Afghanistan, but the former Central Asian Republics (CARs). Granting its agreement for the use of airbases in Uzbekistan and Kyrgyzstan to the US, Russia stressed that the US military presence there should be temporary. Therefore the present situation is that there are about 30 NATO and US military bases deployed in Afghanistan, which could be used not so much as for fighting terrorism, as for exerting military pressure on Russia, China, Iran and India further down the road.

It is worth remembering that even during its military intervention, the Soviet Union built numerous economic installations that were destroyed afterwards. At present, the idea of participating in the industrialisation of Afghanistan is often floated in Russia. It comprises shouldering the restoration and modernisation of the 142 economic facilities built by the Soviet Union. However, this is regarded solely as a business project for Russian companies, rather than assistance in development. Russia will not invest in Afghanistan the way it is investing now; it is only ready to work at the expense of the funds allocated by the international community for the rebuilding of Afghanistan. Where are these funds and where are the security guarantees for Russia's possible investment and its citizens who could take part in restoring the Afghan economy? Where are the guarantees that economic installations to be built or rebuilt by Russia will not to be destroyed again? India, Iran and China are very interested in the restoration of Afghanistan's permanently neutral status, for they hope that increasing economic and political influence in the country will help obtain international legal guarantees of the investment made earlier and create conditions for new economic projects.

The neutral status, if gained by Afghanistan before the withdrawal of the Americans, will become a factor helpful in smoothening out regional antagonisms and finding common ground as well as systemically resolving the most urgent issue—that of foreign military presence in a neutral state. Some believe the neutral status automatically implies the lack of any foreign troops on its soil and precludes the use of its airspace and territorial waters by them. Actually, the situation is not that unambiguous in this respect. As was pointed out above, every state determines the extent of its neutrality policy on its own. There are no compulsory templates and one-size-fits-all solutions. Today, there are a number of problems calling for international coordination, including that of the armed forces, the countering of terrorism, drug production, drug running, arms trafficking and piracy. In Afghanistan, an abrupt termination of foreign military presence without creating the conditions for a peaceful settlement is bound to plunge the nation into civil war. There, one should not demand that the US leave Afghanistan immediately, because this would only lead to the exacerbation of its domestic armed conflict. Therefore, even though the US military presence in Afghanistan runs counter to the national interests of Iran, China, Pakistan and Russia, the leaders of these countries are in no rush to have the US forces pull out immediately.

There is an understanding of the need for creating lasting peace after the US forces have pulled out. If they do so now, Afghanistan may lose its national unity, collapse into several parts, which is far more dangerous to the region than the presence of the US forces in the country. Therefore, these countries are ready to put up with this so far, each independently creating social and political prerequisites for preserving stability, once the

US forces have withdrawn. Although, these activities have been coordinated poorly so far, nevertheless there is a view that the Organisation of Islamic Cooperation (OIC) has certain military-political capabilities in terms of squaring Afghanistan away. The SCO too, will have a certain capability in this sphere in due time. Possibly, the future closer cooperation of the two organisations will be able to facilitate a resolution of the Afghan problem effectively. All the more there is the understanding that further long-term US military presence in the region will jeopardise the interests of many countries, including the CARs, owing to the possibility of direct immediate intervention of the US in their domestic affairs in the first place. In addition, the countries will be faced with social destabilisation if the US decides to spread the Afghan crisis to other states in the region. It is also apparent that the current US administration is heavily dependent on the domestic and global financial situations. If the US administration can disregard the opinion of individual states, a consolidated position of the region's countries, coupled with the public sentiment in the US and other major NATO players, will likely put up a telling argument in favour of the complete withdrawal of troops.

There has been an attempt to improve relations among nations in the region, which have a real influence on the situation in Afghanistan, including Pakistan, Iran, China, India and Russia. In all likelihood, these countries are expected to persuade the US administration to make up its mind on the date of the pull-out of its forces, including the military bases. Therefore, the view that a UN-sponsored international conference be held on Afghanistan's restoration of its permanently neutral status prior to the International Security Assistance Force (ISAF) and US forces withdrawal seems to have the right to exist. Afghanistan's restored permanent neutrality would enable the country to not only reduce the foreign policy pressure exerted on it, but also serve as the basis for a drastically novel security system in the Central Asian region, including resolving the foreign military presence issue in a planned manner under international supervision.

Coming up with the aforesaid conceptual proposals, it may be noted that Russia takes both the political authority of India and its expertise pertinent to the Afghan problem into account so that they can be discussed. Indian experts are known in Russia and consulted regularly. In particular, the bilateral Indian-Russian symposium on "Political, Security and Economic Developments in Afghanistan: Prospects of Regional Cooperation" took place at the Observer Research Foundation, New Delhi in late May 2010. Russian experts attending the symposium appreciated the capabilities of Indian experts as far as the problems of Afghanistan are concerned. Shri S.

K. Lambah, the Prime Minister's special envoy to Pakistan and Afghanistan, Anand K. Sahay, coordinating editor, *Asian Age*, Lt.-Gen. (Retd.) R. K. Sawhney, former Deputy Chief of Army Staff and Director General of Military Intelligence, and Brig. (Retd.) R. K. Bhonsle, Director, Sasia Security-Risks.com Pvt. Ltd., who represented India during the symposium, made a very good impression on the Russian participants. In this connection, Russia hopes to deepen the cooperation between Russian and Indian experts in Afghanistan. This would enable quality expert interaction and an examination of political initiatives as well as creation of an approach for their implementation, including the Afghanistan neutrality initiative that has been mentioned earlier.

RESEARCH NOTE

3. Silk Road Comes to Afghanistan Again

Sreemati Ganguli

Afghanistan was one of the trade centres in the route, stretching from China to the Mediterranean through India and today's Central Asia, which together built up the ancient Silk Road. Since the post-2001 period, Afghanistan has become the focus in a number of Silk Road initiatives as the bridge of inter-regional trade cooperation between South and Central Asia, which may be considered as a welcome change from its stigma of being the centre of insecurity for the last thirty years.

The Initiatives

The first such initiative is the one by the United States (US) to promote the broad idea of a "revival of the fundamental basis for the Silk Road" in the Central and South Asian region that has gained momentum since the then Secretary of State, Condoleezza Rice's visit to the region in October 2005. For the US, such a revival is likely to create new areas of cooperation like trade, transport, energy, democracy and communications among the states of Central and South Asia and will expand relations among these states and Europe, Turkey, Japan, North Atlantic Treaty Organisation (NATO) and the Organisation for Security and Cooperation in Europe (OSCE).[1] The stated goals of this initiative for the regional states are to get more connected, to cater to more than one market and to create a fully integrated Greater Central Asia-South Asia region. For the US, the initiative will help achieve its regional goals, which is to strengthen democratic stability and economic reforms, to foster regional security and cooperation on the war against terrorism and drug menace, and promote economic growth and cooperation in the region.

The Central Asia Regional Economic Cooperation–Asian Development Bank (CAREC–ADB) initiative[2] is another project of transport corridors along Eurasia to promote regional cooperation, under the identical name of Silk Road. The programme gathers together the five Central Asian states, as well as Afghanistan, Mongolia and Azerbaijan and six international financial institutions: the ADB, the European Bank for Reconstruction and Development (IBRD), the International Monetary Fund (IMF), the Islamic Development Bank (IDB), the World Bank, and the United Nations Development Programme (UNDP). CAREC is not only involved in the construction of transport corridors (like feasibility studies, financing for the renovation, etc.) but also seeks to modify the commercial policies of the states and their legislation to facilitate flow of interactions.

In an interesting development, NATO termed its project to provide high-speed and effective satellite channel access to the Internet and to the European Scientific and Educational Networks in the region as the "Virtual Silk Highway."[3] The beneficiary states are Azerbaijan, Armenia, Afghanistan, Georgia, Kazakhstan, Kyrgyzstan, Tajikistan, Turkmenistan, and Uzbekistan.

As a follow-up to the First Kabul Conference on Partnership, Trade and Development in Greater Central Asia (April 2006), the Central Asia-Caucasus Institute organised a panel discussion on "The New Silk Roads: Transport and Trade in Greater Central Asia" in Washington DC, on July 18, 2006. The panelists expressed the hope that new silk roads in the form of new trade and transit opportunities in Greater Central Asia would help promote regional stability. In the Introduction to the volume that followed, S. Frederick Starr commented that the "New Silk Roads," in the countries of Russia, Kazakhstan, Kyrgyzstan, Uzbekistan, Tajikistan, Turkmenistan, Azerbaijan, Iran, Turkey, China, India and Pakistan, "have enormous potential for the entire Eurasian continent, and especially for the countries of 'Greater Central Asia' which they must traverse." He also noted a significant development that "for the first time in centuries, New Silk Roads across the Eurasian continent are on the cutting edge of change, rather than its victim."[4]

Frederick Starr and Andrew Kuchins put forward a Modern Silk Road (MSR) Strategy involving Afghanistan in May 2010. This strategy focuses on the re-establishment of Afghanistan's traditional role as a hub of transport and trade linking Europe and the Middle East with the Indian subcontinent and the whole of South and Southeast Asia. To them, the US-led Operation Enduring Freedom opened up Afghanistan's northern and eastern borders to long-distance trade for the first time since 1936. It is one of the most transformative developments on the Eurasian landmass in the past century and they suggested that America carry on with this "transformative transport-based strategy." If America does not embrace this MSR Strategy, then "gains in the security area will prove short-lived; secondly, it will tell Afghans that US interests are too self-centred to accommodate their own goal of economic betterment; thirdly, it will fan the growing conviction in the region that the US's presence there will end soon; and, finally, it will undercut the willingness of NATO partners to join American-led missions in the future."[5]

In September 2011, Secretary of State Hillary Rodham Clinton, Afghan Foreign Minister Zalmay Rassoul and German Foreign Minister Guido Westerwelle co-chaired the New Silk Road Ministerial, hosted by the German Mission in New York City on September 22, 2011. It was a follow-up of what Secretary Clinton outlined in a speech in Chennai, India, on July 20, 2011 about her vision of a "New Silk Road" linking markets in South and Central Asia, with Afghanistan at its heart. The idea was that "lasting stability and security go hand in hand with economic opportunity" and so, an Afghanistan with better economic partnership with its neighbours would become the reason for enhanced security and stability for the region covering Central and South Asia as a whole.

Robert Hormats[6] discussed the entire gamut of the US strategy for New Silk Road initiative in Afghanistan. He commented that, "We cannot forget that, as history has shown us, simply abandoning Afghanistan could potentially have terrible consequences for the American global and regional security concerns." Further he said that the transition in Afghanistan "must be sustainable—and the political and security efforts must be complemented by progress towards increasing economic opportunities for Afghanistan and the broader region." For him, Secretary of State Clinton's diplomatic efforts were aimed at bringing about a political end to this decade-long conflict and she considered the vision to integrate Afghanistan into the regional economy as a key component. Hormats further elaborated that "the basis for the New Silk Road vision is that—if Afghanistan is firmly embedded in the economic life of the region, it will be better able to attract new investment, benefit from its resource potential, and provide economic opportunity and hope for its people." Such a Silk Road strategy can provide a critical economic boost for all of Afghanistan's neighbours.

Andrew Kuchins[7] analysed the context in which the vision of a Silk Road emerged. The US, "as part of its broader transition strategy in Afghanistan, has embraced the promotion of regional trade and transportation as a way of fostering sustainable economic growth in the country. More broadly, this strategy would also lead to greater economic and political interdependence between Afghanistan and its neighbours." He talked about the past role of Afghanistan in interconnecting the regional and global markets and suggested that, "it is now essential for Afghanistan's economic development, as well as its political and military security, that this role be renewed in a

New Silk Road."

During the post-withdrawal phase after 2014, the promotion of Silk Road initiatives will project an alternative scenario for the US, the region and most importantly, for Afghanistan. For the US, the strategic dilemma remains how to engage itself in Afghanistan and in the wider region, after the completion of its military withdrawal from the country. A number of alternate futures are discussed and deliberated upon—one bleaker than the other. Zalmay Khalilzad deliberated upon the most vital goals before Afghanistan, which are, "defeating the remnants of Al Qaeda in Pakistan, preventing the re-emergence of terrorist sanctuaries in Afghanistan, ensuring the security of Pakistan's nuclear weapons, and discouraging Pakistan's use of extremism and terror as a policy instrument." He also pointed out at three approaches which the US might pursue and which could result in three different futures for Afghanistan. First, if the US adopts the policy of "immediate departure and reallocation of resources," then after "decade's effort in blood and treasure, Afghanistan could face the 1990s all over again." Second, if the approach is "phased drawdown" and "internationalisation of the effort" then, the existing problems will get "worse," as "the US is the sole power capable of galvanising and incentivising international cooperation behind economic integration and a regional settlement." To him, the best strategy is a "sustained, determined US Engagement" as "for now, sustained US engagement is the strategy most likely to ensure regional security. Heavy combat operations need not continue indefinitely, but core US interests would require the US to remain in Afghanistan for another decade to build up and train Afghan forces, conduct counterterrorism operations, and respond to regional contingencies" like "a Pakistani state collapse in which nuclear weapons fall into the hands of extremists."[8] The promotion of Silk Road initiatives is a better strategy for prolonged engagement with Afghanistan.

Thomas Nides commented with regard to the New Silk Road initiative of the US, saying that "a secure, stable and prosperous Afghanistan can exist only in the context of a secure, stable and prosperous neighbourhood." He also suggested, in line with the views of Khalilzad that "this is the beginning—not the end of the effort to wind down the war in Afghanistan ... Washington and our allies and partners must continue to lay the groundwork for long-term support for Afghanistan's future to ensure that transition is irreversible and that the hard-fought gains of the last ten years are sustained." To him, it is necessary that "the countries of the region must choose cooperation over conflict."[9]

Conclusion

For the South Asian region, apart from South Asian Association of Regional Cooperation (SAARC), the initiatives offer another opportunity to connect and cooperate in areas of trade and transport. A region where past memories of partition and present politics of distrust are the main impediments to cooperation and development, the Silk Road initiatives might offer prospects for a better future and this historical metaphor of Silk Road that stands for regional and inter-regional cooperation might help the countries of South Asia to be rid of their historical baggage. For the Central Asian region also, better connectivity with Afghanistan and South Asia would result in better trade and prosperity. As Robert O. Blake, Jr.[10] commented: "Our hope is to encourage all of the countries of the region (meaning Central Asian states) and beyond to help build a network of roads, bridges, pipelines and rail lines to facilitate the goal of embedding Afghanistan more firmly into its neighbourhood and to help Afghanistan realise its goal of creating an economy based more on trade than aid. We must also seek to reduce barriers to the efficient exchange of goods across borders, open markets, and promote private sector investment in the region."

The security situation in Afghanistan is evolving. There is insecurity at present and uncertainty about the future. The main challenge is as much to ensure peace and development, as to handle this task simultaneously. It is not about which would be the first task to accomplish; but about the way to balance these twin tasks at the same time, even if not at the same pace. The successful accomplishment of this complex task in Afghanistan demands involvement of regional and global powers, as the making of the current situation there has had the fair, or rather unfair, share of regional and global power rivalries. The Silk Road initiatives offer possibilities of cooperation in the same direction in a new way. First, Afghanistan would be the centre of activity for the trade and transport corridors and the energy pipelines linking South and Central Asia, leading to China in the east and Turkey to the west, and then eventually to Europe. Second, the development in the area of national and regional infrastructure would help economic reconstruction and political stabilisation in Afghanistan in the long run. Economic benefits would help ensure the active involvement of the other countries in the region, as the stakeholders in the process of development and not as powerbrokers in a new geopolitical game. The most serious challenges that Afghanistan faces are those of security and development. The Silk Road Initiatives attempt to secure Afghanistan on a long-term basis through regional economic cooperation and development.

Notes

1. A. Lee Boyer, "Recreating the Silk Road: The Challenge of Overcoming Transaction Costs," *The China and Eurasia Forum Quarterly*, 4 (4), 2006, p. 73.
2. See www.adb.og/projects.
3. See http://www.nato.int/science/virtual-silk/ 2003.
4. Frederick Starr (ed.), *The New Silk Roads: Transport and Trade in Greater Central Asia*, 2007 at www.silkroadstudies.org.
5. Frederick Starr and Andrew Kuchins, "The Key to Success in Afghanistan: A Modern Silk Road Strategy," at www.silkroadstudies.org/new/docs/silkroadpapers/1005Afghan.pdf, 2010 (Accessed on October 3, 2011).
6. Robert D. Hormats, Under-Secretary for Economic, Energy and Agricultural Affairs on "The United States' 'New Silk Road' Strategy: What is it? Where is it Headed?" Address to the SAIS Central Asia-Caucasus Institute and CSIS Forum, September, 29, 2011.
7. Andrew Kuchins, "Laying the Groundwork for Afghanistan's New Silk Road: How Washington and Kabul Can Turn a Vision into a Plan," December 5, 2011, at www.foreignaffairs.com/articles/andrew-c-kuchins (Accessed on January 18, 2012).
8. Zalmay Khalilzad, "The Three Futures for Afghanistan: Why the country Needs a Long-Term Commitment from the United States," December 16, 2011, at www.foreignaffairs.com/articles/zalmay-khalilzad (Accessed on January 18, 2012).
9. Thomas Nides, "The Silk Road Through Afghanistan: The Country's Economic Future Lies in Its Region," *Foreign Affairs*, December 5, 2011, at www.foreignaffairs.com/articles/ thomas-r-nides (Accessed on January 18, 2012).
10. Remarks by Robert O. Blake, Jr., Assistant Secretary, Bureau of South and Central Asian Affairs, on "US Policy in Central Asia," Forum of the Central Asia-Caucasus Institute, SAIS, January 25, 2012.

RESEARCH NOTE

4. Withdrawal of Foreign Troops from Afghanistan and Preparedness of Its Security Forces

Abdul Hadi Khalid

The issue of transition of security to Afghans and the withdrawal of foreign troops—initially brought up in an election campaign by the current President of United States (US) Barack Obama—has become a part of the US security strategy in Afghanistan. In keeping with this line of reasoning, the US and the international forces withdrew from Iraq towards the end of 2011. In Afghanistan, the transition process started in July 2011 and is set to be completed in 2014. Seven locations (including Mehterlam and Lashkar Gah in the restive provinces of Laghman and Helmand respectively) underwent transition in the first round; so far, in the second round, the transition cycle has been set in motion for a further 18 locations. With this, it is believed that the process of transition has been initiated in more than half of the country.

Preparations by the Afghan Security Forces

According to plans made by the Transition Coordination Committee in collaboration with their international partners and relevant ministries, the combined total of both the Afghan National Army (ANA) and the Afghan National Police (ANP) personnel is scheduled to reach 352,000 (ANA=195,000 and ANP=157,000) by the end of 2014. However, the international community (barring a few nations like France, the UK and Italy, which have entered into strategic partnerships with the Afghan government) is yet to reach a consensus on whether and to what extent they will support Afghan security forces beyond 2014. At present, the numbers of ANA and ANP personnel are 176,000 and 151,000 respectively. The National Directorate of Security of Afghanistan (NDS) too is set to grow proportionally.

Threats and Challenges

The following are the threats and challenges that could hamper a smooth transition of security responsibilities to the Afghan National Security Force (ANSF) and to overall security in Afghanistan:

i. Influence of armed insurgent groups including the different factions of the Taliban, Hezb-i-Islami and the Haqqani Network, Pakistani groups such as Tehrik-i-Taliban Pakistan (or Pakistani Taliban, led by Mawlawi Fazalullah and Hakimullah Mehsud), Lashkar-e-Taiba, Jaish-i-Mohammad, armed groups in Central Asia (most prominently, Islamic Movement of Uzbekistan, and those based in the Xinxiang Uyghur Autonomous Region in China), Al Qaeda and Arab terrorists;

ii. Illegal armed groups—mainly consisting of drug traffickers and organised criminals—have as much influence as the Taliban and can disrupt law and order. They also draw financial support from illicit sources;

iii. Antagonism between various ethnic groups is a remnant of the civil war years and has been exacerbated by ethnically-organised political parties that fuel tensions and orchestrate a sense of disenchantment among their supporters to suit their own purposes. In many cases, patrons and power holders at the local level are closely linked with members of the Afghan diaspora and wield influence in political circles. National unity has been affected in the process;

iv. Conservative estimates suggest that around 35,000 families in Afghanistan live on income generated from poppy cultivation. There are around 3,000 local level drug traffickers and 50 kingpins. This not only contributes further to corruption, but also has an incentive in prolonging the conflict and maintaining insecurity on the ground. It is also estimated that there are one to one and half a million drug addicts in the country. This alone is illustrative of the extent of lawlessness and the depth to which the drug trade is embedded in Afghanistan;

v. Administrative corruption is widespread in the government and has permeated to subnational levels and the banking and financial services sector as well. This claim is amply supported by the manner in which money launderers were allowed to act with impunity and the trust of the common people was dishonoured during the Kabul Bank fiasco;

vi. Social backwardness, widespread poverty and unemployment, especially among peasants and the young, have contributed to a sense of disenchantment thereby hurting the legitimacy of the Afghan government and in extreme cases, allowing armed insurgent groups to recruit in higher numbers; and

vii. Presence of malevolent neighbours.

Risks and Limitations

The following are some of the factors that could pose risks to the smooth transition of security responsibilities from international forces to the Afghan National Security Force (ANSF), and to overall security in Afghanistan:

i. Lack of government access to funding sources and its inability to equip security forces by using national income has resulted in a weak Afghan security force that has to contend with poor quality arms and ammunition. This state of affairs has been further complicated by the lack of a firm commitment from the international community to support Afghan forces beyond 2014;
ii. There exists a lack of coordination in the approach adopted by various stakeholders to improve the security and law and order situation in Afghanistan. While some (like the US Special Forces) have supported and sponsored the formation of the Afghan Local Police that are security forces largely unacquainted with war, others have made efforts to improve the quality of the ANSF. Consequently, the army and the police—which should have been able to serve as the main forces to tackle insecurity and security threats—remain weak;
iii. Poor coordination between different components of the ANSF and the prevailing confusion in respect of whether Afghanistan is tackling a conflict or a post-conflict scenario. Similar doubts also prevail over the mode of operation of the Afghan government;
iv. ANA and ANP have been politicised and, in certain areas, are closely linked to tribal armed groups and intelligence networks thereby inhibiting their normal operation;
v. Corruption is widespread in political circles and nepotism is the norm rather than the exception. The selection of personnel who lack merit has failed to set an example for the generations to follow;
vi. Lack of transparency in respect of the mechanisms being adopted during the peace and reconciliation process with the Taliban and other armed opposition groups;
vii. Lack of clarity over the transition strategy and date by which withdrawal of foreign forces will be completed; and
viii. Lack of cooperation and support for the security sector from civilians.

Probable Scenarios

Listed below are four probable scenarios that may play out, depending on how the transition of security responsibilities and reforms in the governance sector are managed:

i. If the government leadership adopts reforms and manages to mend relations between the government and large sections of the population, the international community continues to support Afghanistan, and Pakistan stops intervening in the internal affairs of Afghanistan, the situation in the country will stabilise and insecurity will be severely limited.
ii. If the reconciliation process between the government and Taliban results in a favourable truce, and if the support from the international community continues to Afghanistan or if there is a decrease in foreign intervention, and the necessary reforms brought about, the tensions will recede, and the security situation will still improve considerably.
iii. If the present government is further weakened by charges of corruption and injustice thereby hurting its legitimacy, and the international community continues to support Afghanistan, a new President could be elected in 2014 replacing the incumbent. The conflict in Afghanistan will then play out depending on how the President then chooses to operate. Even if Pakistan continues to interfere in the internal affairs of the country, Afghans will likely emerge victorious.
iv. If the government continues to be corrupt and the international community stops supporting Afghanistan, corruption will be rampant in the government beyond 2014. If, in such a situation, interference by neighbours continues unabated, the security situation will get worse and a civil war (even more protracted than the last) would likely break out.